The Texas Aggie Bonfire

Tradition and Tragedy at Texas A&M

By Irwin A. Tang

The Texas Aggie Bonfire
Tradition and Tragedy at Texas A&M

First Edition

Third Printing August 2000
Page Design by Blake Mitchell

Library of Congress Cataloging-in Publication Data

Tang, Irwin.
    The Texas Aggie Bonfire
    Tradition and Tragedy at Texas A&M/by Irwin Tang.

ISBN 0-9679433-0-2

Printed in the United States of America
at Morgan Printing in Austin, Texas

to lives lost

Acknowledgments and About the Publishing Company

I would like to thank my parents and my sister for supporting me through these efforts. Thank you to Angus Martin and all the helpful people at the Cushing Memorial Library at Texas A&M. Appreciation goes to the reporters that covered the Bonfire tragedy and its aftermath – Kelly Brown at *The Bryan-College Station Eagle*, Mike Ward and Suzanne Gamboa at *The Austin American-Statesman*, Pete Slover and Christopher Lee at *The Dallas Morning News*, and John Williams at *The Houston Chronicle*. Thanks to Andrea Braendlin for being a great reader. And I especially appreciate my interviewees for their desire to contribute to the process of debate and discussion.

This book is the first publication of The it Works. Our company specializes in amplifying the voices, issues, and debates ignored, distorted, or unheard in the mainstream corporate media. In the future, we may publish books on Asian Americans, the American education system, or a number of different subjects. Fiction is also a possibility. Correspondence should be sent to the addresses on the copyright information page.

Table of Contents

Introduction

Heaven

It is like heaven. Tens of thousands of stars, each one flickering beneath the breath of a person. Each star is the flame of a maroon candle or a white candle. Each breath belongs to an Aggie or a member of the Aggie community, commonly known as Aggieland.

It is quiet. Not silent, but quiet. We can hear the quiet, and it is an expectant respite. We are here in College Station, on the campus of Texas A&M, on the field known as the polo fields, where the annual Texas Aggie Bonfire is built, and where it collapsed at 2:30 in the morning on November 18, 1999, killing twelve A&M students who were at the time working atop the four tiers of logs of Bonfire. College Station used to be nothing but a train station and a college, and right now, on Thanksgiving night, exactly one week after the accident, it is a quiet full of peace and waiting, as if one train had gone and another was still coming.

Tonight the Bonfire was supposed to burn. Instead we stand around a deconstructed Bonfire, the logs lying on their sides under the moon and stars as if they were asleep. As we contemplate the quietness, John Comstock is on our minds. Of the twenty-seven injured students, he was the worst injured and the one who had stayed buried beneath the logs the longest – six-and-a-half hours. His excruciating pain is now replaced with sedative-induced numbness and the mechanical rhythm of a respirator.

1

I am here with my sister Irene. My parents and our extended family and friends are waiting in our College Station home for us to come back and share in the Thanksgiving feast, Chinese style. Duck, squid, all the fixings. My sister is cold. If it were the real Bonfire, she would be warm. The real Bonfire is the biggest fire in the world. Right here at Texas A&M. The biggest fire in the world, and now it's multiplied into a hundred thousand little fires, and it belongs to each one of us. There is no pep rally, nobody to tell us what it all means, like there usually is on Bonfire night, nobody screaming about beating the hell out of t.u., the University of Texas. It is quiet. It is starry. And it looks like heaven.

Once an Aggie

The Texas A&M University students are known as Aggies—as in farmers. A&M stands for "Agricultural and Mechanical." I was once an Aggie. Still am. Once an Aggie always an Aggie.

I was born an Aggie in Aggieland. I grew up here, the son of a Texas A&M chemistry professor and a Texas A&M librarian. I went to Aggieland's public schools—College Hills Elementary, Oakwood Middle, A&M Junior High, and A&M Consolidated High; even in their names local public schooling was a preamble to Texas A&M. When I came of age, I went to "the University" on scholarship. I graduated Magna Cum Laude in 1992 with an appropriately entitled B.S. in Political Science. I went on to earn a Master's degree in Asian Studies from arch-rival UT Austin, and then a Master's Degree in Professional Writing from a neutral school—the University of Southern California, in Los Angeles.

At the time of the Bonfire collapse, I had been back from Los Angeles for only two months. Los Angeles in a lot of ways is the anti-A&M. It is a city of immigrants, while at the same time a city of big money, flash, and plastic beauty, while A&M is vastly white, homogenous, and ostensibly down-home. In a lot of ways, though, L.A. and A&M are alike in that the prevailing culture is carried forth with a muscular confidence and an utter lack of self-conscious irony.

I work as a substitute teacher in Austin. On the morning of November 18th, my house-mate, also an Aggie alum, told me that the Bonfire had fallen and killed four people. What followed from out of my mouth was a litany of disbelief. "What?" "Are you serious?" "Quit messing with me." "Are you sure?" It wasn't just me. No one could believe it. Of course, if you lived, say in New Jersey, and you heard about a giant tower consisting of logs standing on their ends stacked on top of each other, you might think it was a risk-prone structure. But if you lived in College Station, if

2

you were an Aggie, if you had SEEN the bonfire go up and burn down year after year, you would know its solidity. You would see that it is a powerful, beautiful thing. A magnificent edifice, whether you liked it or not. It could never snap before being lit.

But it did. And it wasn't the first time it collapsed. It fell while being built in 1957. Luckily the Aggies were all eating lunch at the time. In 1994, it began leaning and falling apart one morning, and it had to be torn down for safety's sake. But neither the University nor the students ever seemed alarmed.

After the death count reached six and then eleven, I believed it. After seeing pictures of the stack, saw it looking like a dead man lying on the ground in an awkward and broken heap, I believed it. And I wanted to go home.

Texas A&M gave me a lot, and I gave it back in academic effort. And yet, going back right at the announcement of catastrophe seemed somehow wrong. What was I going to do? Stand there and watch people grieve? I couldn't explain to myself why I wanted to go back home, I just wanted to, and so I assumed the urge was a voyeuristic compulsion. And I repressed it. I stayed in Austin until the starry candlelight vigil.

By the time I came back home to Aggieland, I had it in my head that someone had to write a book about the Bonfire, but I wasn't sure who or why. After spending a few days at home, I realized that whoever were to write such a thing could not romanticize the tragedy or the Aggie mythology. But whoever dared to take a straight, unromantic look at Aggieland had better not caricaturize the folks here as dumb rednecks who throw dangerous parties. And it had to be someone who loved Aggieland enough to be starkly honest with it. Upon some pontification, and a review of my life, it became obvious that I had to write the book.

This Book

The question, it seems, on everyone's mind is "What caused the Bonfire to collapse?" Texas A&M established a commission in December 1999 to find the answers to this seemingly simple question. The commission's report is scheduled to be turned in to A&M officials on March 31, 2000, but will likely miss this deadline. As the commission has researched the collapse, the University has released thousands of documents concerning Bonfire, from post-collapse reports to emails to fifteen year-old memoranda. The press and public have used this information to put together a picture of the various possible causes of the Bonfire collapse.

As I finish writing this book, a front page article in The Eagle, the local Bryan-College Station newspaper, features speculation by a former

Texas A&M engineering professor who used to help advise students on the construction of Bonfire. Larry Grosse, now a professor at Colorado State University, says that builders of the 1999 Bonfire did not tie a steel cable around the lowest two tiers of logs, and that this omission may have allowed the Bonfire to collapse as suddenly as it did.

But the steel cable is not used every year, and the Bonfire has stood fine without it in the past. Furthermore, there are no rules to Bonfire construction; methods and instructions are passed down from one generation of student leaders to the next. And the University assigns no construction expert or engineer to oversee the project.

From this short discussion then, the reasons why the Bonfire collapsed are already becoming clear. This book deals with the direct causes of the collapse, and surely the commission will also develop its own conclusions about why the Bonfire collapsed. They will outline the various design, training, and oversight problems, and the University will assure the public that those problems will be taken care of for construction of the next Bonfire.

I propose that the root cause of the Bonfire collapse will be barely touched upon by the press and the Bonfire commission. The root cause of the Bonfire collapse is the Aggie culture itself. Many Aggies will tell you that the culture of Aggieland—the university and its local community—is based on "Tradition." They can list for you various rituals and vocabulary that make up the traditions. But tradition is of course only a manifestation of the spirit of a culture. So, as many Aggies would say, it's not about building a Bonfire; it's about the spirit of Aggieland.

I propose that the spirit of Aggieland and the spirit of the students of Aggieland is a great spirit. I will not go into the details here because, after all, it is a subject complicated by the fact that it is a "spirit that can never be told." But because perhaps it is never told, the traditions that manifest this spirit, and the culture that claims this spirit its own have often not been faithful to it.

Aspects of the Aggieland culture gave rise to the factors that caused the Bonfire collapse. These aspects of the culture allow tradition to trump common sense, which in turn allows for extreme levels of student independence even in dangerous traditions like the construction of Bonfire. The traditional tension, even animosity, between students and student leadership/university administration combined with the tradition of student independence allowed for flagrant and frequent violations of university safety, alcohol, and hazing rules. The tradition of hazing itself intrudes upon the safety of Bonfire construction. The organizational cultural tradition of crisis management/damage control (as opposed to

4

pro-active management/damage prevention) allows for dangerous practices to continue until they cause injury and death, and even then, because of the organizational culture, problems are not solved permanently. The suppression of two-percenters (dissenters or ignorers of Aggie tradition) allowed for A&M administrators to ignore engineers' warning of the instability of the Bonfire design.

Digging even deeper into the relationship between Aggie culture and the quality and safety of Aggie life, many of the same aspects of Aggie culture that caused Bonfire to collapse also betray the spirit of Aggieland by making life in Aggieland difficult for many of its citizens. The culture of violence; the sexual discrimination, harassment and violence against women; the "boys will be boys" attitude; the suppression of dissent and intolerance of nontraditional viewpoints; the historical racism; and the repeated need to validate manhood by any means necessary have not only betrayed the tradition of Bonfire as a unifying force, but have also alienated and betrayed even those members of Aggieland who believe in the Aggie Spirit.

The collapse of Bonfire and the death of twelve students signify the collapse of the Aggie culture. Of course this doesn't mean that we need to get new students and re-educate the community. The spirit of Aggieland lives on in the good people of Aggieland. But that does not mean that those same good people could be caught up in a bad way of doing things. What is needed now is a re-examination of the Aggie culture and the Aggie Spirit. And upon such a philosophical examination and as we constantly question our traditions and culture, we must make the Aggie culture and Aggieland look like, smell like, sound like, feel like, act like, and simply be the Aggie Spirit.

The first section of the book tells the story of the 1999 Texas Aggie Bonfire tragedy. It examines both design/construction flaws, and cultural aspects that allowed for the collapse. The last part of the section does assign responsibility for this preventable accident.

The second section of the book takes a deeper look at Aggie and Bonfire culture and history. It begins with a selective history of Texas A&M, concentrating on aspects of A&M culture that contribute to its dysfunctional characteristics. After that, I present a history of the Bonfire and all its controversies. Thirdly comes six interviews conducted with various members of the Aggie community concerning Bonfire and Aggie culture. Among those interviewed are one former Corps Commander, two students who worked on Bonfire the past three years, one African-American graduate student proposing a memorial for the Bonfire victims, the editor of the local alternative magazine, and the leading anti-Bonfire faculty member.

The third and final section includes a chapter which sums up the Bonfire debate, a chapter on the cultural collapse represented by the Bonfire collapse, an essay about the meanings of Bonfire, and a conclusive essay about Bonfire and the Aggie Spirit.

It ain't about Bonfire. It's about the Aggie Spirit. This book, I hope, will facilitate a re-examination and renaissance of the Spirit of Aggieland.

An Introduction to Bonfire
and Other Aggie Traditions

Bonfire is a big fire. A humongous fire. Bonfire is bigger than the fire itself. Because Bonfire is a manifestation of the Aggie Spirit.

Bonfire is built each year by the students of Texas A&M University in College Station, Texas. The students are known as the Fightin' Texas Aggies, or farmers. The community of Texas A&M and surrounding communities, which, to the north, includes Bryan, Texas, is referred to as Aggieland. The Texas Aggie Bonfire is burned each year at the heart of Aggieland, on the Texas A&M campus.

Since the late 1970's, the Texas Aggie Bonfire has been limited to 55 feet in height and about 45 or 55 feet in width at its base. It is built in the shape of a six-layered wedding cake, with each layer smaller in size than the one below. At the center of the Bonfire is a pole. This is called centerpole. Each layer is built around centerpole. The layers consist of freshly-cut logs standing lengthwise. Every year, depending on who you ask and why you ask, 7,000, 8000, or 9,000 trees are cut down to build Bonfire. Seven hundred gallons of diesel fuel are poured on it in order to light it and to make it burn brightly.

Bonfire is spelled with a capital B, like Super Bowl, which it is comparable to when it comes to Aggie traditions. Traditions, and the value of Tradition, dictate Texas A&M culture. In this section, I will describe how the current Bonfire is built, and introduce you to Texas A&M and some of its culture.

The Bonfire is burned every year on the night before the annual grudge football game against the University of Texas at Austin, which used to take place on Thanksgiving, but now takes place on the Friday or Saturday afterwards. The rivalry between the two schools is over a century old and goes far beyond the football field. Bonfire represents every Aggie's undying love for his university and every Aggies' burning desire to beat the hell outta t.u. Aggies call the University of Texas "t.u." out of playful disrespect. If the burning Bonfire stands erect beyond midnight, tradition has it, the Aggies will win the football game.

Bonfire has changed greatly throughout the years (see History). It started out as a pile of trash in 1909. It grew to a monster log stack of almost 110 feet in 1969. And it has been limited in height to about half that record size since the late 1970's. Of course, what the students actually build may exceed the height limit (see Tragedy). The only years in which Bonfire was not burned are 1963 (in honor of President Kennedy, who had been assassinated that same month) and in the tragic year of 1999.

How Bonfire is Built

In April of 1990, Tony Godinez, Carlos Tamez, and Ben Benton made available for students their "Instructional Manual on the Construction of Aggie Bonfire." The title page states, "This is an instructional manual on the construction methods of Aggie Bonfire. It is directed towards the students of Texas A&M University who will be involved in the construction process." Much of the information provided herein about the Bonfire building process and its hierarchy comes from this manual.

Cut

The first part of the Bonfire-building process is called cut, wherein students cut down thousands of trees and haul them back to the campus in trucks. Each year, a landowner who needs or wants his land cleared donates hundreds of acres of forest to the Bonfire. The land is not given to Texas A&M, but students are allowed to clear it, and they do so for free. The land is usually located in an adjacent county, and students often drive an hour or more to get to it.

Equipment needed for cut includes jeans, leather boots, pots, axes, and machetes. Each student or student team must carry out four steps in chopping down and loading each tree.

First, the student must pick an oak or other hardwood tree with a 1-24 inch diameter, and a height usually between 5 and 20 feet. The tree should be as tall and as straight as possible. The tree must also be accessible to be chopped and removed. Second, the student must clear the area around the tree so that he/she can swing an axe at the tree. The third step is called "killing the tree," which simply means chopping the tree down. When the tree falls, the student must yell "headache" several times. The final step is called "topping the tree" and involves chopping the top of the tree off. The tree should be topped off as tall as possible.

The log is then lifted by a group of students and carried to a tractor path. The lifting and setting down of logs is coordinated through a set of "calls." For example, calling a log up includes the following: "Hands on Top," "Hands Underneath" or "Take a Bite;" "1-2-Halfway- Up," "3-4-All-The-Way-UP." Once a log is set down on a tractor path, a tractor comes and pulls the log to the loading site, where a 40-foot flatbed trailer is loaded with two rows of logs. The logs are then driven to the Texas A&M Polo Field, the present Bonfire site.

Stack

The first step in building the Bonfire is the construction and erection of the centerpole. Two telephone poles arrive from the Lufkin Creosote Company (in Lufkin, Texas). The two poles are cut with matching notches so that ten feet of one pole can be spliced together with ten feet of the other pole. The surfaces of the notches are layered with five gallons of wood glue. The connection is then reinforced with steel bolts, and wrapped with four steel plates and 700-800 feet of 3/8-inch steel cable, secured by 1.5 inch steel staples. A ten foot hole in the ground is dug wherein the centerpole is planted.

Four perimeter poles 150 feet from the Bonfire form a square known as "perimeter." These perimeter poles pull taut the guy ropes that will be connected to the centerpole, to help keep it up and straight. For most of the Bonfire history, women were not allowed to enter the perimeter area.

About a week after the poles arrive on campus, the centerpole is raised at exactly 4:03 in the afternoon, signaling the official beginning of the second fundamental phase of Bonfire construction: stack.

According to the building manual, stacking may involve the following equipment: ropes, chains, brooms, chain saws, chain boomers, cant sticks, tractors, axes, axe handles, pulleys, and shovels. The manual states that "more sophisticated and hazardous types of machinery require a full working day of training."

At stack, workers are divided into separate crews according to what tasks they perform. The swamping crew sets the logs parallel and elevated four inches at one end. The butting crew uses chainsaws to cut the stumps off of logs, so that the bottoms are flat; thus, they may stand up with greater balance.

Building the bonfire stack involves wiring six different layers of logs to the centerpole. Logs are moved onto the stack either manually, with a crane, or by pulley. Pulley ropes are run through the top of the centerpole.

The wiring is done with baling wire; about one ton of the wire goes into Bonfire. Each log is wired with three other logs—the log behind it (closer to the centerpole), and two logs beside it. Both the tops and the bottoms of the logs are supposed to be wired together. The logs are wired together by wrapping the wire around the two logs in a figure-8. The wire is tightened with the leverage of a large nail.

Of course, not all wiring can be done from the ground. Students do work above head level by climbing the stack or by sitting on "swings." Benches are suspended from ropes connected to the top of the centerpole. While a student sits on a swing, a log is positioned against the stack. The "swing man" must then cover the log by straddling the log with his/her legs. "This insures that the log will not fall," says the manual. The swing man then wires the log.

Over seventy people can work on the stack at once, according to the manual, if all six stacks are being worked on, and on all four sides of the Bonfire.

Logs on the first stack may be "slammed" by punching them in with the end of another log. This is done to make sure the log is standing even and snug with the other logs.

During the first two weeks of construction, students may work on the Bonfire between 6 P.M. and 6 A.M. The last two weeks or so are known as "Push," during which students work on Bonfire in six-hour shifts around the clock.

The final touches are added on the last two days of construction. The fifth stack is built by the Junior Redpots and the sixth stack is built by the Senior Redpots. The Redpots are the leaders of the Bonfire effort. Finally, an outhouse is placed at the top of the stack. The outhouse is constructed by sophomores in the Aggie Band, and is known as the t.u. tea-house or frat-house. An Austin City Limits sign, which used to be stolen each year, is now painted by Aggie supporters and placed atop the stack. The population on the sign is the year of the sophomore class's graduation.

Burn

The local Texas Engineering Extension Service Fire Training School hoses seven hundred gallons of diesel fuel onto the Bonfire. At dark-thirty (thirty minutes after dark), students march into the perimeter with torches and throw them onto the stack, setting it ablaze. A yell practice is held as the Bonfire burns, during which the football coach and some players make rousing speeches. As many as 70,000 onlookers come to witness Bonfire each year.

Cushing Memorial Library, Texas A&M University

At cut, workers must sometimes use smaller trees to lift bigger trees. This tree required about forty men to carry (1978).

Cushing Memorial Library, Texas A&M University

At Bonfire cut 1979, two cadets grip the neck of a freshman cadet as he strains to do push-ups. "People in the Corps don't think about hazing as hazing. It's just part of being in the Corps."

*With the help of a crane,
Bonfire pots sink centerpole
into its ten-foot hole.*

Cushing Memorial Library, Texas A&M University

Cushing Memorial Library, Texas A&M University

*An Aggie wires logs into the
stack while sitting on a
"swing" hanging from the
top of the centerpole (1987).*

The Bonfire Hierarchy

The student leaders and organizers of the Bonfire effort are known as Redpots. There are nine senior Redpots and nine junior Redpots. Pots, in Bonfire language, are the helmets worn on the heads of Bonfire workers. Redpots wear red helmets. The senior redpots are the true leaders of Bonfire, and the chief of the Redpots is known as Head Stack. The Redpots coordinate the overall effort with an emphasis on public relations and safety. The Junior Redpots, according to one crew chief, are the "workhorses" of the Bonfire, handling all myriad things from fund raising to cutting site preparation.

Beneath the Redpots are five Brownpots, who take care of the equipment and the Bonfire field, among other various things. Other important positions are the two senior centerpole Pots, the two Junior Centepole Pots, the three Climbers, and the three Junior Climbers. Yellowpots coordinate their respective dormitory's participation in Bonfire erection. Buttpots are the Bonfire leaders for each individual Corps unit. The Women's Bonfire Committee (WBC), Bonfire Reload Crew (BRC) and the Emergency Medical Team (EMT) also play integral roles. The Pink Pot coordinates women in providing refreshments for Bonfire workers.

The Student Bonfire Committee consists of the Redpots, the Junior Redpots, Centerpole Pots, Brown Pots, Yellowpots, Buttpots, and the directors of WBC, BRC, and EMT. The senior Redpots are "ultimately responsible for the actions of the committee as a whole."

The primary purposes of the Committee, as written in their constitution, includes fostering "unity, friendship, and school spirit among the students of Texas A&M University," as well as ensuring that "safety is a primary consideration of those participating in and observing the construction and burning of Texas Aggie Bonfire."

The Bonfire Advisory Committee is appointed by the office of the Vice-President of Student Affairs, and includes Head Stack, a Redpot, university advisors, and representatives from BRC, WBC, EMT and the Alcohol Awareness Committee.

The Bonfire Advisor works in the Student Affairs Office, which is under the jurisdiction of the vice-president of student affairs. Of course the v.p. works under the president. The people in charge of Bonfire in 1999 were:

- University President Ray Bowen

- Vice-President for Student Affairs J. Malon Southerland

- Associate Vice-President for Student Affairs (and Former Bonfire Adviser) William Kibler

• Bonfire Adviser Rusty Thompson

• Head Stack, Red Pot Travis Johnson (senior finance major)

Below the pot level are Crew Chiefs and Bonfire Committee Chairs, who are residence hall members who aid Yellow Pots in organizing dorm Bonfire efforts. And then there are the Dead Pots, former pots that may or may not be enrolled at A&M. The Dead Pots help to "maintain traditions" according to the Bonfire Committee; they help to encourage participation in Bonfire activities.

Pot positions are passed down from one generation of Pot to the next by the handing down of the actual helmet from the current Pot to the newly appointed Pot. This new Pot has been working and learning his position for at least a year. Every Pot writes something on his pot, so some pots have many things written on them, some dating back for many years. The new pot-wearer refers to the one who passed him/her the pot as "father" or "mother." The new pot-wearer is then the "son" or "daughter." Thus, there are also grandparents and grandchildren. In this way, Bonfire is a big family, and one with a long history.

Texas A&M Traditions and Institutions

Texas is the only state of the union that was ever its own republic with its own presidents, and national government. Texas's original constitution had a clause that allowed it to secede from the union and revert to independence. This independent nature is mirrored and sustained at Texas A&M, which possesses if not its own sovereign government, at least its own independent-minded culture. Having developed with a unique mission to educate farm boys and also deliver ready-trained men to the U.S. military, and doing so in relative geographic obscurity, A&M culture developed traditions that have been strictly adhered to, despite their constant evolution. A history of Texas A&M is provided in a later chapter. But to read about Bonfire, one has to know of some of the basic traditions of Texas A&M.

First, there is the Aggie Spirit. We will talk more about this in a later chapter. For now, simply understand that it is the inexplicable, indescribable spirit that makes Aggieland what it is.

The Twelfth Man tradition is an incarnation of the Aggie Spirit. Legend has it that during the 1922 Dixie Classic Football Game—played between Texas A&M and national champions, Centre College—the A&M team was so battered that Coach Dana X. Bible faced a player shortage, and may not have had enough players to finish the game. He looked up into the stands at A&M student E. King Gill, a former football and basketball player. Gill walked down from the stands and put on the uniform of an injured player.

Gill never had to enter the game, and the Aggies won the game 22-14. But Gill's readiness to contribute and help the Aggie cause, his readiness to enter the game at any moment, is now referred to as the spirit of the 12th Man. It should be noted that Gill's volunteerism is no small act. In the early days of football, college and high school players died from injuries at an alarming rate.

The Corps of Cadets

To understand Texas A&M, one must understand the Corps of Cadets. For most of Texas A&M history, every student of the University was required to belong to the Corps of Cadets. The Corps is an ROTC program that trains college students for military duty and military office. But most will tell you that the Corps of Cadets is more than an ROTC program.

ROTC programs are most often only two years long, and the Corps is a four-year program. Furthermore, only thirty-five percent of the students in the Corps are contracted with the U.S. government to enter the U.S. military after Corps careers. Many A&M students thus enter and stay in the Corps in order to be a more integral part of A&M traditions and to participate in uniquely Corps of Cadets activities.

The Corps does have a proud military history though. The Corps supplies the U.S. military with more officers than any other military school that is not run by the military itself.

Every major Texas A&M tradition originated from the Corps of Cadets and their members.

Spirit Yells and Midnight Yell Practice

The University, which opened its doors in 1876, did not officially allow women to attend until the 1960's. So it would have been mighty funny if Texas A&M had cheerleaders. Instead, A&M has yell leaders, who lead the crowd in various spirit yells. With a system of hand signals, the next yell is identified to the crowd. Then the students "hump it" by bending over and putting their hands on their knees. They then recite the yells in unison with the yell leaders.

One yell goes "Farmers fight, farmers fight, farmers, farmers fight!" Another goes "Beat the hell outta t.u. (or whoever A&M is playing)." One yell is called up when the opposing coach is standing up, red-faced, and yelling at the referee. The yell is signaled by rotating an imaginary steering wheel, and goes, "Sit down, bus driver!"

Instead of pep rallies, Aggies have yell practice. Midnight Yell Practice occurs at midnight the night before the game. The five yell Leaders are elected by the student body. Yell Leaders used to be the coordinators of the university Bonfire-building effort. The Head Yell Leader used to light Bonfire.

Silver Taps, Muster, and the Memorial Student Center

Silver Taps occurs only if a current Texas A&M student has died since the previous Silver Taps. The ceremony begins at 10:30 pm on the first Tuesday of the month. All the lights of the campus are turned off. The elite Ross Volunteers, a group within the Corps of Cadets, honor the deceased with a 21-gun salute. From the top of the Academic Building, Taps is played in three directions—north, south, and west, "because those who have died will never see the sun rise in the east again."

Muster is a roll call for the dead that occurs every year on April 21. On this date in 1836, the decisive Battle of San Jacinto occurred, "liberating" the new republic of Texas from Mexico. In the late 1890's, the Corps of Cadets used to practice war drills, maneuvers, and games every April 21 at the site of the San Jacinto battlefield. Afterwards, there were parades, and it was decided that on this day, Aggies would honor those who had died during the year.

At Muster, the names of students past and present are called out in a roll call, and a friend of the dead, calls "Here" in his/her place. Muster takes place each year at around four hundred places throughout the world, wherever Aggies are present.

The Memorial Student Center is the student center, and it is dedicated to those Aggies who have died in war. People are asked to remove their hats, caps, and head gear while in the center, in honor of the dead. Because Texas A&M has sent so many men and women to war, and because so many have died, the University has a unique panoply of ceremonies, rituals and memorials for the dead.

Elephant Walk

Another death-related tradition, but in a more figurative sense. On the Tuesday before Bonfire, seniors gather at Kyle Field, and at exactly 99 minutes after noon, they begin to wander the campus "like elephants seeking a place to die because their usefulness to the 12th Man is about to end." The seniors hold mini-yell practices as they lumber their way to the Bonfire site. Meanwhile, the juniors walk from the Bonfire site to Kyle Field.

Hazing

One A&M graduate speaking on a Dallas radio talk show recently referred to Texas A&M as the hazing capital of the world. The Corps of Cadets has long had its own elaborate system of hazing. Some involve Bonfire, and most don't. One of the more interesting acts of hazing is called "quadding," which involves being stripped to one's underwear and having water poured on one's genitals from an upper-story window. As a cadet, former U.S. Secretary of Housing and Urban Development Henry Cisneros was quadded by his "best friends." He called the mindset "primitive but not in a pejorative way."

Dorms and Corps outfits all have their own individual traditional forms of Bonfire hazing. "Groding" in the name of Bonfire is practiced ubiquitously. Students are dragged and plunged into a mud pit known as a "grode hole" in order to get them excited about Bonfire, or simply as a form of initiation. In the past, these grode holes have often contained ingredients other than mud. In fact, the University recently considered designating official grode holes to prevent injuries and holes in the landscaping.

Although hazing is officially prohibited by University rules, it is largely tolerated by the Texas A&M administration. It seems that only when an Aggie is seriously injured does the rule get dragged out and brandished.

Vocabulary

Every distinctive culture has its own language. Here are some key terms you might find useful in reading this text. There are hundreds of other living and dead Aggie slang terms. There is an especially complex system of food vocabulary applied when eating at the Corps mess halls.

> Band Queer (BQ) – Aggie Band member. The Aggie Band is part of the Corps of Cadets.
>
> The Batt – *The Battalion*, the school newspaper.
>
> Corps Turd (CT) – Member of the Corps of Cadets.
>
> Fish Camp – a camp where incoming freshman bond and learn Aggie Traditions.
>
> Good Bull – Something good, funny, or fitting well with Aggie ways.
>
> Non-reg – a student not belonging to the Corps of Cadets.
>
> Old Army – the old days and the way things used to be done.
>
> Old lady – roommate.

Red Ass – something/someone Aggie-traditional; expressing the Aggie Spirit.

Squeeze – squeezing of the left testicle at critical moments of a sports event, to share the team's pain.

Teasip or T-sip – a student of the University of Texas at Austin.

Two-percenter – a person who does not participate in Aggie traditions. Possibly also a dissenter to Aggie culture.

Waggie – female Corps of Cadet member.

Wildcat – the way Aggies "whoop" it up and express excitement.

The 1999
Texas Aggie
Bonfire
Tragedy

The Tragedy

The Fall Semester

It had been a pretty typical Bonfire season. The fall 1999 semester began at Texas A&M. And the Bonfire controversies began.

In late September, even before cut officially began, one of Texas A&M's more red-ass dormitories, Walton Hall, was banned from the building of Bonfire 1999. According to the University, students from Walton had hazed other students from the same dormitory during cut for Bonfire 1998. Specifically, Walton students were cited for forcing new crew chiefs to hug trees while being harassed physically and verbally. According to A&M officials, alcohol, which is prohibited at Bonfire activities, may have played a role in the hazing. Despite the ruling, members of Walton Hall would participate in the building of Bonfire 1999, and even get sent home by Redpots for being intoxicated.

On October 1, Ramiro Reyes, an Aggie senior political science major, was walking home from work. It was around 11 A.M. on a Friday. As Reyes cut across a corner of the polo field, about 200 yards from the Bonfire stack, a student ran up to him screaming obscenities. The student pushed and shoved Reyes off the polo fields, tearing his shirt. As Reyes was being forced off the field, he asked his assailant why he was being attacked. The assailant answered, "Because you're on my field, and I'm a junior Redpot."

Josh Broach, a junior Redpot and industrial distribution major, and

21

Clayton Frady, a junior Centerpole pot and construction science major, were accused of the assault. University Police Chief Bob Wiatt said that Reyes' evidence would not hold up in a court of law, and charges were not pressed. "It was really just my word against theirs, so it's almost what you expect," Reyes told *The Battalion*. "I mean, I love A&M and its traditions, but what I don't like—what it comes down to—is that more respect is given to traditions than people."

Reyes wrote a letter to the administration about the incident, placing it in the context of the general treatment of minority students on the Texas A&M campus. Reyes then met with Vice President of Student Affairs Malon Southerland about the assault, with no tangible results.

Cut officially began on October 2 and continued through early November. Thousands of students drove out to forested land owned by Alternative Fuels, Inc. in adjacent Burleson County to cut down seven thousand trees. According to some workers (in post-collapse witness statements), these trees were noticeably shorter and more crooked than those of previous years. Students would notice during stack unusually large gaps among the oak logs because of their crookedness. Alternative Fuels planned on building a power plant on the land the Aggies cleared.

Like so many October's and November's of the past, Aggies took in the unique pleasures of building the world's largest Bonfire. Of course it was hard work, but therein lay the glory. November, which is usually kind of a monsoon season for East Texas, was this year unusually dry, making the work of Bonfire even more pleasurable, except for those hardcore builders who might revel in the grime and mud of rainy Bonfire work days.

As usual, some students were injured both at cut and stack. Some got bruised up. Others cut or sliced their feet with axes. One student walked into a log being carried by other students and knocked out his two front teeth. Usually, most of the injuries occur at cut, where swinging ax blades and falling logs invariably squash, slice, and break appendages. Furthermore, all three deaths that had been associated with Bonfire had involved cars and tractors. Once the logs had been transported to the campus without any serious traffic accidents, a sigh of relief was usually released.

On November 1, Senior Redpots stood on centerpole as it was lifted by other Bonfire workers. On November 5, the 100-foot centerpole was raised—plunged into a ten-foot hole and stood erect—at precisely 4:03 pm, as is tradition.

Stack began. Somehow, a student's head became wedged between the first level of stack and a log that was being prepared for wiring. The Aggie suffered a minor concussion and cuts. But injuries are to be expected. What seemed unusual was the high rate of mortality among Aggies thus far that fall, as seven Texas A&M students had died as a result of skydiving and traffic accidents. The final cut was done on Saturday November 13. Push began. The Bonfire was set to burn on Thanksgiving night, November 25.

Tuesday November 16, 1999

Between 10 p.m. and 11:30 p.m., student Luigi Angelucci was on the fourth stack of Bonfire directing logs. His Texas A&M Police Department post-collapse witness report tells what happened next

> I was asking the other swingman where he wanted to wire in the next log, when I felt a jolt, I grabbed stack, but then realized that nothing was going to happen, it wasn't falling over or anything. I immediately looked to my left, that's where the noise came from. I saw the end of the crane hitting the cross tie, and knocking off 3-5 inches of wood off the end . . .

The cross ties are a cross of planks nailed into the centerpole above each tier of logs. Logs in each tier are sawed off at each cross tie to give each tier a look of evenness. Hitting a cross tie with enough force could have damaged, or perhaps even fractured, the center pole. The Redpots ascertained, however, that work could continue. According to Vincent Kessler, "We were told that the crane hit one of the cross-ties. Everyone cussed, shook their heads, and got back to work, but everyone said that it was one of the younger guys working on the crane."

Thursday November 18, 1999

On the evening of Wednesday November 17, some Texas newspaper reporters turned in Bonfire stories to be published the next morning, not knowing that their reports on Bonfire hazing by Hart Hall would become almost irrelevant because of what would happen later that night. Battalion photographers had taken pictures of Hart Hall crew chiefs with their wrists and ankles bound while other students poured honey, cat food, and other substances on them.

On the night of Wednesday November 17, at about 10:30 pm, Rusty Thompson, the Texas A&M University Bonfire Advisor, examined the Bonfire. Everything seemed fine. An hour or two later, the four lower guy wires attaching the centerpole to the perimeter poles were cut, so that they would not get in the way of constructing the stack. The four higher ropes remained attached to the centerpole.

Midnight passed. It was now Thursday the 18th, exactly one week until the day of the burning. As the late night shift replaced the evening shift, some students noticed that something didn't quite seem right about the Bonfire. They talked about it for a moment, but no big deal was made about it. Jaclyn Gold, however, had been complaining for days that the stack looked like it was leaning; she had been told by Redpots that it was not leaning. The festive mood was not killed, however, as some students mooned each other.

For almost two and a half hours beyond midnight, seventy or so students worked on the stack of logs while dozens of others worked around it. Students from Corps of Cadets Company K-2, Company D-2, Company C-2, Squadron 16 and Squadron 17, as well as dorm crews from Moses Hall, Mosher Hall, Aston Hall, Dunn Hall, and the Fowler Hughes Keathley complex carried, placed, "slammed," and wired logs onto the stack. Although Walton Hall was officially banned, some of its students were present. Students wired logs to each of the first four tiers, the fourth one towering to 59 feet in the air, around six stories up. It is unclear whether students knew at that time that the Bonfire had already exceeded its height limit.

The final two stacks are not wired until the last two days of construction; the students were well on their way to completing the 89th Bonfire to be burned, and the 92nd Bonfire overall. Three previous ones had not burned. Two of those (1957 and 1994) had fallen before they were completed, and those were rebuilt and burned. The 1963 Bonfire was completely constructed but not burned in honor of President John F. Kennedy, who had been assassinated days before. That Bonfire was dismantled and not rebuilt.

Many of the students, even if they did not know the precise history of Bonfire, were acutely aware of their being at the cutting edge of history, as its blade swept forward through time. Even as they concentrated on such purely physical tasks as wiring trios of fresh logs together, they knew, if only in their hearts, that they were carrying forth a tradition and a ritual of varied but vastly important meanings—meanings perhaps quite slippery to verbal grasping and expression. Perhaps only a few, in their exhaustion and their intoxication with the work itself, could articulate at that hour an eloquent summation of the meaning of Bonfire and the Aggie Spirit. It didn't matter. The meaning and history of Bonfire was felt, at that moment, as it had been felt by dozens of Bonfire generations past.

Head Stack Travis Johnson and Redpot Zac Dietrich had been walking the stack since 10:30. Everything was going well, and Johnson would later report that he saw no alcohol at the site. Some workers were moving smaller logs to behind the Redpot shack; these were to be used for the fifth and sixth stacks of Bonfire. A crane operated by student Mike Rusek was helping students place logs on the south and east sides as the north side had been overloaded with logs. Some students were "slamming" logs into place, swinging the butt end of a log into the lower half of a log so that it stands even and snug with the others on stack. According to Nathan Knowles, a majority of the logs were double-wired onto stack. Some would comment later that the wiring was shoddy and loose.

William Richard Stepler IV told A&M police that he "showed up at midnight and was talking with some of the JRP's and we comment on how [Bonfire] was looking good just a slight lean, but symmetrical." Apparently the Junior Redpots did notice a tilt in the stack.

At about 1:50 or 2:00, according to his witness report, Jonathon Wilson made a comment to a Junior Redpot and to those around him that the Bonfire was shaking slightly. The Junior Redpot told Wilson that the Bonfire shakes a little when a log is placed on first or second stack. Wilson took his word for it, but thought the shaking unusual because he had never recalled such movement before.

Meanwhile, junior engineering technology major Jerry Self had just been named a Brownpot. Jerry Self, senior Brownpot Jeremy Frampton (Self's "father"), Christopher Breen '97 (a former Brownpot), Milton "Chip" Thiel, and possibly one or more Redpots (according to one report) climbed up to the top of the fourth stack in order to hold a ritual for the passing of the brown pot from one generation to another. Cashell Donahoe stated later, "When I was working on stack, an old Brown pot climbed past me, and I could smell the alcohol on him."

Jim Daniel, who was working on the fourth stack, said that each of the pots on the fourth stack "had one beer. However, none of the ones I talked to—3 of them—were intoxicated. We had clear, lucid conversations." Another student said that the pots on the fourth stack "were talking and joking and there was a little horseplay, but nothing dangerous."

It was Brittny Allison's first time on stack. Her friend from the Corps of Cadets was to teach her how to wire logs in. They took the first available swing "and chose the one that was on 2nd stack." Her friend instructed her "on how to cut the wire and make figure eights and told me to wait for a log." He then left her, as he did something on the ground. Brittny Allison was ready to wire logs in after this short training session, except that it took a long time for the log to be delivered by the crane. In the meantime, she said hello to friends below her "to show them I was up in a swing."

At about 2:28 A.M., Centerpole pot Thomas Kilgore was patrolling the base of the stack, enforcing safety standards:

> I was 3-4 ft away when I noticed first stack logs start to move
> slowly away from me. That night I was a little tired and a bit hungry

so I thought I was going to faint. I shook my head and took a few steps back to get a better view to see if it was actually moving. There was NO noise at all when it first started moving. There were at least three seconds when it was moving and no one knew it was actually falling. At this point I ran along stack on the SW side to get a better view. After 2-3 seconds the whole stack hit a certain angle, plane, and started to fall fast [. . .] There were not any noises until it hit that angle.

Some students heard nothing at all. Some heard one loud crack or pop. Others heard two in quick succession. The northwestern guy rope snapped as Bonfire tilted toward the southeast. Just as Paul Fulham slammed a log into the first stack, according to his witness report, the first stack twisted clockwise and the second stack counterclockwise as the whole stack toppled over. It fell "like a domino," according to a student standing outside of perimeter.

Some students fell from as high as the fourth stack. Others elected to jump from where they were. Many made a split-second decision to hold onto the nearest log and ride the Bonfire down. Within a few seconds after the loud pop, the entire Bonfire stack, partially fallen apart and partially intact, crashed into the ground. Dust kicked up everywhere and the perimeter lights flickered out within seconds. In this darkness, some survivors screamed in terror while others called out the names of their friends. Some struggled to remove themselves from under the logs and ropes while still others could not.

At the time of the accident, two men were each operating a crane to help place logs on the stack. One was an employee of H.B. Zachry, a construction company that had donated equipment and personnel to help build Bonfire. The other operator was student Michael Rusek, and his witness report follows.

> Was operating crane on S. side of stack. Had just picked up log from SW side of stack. Picked log up, I heard a loud cracking and popping and saw stack falling towards my crane. I jumped out and then set the log down and turned machine off. The logs fell through the front windshield and land on roof.

Rachael Rene Hines of Keathley dormitory described to police what happened at 2:28 A.M.:

> I was wiring in a log when I heard a cracking noise. The log I had my arms wrapped around began to move away from me. I looked up to my swingman (I was standing on the ground) to tell him to hold the log when I realized the whole stack was falling away from me.

Knowing all of my dorm was on the top on the opposite (falling) side, I didn't hesitate in running around the right side to find them. Stack had fallen on the crane, and as I walked around it I came upon two people I believe were already dead. Neither was moving, both were bloody and broken-looking. I saw many others trapped before being taken away by friends.

Most all of those who were able to helped and comforted the injured and trapped. One Aston student took his own shirt off to warm Caleb Hill as he went into shock. Others helped those with broken bones climb off of stack. Unfortunately, many of those who were pinned by logs were beyond help. One student described coming upon a student struggling to breathe because his chest was pinned by the knot of a log. The first student called out for help and when help came, he walked away because he thought that the entrapped student would not be extricated in time, and could not bear to watch him die.

Other students reported walking into a "cave" that had formed between the fallen stack and the ground. By crawling into this space, students could look up and see two fellow students entrapped within the logs of the Bonfire. One had died instantly. The other was still alive, but died by the time rescuers arrived.

The Rescue Effort

University policeman Scott Chambless arrived at the stack site at 2:31 A.M., and officer Al Guttierez arrived within a few minutes thereafter. When Guttierez got there, the first thing he saw was "approximately 20 to 40 people running around screaming." Chambless had already started moving people away from stack, which he thought could continue falling. More officers arrived immediately after Guttierez, and they began to draw a perimeter around the northeast side of Bonfire. According to Guttierez, "there was a minor flare up of the students" but the conflict "was handled."

As Chambless and Guttierez arrived on the scene, ambulances were on their way. Graduate student Mandy Neill, who lives near the campus, recalls waking up at 2:30 to hear what sounded like "every ambulance in the city" rushing past. Even people several miles away at the Texas A&M Riverside campus had heard the crack of the center pole and the collapse of the thousands of tons of logs.

One College Station policeman had seen a student trapped underneath a log. He was still alive. The officer, unable to do anything, asked the student to give a sign that he could hear the officer. "He gave me thumbs up, but his eyes went blank and he passed away," the officer later reported, "I checked for a pulse, but could not find one, and there was no way to perform CPR."

The first ambulances and fire trucks arrived as police were securing a perimeter around the fallen stack. They found twenty-three students who were injured but free from the stack. Triage was set up immediately. Emergency medical personnel found three deceased students beside the stack. They were the three Brownpots—Jerry Don Self, Jeremy Richard Frampton, and Christopher David Breen—who had been standing on the highest constructed stack of logs. Emergency personnel were told of another eight deceased students trapped within the wreckage. And there were six students trapped alive.

Texas A&M police officer Roger Paxton was one of the first on the scene. In a November 24 report, he wrote that he was alerted to the Bonfire collapse at 2:42 A.M. When he got there, his first assignment was to maintain the east perimeter. "During that time," he reported, "I had several red pots and brown pots approach me to ask if there was anything they could do. Several of the individuals I spoke with had an odor of an alcoholic beverage on their breath. One of the red pots wanted to know when they could start stacking Bonfire again."

At 3:15 A.M., Billy Parker of the Texas Task Force Urban Search and Rescue team arrived on the scene. The team specializes in rescue operations involving collapsed structures. With Bryan's Assistant Fire Chief Mike Donoho, Parker began devising a plan to remove the students trapped within the stack. Some local members of the team, from the Bryan and College Station fire departments, had already arrived and more were to come.

Lieutenant Stanley of the Bryan Fire Department sized up the situation to the rescue team. Five students were trapped under the logs (apparently one having been removed). The stack had fallen in a southeastern direction. Three of the trapped were on the east side of the stack, and two were on the west side. One student on the east side had his pelvis pinned by logs, and was on his way to being freed by College Station Firemen. Other students had their legs and arms pinned. On the west side, a student referred to as Patient #5 had his entire right side pinned by logs, and only his left arm was visible to rescuers.

Because of the structure of Bonfire, with its clusters of logs wired together, it didn't collapse like a pile of matches, according to Kem Bennett, director of the Texas Engineering Extension Service and Texas Task Force I. There were pockets of space in which survivors could have avoided being crushed. But it was a matter of getting to any survivors before their injuries killed them. The Texas Task Force reported that "with the Bonfire collapse,

28

the construction of the stack posed a variety of problems that had to be addressed to include but not limited to: how the logs were wired together; the stability of the collapse; likely survival places; the shear amount of logs to be moved or cut to effect the rescues."

"It's a slow, slow process," College Station Fire Department spokesperson Bart Humphreys said. "It's like pick-up sticks. Lifting each log is critical and every move affects another log. We don't want to further injure anyone or risk hurting the workers. They are taking this apart log by log." Some logs were pinned in the ground in such a way that moving them or logs sitting on them might cause a major secondary collapse.

Rescuers cut wires and removing logs by hand, one by one. When Corps of Cadet members heard about the collapse, they rushed to the scene with pliers and pots, but they were told that it would be better for them to stay outside of the perimeter and watch the excruciatingly slow process. The first two trapped living students (both on the east side) were removed at 3:30 A.M. and 4:00 A.M. and rushed to the hospital.

At 4:18 A.M. the third student was removed from the east side. At this time, Redpots, who had been allowed inside the police perimeter to help with rescue efforts, asked for further assistance from students to help remove the logs. Redpots gave orders through the Bonfire chain of command, and while lifting logs, Bonfire workers used their traditional coordinating calls. Thousands of A&M students gathered around the perimeter throughout the morning, afternoon and following night, but only some were allowed to help. Texas A&M engineering professor Pete Keating was called to the scene to help with devising ways to rescue students safely.

By 6:37, the fourth trapped student, who had his arm pinned, was extricated from the west side of the stack. The final student, Patient #5, was John Comstock, a nineteen year-old freshman from Richardson, Texas. He had been working on the fourth tier of the stack when it shook and fell. When rescuers found him, they asked him for his phone number. Using the only exposed part of his body, his left hand and arm, he signaled his mother's number. He could not speak well because the log he had ridden fifty-five feet down to the ground was now on his head. Comstock would occasionally give the thumbs-up "gig'em, Aggies" sign with his free left hand.

By the time the fourth student had been removed, Comstock had been in excruciating pain for four hours. But at least he was still alive; when a tag was first put on him, he thought that rescuers might "sacrifice" him in order to save the others. College Station Lieutenant Paul Gunnels tried to help Comstock accept the fact that "he would be here for several hours and he needed to relax as much as possible." Hot packs kept his body temperature up, oxygen was administered, and goggles protected his eyes from dust.

As log after log was removed from the pile atop Comstock, more and more rescue workers filed in from throughout the state. More than a hundred rescue workers from around the state worked in shifts throughout the first twenty-four hours after the accident. Rescuers came from the College Station and Bryan police departments, the Austin Police's K-9 Search and Rescue unit, the Army National Guard Bryan Unit, the U.S. Army Reserve 420th Engineering Brigade, and the A&M Emergency Medical Service. Log moving equipment was donated by Steely Lumber Co. of Huntsville.

At 7 A.M., log removal stopped. Comstock waited. Rescuers were concerned that further movement might cause the stack to collapse further. Structures called "rakers" were set up by the Urban Search and Rescue Team to stabilize the stack as they removed logs. These rakers were constructed on site in the hours after the accident.

Shortly after 7 A.M., Alton Rogers of Rogers Engineering Services of College Station was called by David Godbey, Assistant Director of the Physical Plant, to assist with log removal and the rescue of Comstock. According to Rogers' report, "the extraction of John was complicated by the fact that one victim was pinned next and slightly above his position in the stack." This deceased victim had to be removed first before getting to Comstock. The process was "painstakingly slow," according to Rogers, but the slow pace was "necessary for the safety of the rescue crews and for John Comstock."

By 7:45, with the "raker" structures set up to prevent collapse, log removal began again. At 8:58, the dead student near Comstock was extricated from the stack. At 9:04 A.M., six and a half hours after the collapse, John Comstock was pulled out from the collapsed Bonfire stack. Lt. Gunnels asked Comstock "to show them the thumbs up (Gig'em Sign), he did and all the aggies started clapping and yelling with happiness." He was rushed off to College Station Medical Center.

At 9:15, the rescuers stopped all activity and moved all nonessential personnel to the outer perimeter. They planted detection devices among the logs, and asked for silence from the crowd. These devices produce electrical charges from minute motion, and can detect sounds as faint as breathing, tapping or a finger scratching on wood. Once a sound is detected, the devices are moved closer to the sound. This is repeated until the person is located. Using this method, according to the official Bonfire Rescue Operation timeline, it was determined that there was "still possible live patient in south end of stack." Newspapers reported that tapping and moaning could be heard by the listening devices, and that rescuers honed in on these

Photo credit: Wilber A. Williams

Students arrived at the site of the accident and could only watch and wait as rescue workers tried to save the lives of their friends and fellow Aggies.

Cushing Memorial Library, Texas A&M University

Collapsing in a southeasterly direction, some of the Bonfire logs fell on a crane operated by a student. The crane was in the process of lifting a log to the stack; the log hangs vertically in the foreground.

Rescue workers work frantically to remove a survivor from the wreckage. A female student Bonfire worker helps them.

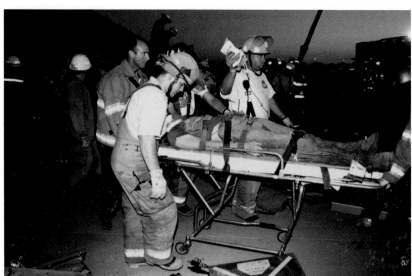

With his neck in a brace and his body strapped into a stretcher, the injured student is taken to an awaiting ambulance.

Photo credit: Wilber A. Williams

As the Bonfire is being dismantled at an excruciatingly slow pace, students sit through the night awaiting news.

Cushing Memorial Library, Texas A&M University

Rescue workers remove logs from atop one of the deceased students. A white sheet marks where the body lies, and also keeps it out of sight. The broken centerpole stretches along the fallen stack, distinguished by the white tape wrapped around it.

Cushing Memorial Library, Texas A&M University

The centerpole broke where a set of cross-ties had been nailed into it.

A solemn Bonfire builder stands before the parking lot next to the fallen stack on the night of the accident.

Photo credit: Wilber A. Williams

Cushing Memorial Library, Texas A&M University

The 1994 Bonfire should have been a warning. The stack shifted and cracked centerpole. As the stack began falling apart, Texas A&M dismantled it. In an all-out effort, students rebuilt the Bonfire in seven days, in time for the football game against UT Austin.

sounds. It is unclear when or how it was determined that morning that there were no more living students trapped within the wreckage.

Although they thought they had heard tapping, they later discovered that the sounds they heard were probably caused by debris in the stack, "since no additional [living] victims were found," according to Rogers.

At ten o'clock, rescuers met and decided to set up three teams to remove logs from the stack using cranes. A fourth crane would arrive that afternoon. Students were also allowed again to remove logs from the stack. The Texas A&M football team cancelled practice in order to help remove logs from the massive pile. Hundreds of other male and female Aggies helped with the rescue efforts.

Every once in a while, students were asked to step back. A sheet would be lifted to shield a body being removed from the stack and placed on a stretcher. These victims were carried into hearses waiting at the perimeter. Catholic and Episcopalian priests were on hand to give last rites. Bodies that had not been removed from the wreckage but were visible from outside were covered with white sheets as much as possible. More media than Bryan-College Station had ever seen had converged upon the Bonfire site, and they were denied any gruesome pictures.

There were plenty of sad sights. Pots that had been knocked off of the heads of Bonfire workers sat on the ground beneath the fallen logs. Jackets and shirts were strewn along some of the tree trunks.

Five bodies were removed between 11:42 A.M. and 1:40 pm. According to the Rogers report, four or five victims were found in the third and fourth stacks of Bonfire, and the last of these, a female, was removed between 3 and 4 pm. A male and a female student were still trapped between the first and second stacks. A decision was made to allow a knuckle boom loader to remove logs in order to protect rescue workers. The operator, James Gibson, was extremely skilled and expedited the process, picking up three to six logs at a time.

Even so, the number and weight of the logs were immense, and the male victim was not extricated until 10:30 pm. The female victim, Miranda Adams, was located only three to five feet away from the male victim, but it took another two hours or so to remove her body. The knuckle boom operator continued working until the entire stack had been dismantled around 2:30 A.M. Friday November 19, twenty-four hours after the collapse.

Almost two days after being removed from the stack, seventeen year-old freshman Tim Kerlee died of injuries caused by the Bonfire collapse. In the days after his death, news circulated that as he was still trapped amongst the logs, mortally wounded, he directed rescuers to other injured

Aggies. Kerlee's death brought the number killed to twelve. In a sad twist on words, he became the Aggies' Twelfth Man, and many emphasized that he did embody the spirit of the Twelfth Man by his efforts in helping to save the lives of other Aggies.

John Comstock spent 83 days in intensive care in College Station. Most of that time he spent fighting off death. He was sedated and breathing through a respirator for weeks. He had suffered internal injuries requiring surgery, and his left leg had to be amputated under the knee. His right wrist was broken, and it was not until January that he began speaking on a regular basis. On February 8, he was transported to Dallas to rehabilitate for two months and remain close to his mother. He plans on returning to Texas A&M for college, but does not wish to work on another Bonfire.

The Victims

Within the confines of this book, there is not space enough to begin describing the lives and dreams of the twelve Aggie students who died in the collapse of the Bonfire. Upon researching their lives, one comes to the understanding that they were among the best and brightest of the school, and that they embodied the true Aggie Spirit.

> Miranda Denise Adams, 19, sophomore biomedical sciences major, of Santa Fe, Texas.

> Christopher David Breen, 25, graduated from Texas A&M in 1997 with a degree in agricultural development, of Austin, Texas.

> Michael Steven Ebanks, 19, freshman aerospace engineering major, of Carrollton, Texas.

> Jeremy Richard Frampton, 22, senior psychology major, of Turlock, California.

> Jamie Lynn Hand, freshman environmental design major, of Henderson, Texas.

> Christopher Lee Heard, freshman pre-engineering major to pursue ocean engineering, Houston, Texas.

> Timothy Doran Kerlee, 17, freshman mechanical engineering major from Bartlett, Tennessee.

Lucas John Kimmel, 19, biomedical science major as a precursor to veterinary medicine, of Corpus Christi, Texas.

Bryan Allan McClain, 19, freshman agriculture major, of San Antonio, Texas.

Chad Anthony Powell, 19, sophomore computer engineering major, of Keller, Texas.

Jerry Don Self, 20, junior engineering technology major, of Arlington, Texas.

Nathan Scott West, sophomore oceanography major, of Bellaire, Texas.

Coming Together

Within hours after 2:30 A.M. on November 18, the Texas A&M campus, one of the largest in the nation, compressed itself into the block of land known as the Polo Field. The collective heart of the student body seemed to be buried in those fields. Students weeped and sobbed uncontrollably, prayed, and lay prone, in agony. Some cried for friends and loved ones. Others cried for people they knew nothing of—only that they were fellow Aggies. To help each other bear the burdens of grief, Aggies hugged each other, wiped each others tears, and spoke to each other words of comfort.

Some Aggies were lucky enough to help in the rescue efforts. We can never know what contributions this aid might have made to the saving of lives. Were logs removed faster because of Aggies' help? Did the fact that Aggies were close by give a degree of hope and comfort to those trapped beneath the logs?

Whatever the answer to those questions are, the Rescue coordinators from Texas Task Force One certainly thought the rescue plan was executed well, the contributions of Aggies notwithstanding. Urban Search & Rescue Search Team Manager, Pat Barrett wrote in his rescue report that the extrication of the victims was "completed in a 24-hour period with the hard work of many different agencies, as well as the tireless dedication [of] all the workers involved." Task Force One Rescue Program Supervisor/ Rescue Specialist, James Hyles Jr. was more explicit. He wrote about his experience, "Although command was in its early stages everything was working well. There were bonfire staff working right along with the rescue operations. I noticed total leadership among all personnel there. In conclusion, what I saw was that everyone was doing all they could to rescue and help in any way possible. This was totally a TEAM EFFORT everyone pulled together as professionals to overcome this tragedy."

By 2:00 pm, St. Joseph's hospital in Bryan had used over 200 pints of blood in treating Bonfire patients. More blood was to be used in treatment and surgery, including amputations. Thousands of people donated blood from Texas A&M, UT Austin, Dallas, Waco, Tulsa, and various parts of Texas. Alumni and Texas citizen alike lined up sometimes for hours to donate blood. Over 300 people could be seen waiting at the Red Cross center on University Drive in College Station. Even Longhorn Senator Kay Bailey Hutchison was photographed with the tube in her arm. As parents and alumni learned of the tragedy, many drove to College Station to help rescue efforts and to comfort students.

Dozens of restaurants and community members sent food to the rescue site. Sororities passed out hot food, and one student even gave away clothes from his own closet so that those at the rescue site could keep warm. Hotels offered free lodging for families of the killed and injured. A Houston cellular phone company donated fifty phones to the rescue team and to students. Meanwhile, community members flooded the phone lines of the College Station Chamber of Commerce inquiring how they could help.

Student Meghan Smith commented on the efforts, "It just shows how much of a family the Aggies are. When one Aggie is in trouble, there's always someone there. When fifty are in trouble, they have two cities and then some. Everyone pulls together to get through it."

Prayer was one way to deal with the tragedy. Each time a body was carted away from the Bonfire field, hundreds of rescuers and students huddled, kneeled, and prayed. Churches prepared special prayer sessions and masses for students.

By 4pm on the day of the accident, more than a thousand students had spontaneously congregated around Rudder Fountain to pray for the Bonfire victims. Holding hands and pleading and imploring God both silently and aloud, the scene moved Vice-President J. Malon Southerland— who watched from his eighth floor office—to tears.

As students lay in hospital beds struggling for their lives, their friends and dorm-mates set up twenty-four hour vigils to stay by their sides or in the hospitals, supporting their parents.

On the night of the accident, a memorial was held which 14,000 people attended. And on the night of the Bonfire, a candlelight vigil was held in its place. More than 70,000 people attended the vigil and the subsequent yell practice.

On the Monday after the accident, the UT Hex Rally, held annually as a pep rally for the A&M game, was replaced by a Unity Rally, at which A&M and UT students honored and remembered those who had died in the Bonfire tragedy. More than 10,000 students, graduates and administrators from both universities burned white candles—the color shared by both schools—and held up their respective hand gestures (the A&M "gig'em" and the UT "hook'em") in solemn harmony. In the century-long rivalry between the school, no one had ever thought that such a linking of arms could be possible, but, as one Texas Aggie said, "This is a sign of loyalty that can happen with Texans."

At halftime of the A&M-UT football game, the UT Band—instead of stomping out and blasting their usual marching tunes—stood still in the middle of the field and played "Amazing Grace" and "Taps." The UT Band brought down their own orange flags and raised maroon Texas A&M flags. The acts of respect and consolation prompted some A&M students to write in letters and online bulletins that UT students had shown more class than one would ever expect. Aggies and Longhorns reciprocated due respect and helped to strengthen perhaps a permanent newfound bond between the universities.

On the first Tuesday of December, Silver Taps was convened. The lights of the university were turned off. Thousands gathered in pitch darkness and absolute silence in the Academic Mall. The Aggie trumpeter in the Academic Building was to play Taps three times. As he played the second time, a train began lurching by on the tracks along the western edge of the central campus. The train wailed in reponse to the solemn notes of the trumpet. The trumpet and the train exchanged cries as students stood and listened. As the trumpeter finished playing Taps toward the south, the train also rested its voice and lumbered its way out of town.

From Tragedy to Living Myth

As the work of Joseph Campbell has shown, every society and culture—even individual communities—need myths. Myths are those stories that dramatize and make meaning of the world around us. Creation stories are often considered myths. Almost all hero tales are myths. Aggie lore contains a great number of wonderful myths, the greatest probably being the story of the Twelfth Man.

Along with myths, ceremony—which goes hand in hand—helps to lend honor to both life and death. Muster, Silver Taps, the Memorial

Student Center, even the various graves of the Aggie mascots serve to create an air of honor and dignity to the lives and deaths of Aggies. It is partially through these rituals and legends, then, that Texas A&M has created for itself through one hundred and twenty plus years of somewhat isolated existence its own unique system of cultural values and activities.

When the Bonfire tragedy struck, Texas A&M was in complete and utter shock and disbelief. In the wake of the emergency, students, faculty, administration, and community all came together in a truly heroic effort to save as many lives and prevent as much permanent injury as possible.

The vast majority of students had never witnessed so much blood and death in one place before, and the last place they would have expected it was at their university. A good portion of the community and student population assumed that the Bonfire would come to an end. The logic of the "story" that had emerged was that this was a tremendous tragedy, one that few had ever even conceived could occur at an American university, and naturally the community would do whatever it took to prevent anything close to such a calamity from ever happening again—even abolishing Bonfire.

But almost immediately after the tragedy, Aggies began re-interpreting it through the lens of Aggie culture. Furthermore, natural mental defense mechanisms favor less distressing interpretations of extremely emotionally threatening situations. Aggies began interpreting the tragedy through the rituals and through the "legend-making"traditions of Texas A&M.

Right after the accident, at around 3 A.M., Student Body President Will Hurd rushed to the Bonfire site. Only three students killed in the accident had been extricated, but it was obvious that more bodies would be removed. Hurd began helping to account for the living so that rescue workers could figure out who remained under the stack. As he encouraged others to write down who from their dormitories and Corps outfits had survived, he also began to organize a memorial service.

Aggies are known for—and they are rightly proud of—their memorial services. Silver Taps and Muster are honorable ceremonies. Hurd was only following in the Aggie tradition of memorial-making. But did he have to start doing so while bodies were still being extricated from the logs? One student that early morning asked him the same question. He answered, "It's already time for the healing to begin." On this subject, one former student emailed Dr. Bowen the following:

> I am a former student and very proud to call myself an Aggie. However, I do not understand why my beloved university would see fit to have a memorial service for our tragically deceased before all of

our kids are even pulled from the bottom of the stack. I am hurt, and sickened, as I am sure you must be as well. Why?

By 6:50 A.M., the Texas A&M email news service had announced to the community that the location of the memorial service had changed to the Reed Arena, so that more people could be accommodated.

At 7:30 that evening, most local radio and television stations broadcast the memorial service. Within Reed Arena, more than 14,000 people—including President George Bush—packed the space. President Bowen told the crowd, "This has been a day of unspeakable grief and sorrow. Our sorrow is great. Our suffering is immense. We must continue to support one another during these difficult times." He said, "All of us cried as we watched our loved ones being removed from the stacks of logs. We prayed that all would be alive but they were not. We prayed that all of the injuries would be minor, but they were not. We prayed that our agony and our grief would end quickly, but it has not."

Hurd himself addressed the listeners, "A lot of people have asked themselves today why it happened. But together, we have tried to look at this as an opportunity to embrace one another as an Aggie family." He said, "We must celebrate the way in which these Aggies lived."

University of Texas Student Body Vice President Eric Opiela later wrote of the memorial:

> As part of the UT delegation, we sat on the floor of Reed Arena and immediately following the end of the service, I heard this rustling sound behind me.
>
> I looked over my shoulder and saw the sight of close to 20,000 students spontaneously putting their arms on their neighbor's shoulders, forming a great circle around the arena.
>
> The mass stood there in pin-drop silence for close to five minutes, then from somewhere, someone began to hum quietly the hymn, "Amazing Grace." Within seconds, the whole arena was singing.
>
> I tried, too—I choked; I cried. This event brought me to tears. It was one of—if not the—defining moments of my college career. I learned something tonight. For all us Longhorns to discount A&M in our never-ending rivalry, we need to realize one thing. Aggieland is a special place, with special people.
>
> It is infinitely better equipped than we are at dealing with a tragedy such as this for one simple reason. It is a family. It is a family that cares for its own, a family that reaches out, a family that is unified in the face of adversity, a family that moved this Longhorn to tears.

Indeed, Texas A&M, more than any other large American university is a family. But it is also a family that loves to talk about how much of a family it is, and how much each member sacrifices for the benefit of the larger whole. Therein lies the process of myth-creation.

Within hours of the collapse of the Bonfire stack, A&M students and alumni began saying that we must continue to build the hell outta Bonfire now because Aggies had now given their lives so that this Bonfire—and future Bonfires—might burn brightly and proudly. The tradition must live. One Aggie was quoted by U.S. News & World Report as saying that "if not in size, but in spirit, the bonfire will be even bigger now."

The Bonfire was becoming bigger. It was becoming bigger because students, alumni, and probably some politicians and administrators were seeing two types of heroism emerging from the tragedy. First there was the heroism of the deceased students. They had sacrificed their time, their sweat, their grades, and now their lives, so that one of the greatest Aggie traditions could live. The second type of heroism was the student response to the death of the original heroes. The students and the larger community came together to help save the lives of students, serve the injured and the families of the deceased, prop each other up in a time of great pain, honor the dead, and demonstrate to the whole world what it means to be an Aggie.

Aggies knew that a "coming together" of an extreme breed had been created when they joined with UT students to produce the Unity Rally (in place of UT's anti-A&M Hex Rally) at the UT campus. Aggies knew that something special was happening when 70,000 people gathered around the fenced-off Bonfire site on Thanksgiving night for a candlelight vigil. They knew they were coming together for a greater reason than football when they went to the Yell Practice after the candlelight vigil, and they didn't do the traditional, "Beat the Hell outta t.u." yell. The A&M football team and the A&M crowd came together the next day to make a dramatic comeback and win the football game.

"Coming together" became the theme of Bonfire-related ceremonies, remarks made to the press, speeches at major events, and conversations between individual Aggies. Indeed, the moments of unity brought a lump to even the most die-hard two-percenters. Nonetheless, sometimes when Aggies and their representatives spoke of the coming together, it took on the tone of self-congratulation. But it was so much more comfortable to talk about the coming together than it was to talk about one thousand pound logs falling on students, some of whom may have been drunk.

A&M did deserve to pat itself on the back for its cohesiveness during a time of crisis. But praising their own unity not only distracted them, but also put into place a critical piece of the myth, which goes something like this: Twelve heroic Aggies died in order to build the 1999 Bonfire. Aggieland came together to save as many people as possible and to honor the dead. The most important way that Aggieland must now honor the dead is by ensuring that future generations are allowed to burn the Bonfire.

This ongoing myth is beautiful in its simplicity and its tautological internal logic, just as all beautiful stories are. This hero-story will be re-told for generations yet to come, as well it should be. The only problem is that it seems to have developed prematurely, just as the memorial may have been conceived and realized a bit early. The Aggie Spirit is an eager and go-to-it kind of spirit, so that should not be surprising.

Whatever the reason, the new Bonfire myth has become the central force in the debate about the future of the Bonfire. Those who oppose the continuation of the Bonfire are now going against the wishes of martyrs, or at least victims. Those who emphasize that the twelve students died in a preventable accident are now stripping away the meaning of their deaths; after all, they died for Bonfire (they even lived for Bonfire). The myth focuses our attention on the wishes of the dead and their families (all of whom wish understandably that the Bonfire should continue). To a degree, the focus is taken off of the nasty process of determining how the accident occurred, who is responsible, and how in the future it can be prevented. Ironically, if Aggieland does not concentrate on these questions and on the question of what alternatives exist for Bonfire, we will inevitably have to incorporate into the Bonfire mythology yet more myths having to do with young Aggies, death and sacrifice.

Early Lobbying

It seemed the lobbying campaign began immediately after the Bonfire stack collapsed. Students talking to reporters at the site said that they hoped the tradition would continue. By 10 A.M. on the morning of the accident, President Bowen had already received several pleas from students and alumni to continue burning the Bonfire. At 7:08 A.M., a student emailed President Bowen with the following plea (spelling and grammar have been left in their original forms for all emails):

> I know that TAMU had a tragedy today involving bonfire, and several students realize that due to this we may not have bonfire. We would like to request that we have a small bonfire and make it a candle-light vigil to honor those involved in the tradegy. Please consider this before canceling bonfire completely.

This request was a typical one that Dr. Bowen received over the days following the accident. Students and alumni wanted the Bonfire to burn despite the tragedy. Even a small Bonfire would be better than none at all, and many made suggestions as to how the burning could be a tribute to those who had been killed by the accident.

The following email was sent at 8:43 on November 18, about six hours after the accident:

> My prayers and thoughts will be with the Aggies' families who lost their loved ones in this morning's tragedy and with other Aggies

everywhere whose hearts have been wounded. Like Silver Taps, Midnight Yell and even the tradition of saying "Howdy," Bonfire embodies the tradition, a feeling that is unequaled at ANY other university in the country, of our desire to be unified.

I'm certain this question will come up: I do not think we should end the tradition of bonfire. It is a dangerous undertaking, one that those who died surely thought about, at least as much as a young person can fathom such potentially fatal consequences. An investigation should take place, safety and construction procedures should be reviewed and probably stricter working conditions should be enforced. But let's keep things in perspective; of all the dangers we face daily, and through all the years bonfire has been built, today's deadly event is, however difficult this is to grasp at the moment, extremely unusual.

Let's prevent this from happening in the future, and let Aggie traditions, including bonfire, live.

The writer brought up an important point, one that may not serve to bolster his conclusion: Just how much risk could the students' fathom was involved in working on the Bonfire stack? The following email was received by President Bowen at 8:53 on the morning of the accident:

Aggie Bonfire collapsed last night at 2:30 A.M. 4 dead. several still trapped in wreckage. One was just pulled out alive. 30+ injured, but ok. Univ Press release sez Bonfire cancelled. I'm up for a giant Silver Taps the night before the game. Let pray for those still trapped and the families of the deceased Aggies.

The sender then quoted Psalm 23. The tone he took when he wrote that he was "up for a giant Silver Taps" betrayed a sort of pleasure or gratification he might get from attending these Aggie memorials for the dead. The following is an excerpt of an email sent by a recent graduate to President Bowen at 9:05 the morning of the accident:

Their deaths were tragic, but if we allow critics to kill the Bonfire experience, then our brothers died in vain. I would like my children to know what Bonfire is like. I want them to feel the power and camaraderie Bonfire fosters. Bonfire is such an integral part of Texas A&M that I can't imagine a Texas A&M of the future without Bonfire. Please don't rob my children of that experience.

Dr. Bowen, these are troubled times at Texas A&M. Leaders are needed. Friends are required. Its time for the Aggie Family to show why we say, "from the outside looking in you can't understand it . . . from the inside looking out, you can't explain it." Don't let those Aggies deaths go for not. Allow future generations to enjoy the masterpiece that is Texas Aggie Bonfire!

Like many Aggie alumni, a man who graduated in the 1970's (writing at 10:12 A.M. in an email entitled "Bonfire!") offered his help. He then wrote, "My son is a senior in high school and his first question was, is this the end of Bonfire?" Bonfire is of such import that on the morning of the tragedy, the first question of children who have not yet attended A&M is whether or not Bonfire will continue.

At 10:41 A.M., a local medical doctor wrote to Bowen to suggest a two-year moratorium on Bonfire in honor of the victims. He added that this break would still allow all students to have at least two bonfire experiences over a four-year period.

Shortly after noon on the day of the accident, proposals for Bonfire alternatives began pouring in to President Bowen. The first proposal, sent by a true "Ag"—an Agriculture and Life Sciences professor—proposed that the entire Bonfire be rebuilt and varnished as a permanent memorial in place of the annual burning. His argument for such an alternative included the frank inquiry, "Why build the bonfire each year, thus destroying the forests of our children, demanding untold hours of toil from our undergrad students, and posing risk to life and limb of students?"

The following email excerpt (from a recent graduate), received shortly after noon, was typical of those who support the continuation of the Bonfire.

> [Those who died] were giving of their time, dedication, and the ultimate sacrifice so that the entire university could enjoy one night of spirit. Are we saying they did this for nothing? I know they would want a bonfire to burn as usual. Their goal was the fire. Therefore, we need to give them the fire. A bonfire in their memory and honor needs to burn! Those kids wanted to see the bonfire burn. Let them see the bonfire burn!

Like many others, the writer claimed to know what the "kids" want, even now that they are dead. One parent wrote, "Not many sacrifice sleep and GPR's to stack overnight. Bonfire '99 should burn in THEIR honor." The parent, a Ph.D. student in Forest Science, wrote that his/her three year-old daughter awaits a simplistic explanation for why her parent has been crying. "In the years to come, how do I explain that these young people died doing something they cared about and the University . . . cancelled Bonfire? What does that say about respecting their commitment to traditions?"

In the late afternoon, a professor in Family Medicine suggested that the Bonfire be made into a virtual Bonfire—a computer simulation. She went on to write that the Bonfire, in military terms, is comparable to fighting a war in a World War II style as opposed to the modern way, with "smart weapons." She said that "this is a signal to all Aggies that we have to shift our paradigm into the electronic age. We can transform the spirit of the tradition into a new reality."

Of course, the Bonfire could never be replaced by a simulation. Anything that is only virtual simply could not manifest the Aggie Spirit. The writer of the following letter better understands that the Aggie Spirit must manifest itself through something that requires extreme exertion and monumental effort.

> In the coming hours and days, thoughts about today's tragedy will turn to questions about the future of bonfire. Should introspection and evaluation necessitate the end of bonfire there should be something to take it's place. I believe we saw a glimpse of what that might be earlier this semester. Before work on the stack began another structure was erected on the bonfire site; the first all-Aggie built Habitat for Humanity house. Why stop at one!
>
> Let's turn our burning desire to beat the hell out of t.u. into a desire to help more people and build more houses than t.u. We can challenge t.u. to see who can build the most houses in the month prior to Thanksgiving. Can you imagine anything more inspiring than walking out to bonfire site on Thanksgiving day and seeing 10, 20 or 30 houses built with Aggie sweat and pride? On each house there would be a bonfire emblem dedicated to those that have died. Afterwards, instead of just ashes and memories, there will be homes and families. We can turn this tragedy into opportunity—a promise of hope for members of our larger community.
>
> In the years that follow when students return they will have more to point to than just a field where bonfire burned. They can go through the community and see the homes they built and the lives they gave opportunity to.

There emerged two basic schools of thought on the future of the Bonfire. One was to continue the Bonfire as it is with safeguards that would ensure its structural integrity. The second school proposes to erect a memorial in honor of the Bonfire 12 and to establish a new tradition, such as building homes in the local community.

Watch What You Say

Within the first week of Bonfire, some Texas A&M faculty who had been opposed to the Bonfire long before the accident spoke to reporters. Biology professor Hugh Wilson and chemistry professor Danny Yeager were the most active dissenters, their voices and opinions airing on CNN's TalkBack Live, National Public Radio's "All Things Considered," TIME magazine, and The Bryan-College Station Eagle.

Although all of those opposed to Bonfire were saddened and shocked by the tragedy, they perhaps found more reason to oppose the Bonfire as a result of it. Traditional dissenters to the Bonfire tradition believe Bonfire is a tremendous waste of natural and man-made resources, as well as a waste of 125,000 hours of labor. They think that the time and material could be better applied on something constructive. They also see the Bonfire as environmentally irresponsible.

Two professors who have not been as outspoken as Wilson and Yeager, but who spoke to the Eagle were philosophy professors Steve Daniel and Colin Allen. On the day of the tragedy, Allen told the Eagle that "even people who have been critical of Bonfire hate to see what happened today."

However humane these bonfire dissidents seem, apparently they are still a threat to the Texas A&M Administration, specifically to President Bowen.

L.A. gangster-rapper Ice-T says in a rap song, "Freedom of speech, just watch what you say." Such is the case at Texas A&M University.

Obviously, there is no prohibition against speaking one's mind. But speaking publicly against the University's traditions often draws a backlash. The punishment may be as innocuous as a colleague saying, "Hey, Highway 6 runs both ways," which is the Aggie version of "Love it or leave it." Other times, a dissenting comment draws more serious consequences. Most people in the Aggie community understand this, but do not know exactly what those consequences might be.

When the University released thousands of pieces of its email correspondence for the Bonfire, a revealing exchange was made public. On November 22, four days after the Bonfire collapse, a former student emailed President Bowen, asking him to remove Dr. Hugh Wilson from his position as professor. The former student wrote that Dr. Wilson's "Dumb as Dirt" anti-Bonfire web page charges Texas A&M and other public bodies with illegal activities, and that the page calls those who disagree with Wilson "dumb" and "irrational." He felt that these methods of argument warranted Wilson's removal. Bowen answered the former student two days later with the following email.

> Subject: RE: Removal of Dr. Hugh Wilson
>
> Dr. Wilson has spent years criticizing the bonfire. He thrives on controversy and feels rewarded when he is attacked by someone he has offended. We do monitor his activities and he is working within his constitutionally protected rights of communication. If he should cross the line, we will take appropriate action.

The email makes the not-so-implicit threat, "We are watching Wilson closely. Once he takes an errant step we will use it as justification to dismiss him."

The DAN Books

On the day the Bonfire fell, Bonfire Adviser Rusty Thompson told reporters that there was no written blueprint as to how the Bonfire is to be constructed, that the information is passed down from one generation of Redpots to the next. If there were building instructions, Thompson said, they would be in the little notebooks that the Redpots carry with them all day and night.

Those notebooks are called General Dan Faires Communications, and each Junior Redpot carries one. All of the 1999 Communications were turned in to investigators of the accident and made public. Although the books are not particularly informative about the nuts-and-bolts construction of Bonfire, they do provide a great deal of insight into the Redpot culture.

Each book contains a condom taped into an inside divider. Each book contains a section of quotations and sayings of various bonfire workers. Some of the books contain the imperative, "Don't be gay." Others contain the acronym, "NTAFB" and its explanation, "Never trust a Fucking Bitch. Don't tell them anything." One book uses a racial epithet against African-Americans.

Negative comments are made against Pink Pots and Band members. One wrote, "We fuckin hate BQ's [Band Queers] except Mike Ruscek. He will save my ass." The Redpot may have been referring to the student crane operator, Mike Rusek, who was also a band member.

Some books write something similar to this quotation: "It's not about building a goddamn fucking Bonfire. It's about being a fucking Aggie." This demonstrates the common theme among Aggies that building the Bonfire has little to do with simply building a big fire. Building the Bonfire expresses the Aggie Spirit.

The work ethic of the Redpots seems to concentrate on the intensity of one's exertion and the dedication to, even obsession with, building the Bonfire. "Nobody ever drowned in their own sweat." "Never let anyone work harder than you." "Running saves an hour a day." "Eat Sleep Drink Shit Aggie Bonfire." "There is a purpose to everything. It is not a glory job. You want glory be a Yellboy (yell leader)." "Step up intensity—do job better." "Pain is weakness leaving your body."

Safety was a concern, at least on paper. "People not wearing pots we are responsible." "Safety, motivation, key." Safety, however, may have been compromised by such ideas as the one presented in this quotation: "Be decisive even if it means being wrong." Did the Junior Redpots continue building a leaning Bonfire even though it could be "wrong"?

One of the reasons why very few people knew about the many violations of school and Bonfire policy occurring at Bonfire events may have been the apparent distrust of the outside community that Redpots encouraged with each other. "Don't tell nobody nothing." "Never talk shop on campus walls have ears."

And of course, there was, "Aggies Against Bonfire = Aggies Against God."

Official Reaction

November 18, 1999

On the day of the accident, most of the important officials under whose jurisdiction the Bonfire is constructed each year made statements to the press. All of the statements expressed sorrow at the accident, but some revealed other concerns.

Texas A&M University President Ray Bowen announced that the 1999 Bonfire burning would be cancelled. "It is only fitting that the Bonfire not be held next week," he said. "Will it be held next year? That will be answered in the coming weeks or months after careful review of what transpired. We don't have all the answers today. Our primary concern is getting those students all out from underneath the stack."

Bowen also stated that he was "99 percent confident" that safety measures had been adequately carried through. He said that future Bonfires may be different. "It may be a small bonfire. You can imagine where it's actually built by professionals but cut by students, just to be sure that what's up there is meeting every standard."

Rusty Thompson, the Bonfire adviser for the 1998 and 1999 Bonfires, said that although Bonfire is built only by students, three volunteers from construction companies were serving as advisers at the Bonfire site when the accident occurred. It became known later that there was only one volunteer crane operator. Thompson countered rumors of horseplay by saying that the students were not playing on the stack, and he called the Red Pots "true professionals" who "know exactly what they're doing."

When asked why there was so little adult supervision in the construction of Bonfire, Thompson answered that the students are adults, which brought a big "whoop" from the crowd of students. Thompson was active in responding to the media for the first few days after the accident but then grew extremely quiet with the media purportedly because he was busy dealing with the accident aftermath itself.

Bob Wiatt, the University Police Chief, stated that "from what we have gathered at this point, there is no indication that anything inappropriate occurred at Bonfire site the night of the accident. That includes alcohol, rough-housing or careless behavior."

Governor George W. Bush choked back tears at one point as he spoke, "I just can't imagine what that means to have that happen to them. It's sad, it's tough . . . But the university will rally and recover. Right now it's a time of chaos at Texas A&M, but things will be fine." Later, Governor Bush would call Bonfire "a great tradition."

On Friday, the day after the accident, Governor George Bush was asked whether he thought the tradition of Bonfire should continue. He answered, "Absolutely." About the memorial service that had been held the day before, Bush said, "Nobody was urged to come, nobody was told to come and it was a turnout that was unlike anything I've ever seen. People just praying and crying and sharing their grief and concern about the fate of these people, those surviving and those who passed away."

November 22, 1999

On Monday Nov. 22, University administrators met with local law enforcement, fire and rescue organizations, and the U.S. Department of Labor's Occupational Safety and Health Administration (OSHA) to figure out who would conduct the investigation of the accident, and how it would be conducted.

On the Saturday before the meeting, Lieutenant Governor Rick Perry had already said that he and other Senate leaders preferred that the investigation be handled by Texas A&M. "No one has more interest in finding out what happened there than the University," he said. "I have every indication that Texas A&M will look at every aspect of this and do it in a full and proper way and disclose all the facts that need to be disclosed."

George W. Bush decided to let Texas A&M take care of its own business. After a weekend of funerals, President Bowen announced that the university would choose a qualified person to head an independent commission to investigate the Bonfire accident. The commission would be charged with finding the cause of the accident but not making recommendations as to the future of the Bonfire or assigning responsibility for the collapse. Bowen stated that the commission would be expected to turn in its report by March 31, 2000.

By the end of the week, Bowen announced that he had chosen Leo E. Linbeck to organize and chair the commission. Linbeck is the chairman and chief executive officer of Linbeck Construction Corporation. John A. Weese and a team of university staff members were chosen to help Linbeck in his investigation.

Bowen said that he chose Linbeck "because of his reputation for integrity and openness and his vast knowledge and experience in various aspects of construction." Linbeck stated that the investigation would be impartial, open, and thorough. But his integrity was called into question when reporters brought up the fact that Linbeck is the chairman of Texans for Lawsuit Reform, which lobbies the state legislature to limit punitive damages in civil injury and death suits. Further muddying the separation of interests is the fact that Bartell Zachry is also a member of the board of Texans for Lawsuit Reform. Zachry is the head of H.B. Zachry, which may be a target of civil suits because it volunteered a crane and three workers to help build the Bonfire.

December 1999

On December 1, Linbeck chose the other four members of the investigative commission. Allan Shiver, Jr. is the son of the late governor of Texas, Allan Shivers Sr. He runs a consulting and investment company in Austin and helps run an orchard in the Rio Grande Valley. Veronica Kastrin Callaghan of El Paso is vice president of KASKO Ventures, an industrial real estate company. She works in the area of industrial warehouse construction. Hugh G. Robinson is the CEO of a construction management firm called The Tetra Group. He also serves on the board of directors of Belo Corporation, the parent company of *The Bryan-College Station Eagle* newspaper. The final member of the team is William E. Tucker, chancellor emeritus of Texas Christian University, having served as chancellor from 1979-1998. Linbeck, Callaghan and Robinson have all served on the board of the Federal Reserve Bank of Dallas.

According to Bowen, "The commission is to satisfy itself that the truth about what caused the accident is known as far as it can be discovered and to report its findings and conclusions with recommendations for corrective action."

The future of the Bonfire (whether the tradition is to continue and in what way) is to be decided by the University and its students, but soon after the accident, Bowen already had thoughts about that. On November 19, Bowen told *The Eagle* that "it's highly probable bonfire will continue. I can't be more explicit at this point." On November 30, Bowen wrote an email to alumnus Malcolm Hartman Jr. saying, "If I had to bet, I would bet that it continues." Bowen also said that safety issues had to be addressed.

On December 3, the investigative commission met at Texas A&M and came up with a set of preliminary questions that it wanted answered, including:

- Were specific structural designs used to build the bonfire, and was outside expert advice sought?

- What equipment was used, and what kind of training did operators have?

- How were students selected and trained to work on the bonfire—and what role did A&M administrators play in supervising them?

- Who in the A&M administration was responsible for ensuring safety at the site, and what was the attitude of students toward safety concerns?

On December 10, the commission assigned Kent Lietzau and Jon Zagrodzky of management consulting firm McKinsey & Company to assemble the professional investigators and technical experts for the investigation.

Packer Engineering, based near Chicago, was assigned the job of discerning the exact cause of the 1999 Bonfire collapse. They will look for differences between the 1999 Bonfire and previous ones. Fay Engineering will study the evolving structure of the current Bonfire structure, which originated in 1946, when a center pole was first used to build it. Fay Engineering will analyze the materials used and conduct stress tests on the different designs used over the decades. Kroll Associates specializes in business investigations, forensic accounting, security consulting, crisis management and electronic systems protection. Kroll will coordinate investigative teams, maintain a communications and information-sharing system between teams, and conduct interviews.

January 2000

In early January 2000, the commission and its hired investigators announced that a report may not be ready by March 31, 2000, as Bowen had requested. Investigators also estimated that the total cost of the investigation could be $500,000 or more. Linbeck encouraged investigators to not speak to the public during the investigation.

At the January 18 commission meeting, Linbeck stressed again the importance of the March 31 deadline. The commission hired Performance Improvement International to investigate the organizational and historical causes of the accident. In a presentation to the commission, CEO Chong Chiu said that in their experience, the majority of root causes of an accident are "Executive Management Errors" and "Organizational and Programmatic Failures." These failures refer in the case of Texas A&M to failures of the A&M administration and the direct supervisors of Bonfire. For instance, poor wiring of logs may have led to the accident, but poor training programs or rule enforcement may be the root cause of such a problem. Also included in PII's investigation are A&M Bonfire's cultural, social, and behavioral issues, which may affect the "atmosphere of safety," as the commission has termed it.

When asked whether the presidential and vice-presidential offices would be included in the investigation, Chiu said that if the facts led to such an investigation, it would be done. Linbeck stated on the subject that investigations usually start at the bottom and work their way up. Theoretically, the investigation could move its way up to the top. I pressed Chiu on the issue of presidential and vice-presidential responsibility, and he stated that if such administrative fault were found, it could be categorized as either "negligence or ignorance."

In January, the Board of Regents set a spending cap for the commission of $1 million. In February, the commission reported that it needed both more time and money, and was granted both.

Analysis of the Official Reaction

Texas Governor George W. Bush would have shown incredible boldness and leadership had he stated that Texas A&M would have to face state or federal intervention. But that is not the way of George W. Bush. In the past, the state has intervened, especially on issues of hazing, which, like Bonfire, has also resulted in death.

So many times in the past, supporters of the more controversial A&M traditions have said, "let the boys be boys." Now that the school is co-ed, Bush has said, let the Aggies be Aggies. He further distanced himself from making any stand by letting Rick Perry do the honors of telling the press that the state government would not intervene on the issue of Bonfire or its investigation.

President Bowen decided to assign an "independent" commission to investigate the collapse. The companies that are actually investigating the collapse, however, are not fully independent. They have signed contracts with the University, and the University pays them, not the independent commission.

On January 21, 2000, The Wall Street Journal published a scorching front page upper left-hand article analyzing the process by which Texas A&M administrators were able to wrest the responsibility of investigating the Bonfire accident from the D.A.'s office and shoo other investigative bodies away. Because the Bonfire workers were volunteers, OSHA could not get involved. Local D.A. Bill Turner wanted an independent investigation, but he only had two investigators. He asked for help from the Texas Rangers, but the Rangers could find no criminal violation, so declined. Law enforcement officials, according to the articles sources, were told that an investigation on their part was not necessary. The only government entity that could have resisted the power of Texas A&M was the state government, and George Bush decided that Texas A&M could conduct an honest investigation of itself. Texas A&M then creates an investigative commission whose chairman declares himself that it is merely a "fact-finding" organization; only the final report will reveal whether the commission will assign responsibility for this preventable accident.

Meanwhile, the university constantly floats the idea that the Bonfire is a purely student-run activity.

On February 5, seemingly following The Wall Street Journal's lead, the Austin American Statesman published an editorial stating

> What is surprising is that A&M failed to invite outside investigating agencies to study the collapse. By naming its own investigating commission, the university showed greater commitment to self-protection than to truth.
>
> The committee members are respected and undoubtedly honest citizens with excellent intentions. But airlines do not name the commissions that investigate their fatal accidents. Nor do logging companies or construction companies. And, as a recent example of the impartial inquiry into the Seton Hall dormitory fire shows, neither do most universities.

It was revealing that on November 22, 1999, President Bowen, without having assigned even a chair for the investigative commission (much less asked him how long such an investigation might take), set a deadline of March 31, 2000. This deadline no doubt has put time pressures on the investigating companies. The management consultants referred to the possibility of going over the time limit a "sensitive issue." In late February, the commission was granted extra time, but observers are left to wonder why the March 31 deadline was set in the first place. Perhaps the university wanted to finish the investigation in time to get ready for Bonfire 2000, preparation for which would begin in the spring. The university quieted such speculation when it finally hinted in late February that Bonfire 2000 would be suspended.

The investigators are working for the organization they are investigating. If the administration is truly dedicated to the truth, the commission will be given the time, money, and freedom to squeeze out an approximation of the truth.

Causes of the Collapse

If the Bonfire collapse began as a mystery as to what caused it, the mystery soon transformed into farce, as culprit after culprit stood up. A dozen factors emerged, each of them possibly causing or contributing to the accident. Within weeks of the accident, investigators and former builders of Bonfire agreed that the collapse could not be blamed on one factor. Perhaps, however, the accident would have been less severe (and claimed fewer or no lives) in the absence of any one of these factors. What are these factors, and how did they affect the stability of the burgeoning Bonfire stack?

Tradition

Sometimes it is difficult to tell the difference between tradition and sheer inertia.

The Student Tradition

The supposed tradition that contributed most to the collapse of the Bonfire is that of students leading and organizing Bonfire construction. Many have forgotten that the original tradition was for the Corps Commandant and Assistant Commandant to head the Bonfire effort. These are university employees. Anyhow, the tradition transformed into that of the students leading the Bonfire effort. Even so, Texas A&M assigned a Bonfire adviser to guide the whole operation. The adviser in 1999, Rusty

Thompson, was not an engineer, and his previous professional experience involved managing college dormitories. Thompson had recently increased his staff help when the Bonfire collapsed. The university realized that it needed more supervision to control the alcohol and other shenanigans during Bonfire construction.

Too little too late. Tradition caught up with the inert university. There was never an engineer officially assigned to Bonfire construction. When Dr. Larry Grosse left Texas A&M in the mid-1990s, the university lost a professor who had committed himself to helping students build a safe and sound Bonfire structure. The university did not replace Grosse, and so Bonfire construction went on for years without an engineer overseeing the operation. As a result, practices that Grosse had helped to develop such as the use of steel cables and interlocking logs were used less and less. Practices that strengthened the structural integrity of stack degraded.

The tradition also allowed students to do whatever they wanted during Bonfire construction—that is, until someone was hurt or killed, or the police, media, or residents exposed dangerous or unruly practices. No university official regularly monitored Bonfire construction. Neither the stability of the stack, nor the stability of the students were regulated.

The Oral Tradition

Because there is no written blueprint or instruction manual as to how to build the Bonfire, practices change every year, making Bonfire a tradition that evolves with each set of leaders and how they want to build Bonfire. Bonfire leaders learn the Bonfire design and construction methods from the previous years' leaders, through experience and word of mouth. "The scary thing is the process probably leads to a cumulative variation," said Texas A&M engineer Ray James during the post-collapse discussion. "They learn from the previous leaders so if the previous leaders decides to do something different, the next year they do it that way." In this way, slightly dangerous practices can be compounded year to year until they contribute to a fatal accident.

Two collapses previous to the 1999 disaster (1957 and 1994) demonstrate that the constantly evolving design often evolves into dangerous configurations.

Imbalance

The Bonfire began as a pile of trash and scrap being burned on the A&M campus. In the 1940's, it transformed into a conical "teepee" of logs stacked up against the center pole. The wedding cake style of six tiers of

61

logs may be the most unstable design that the Bonfire has ever employed. Logs are not necessarily pushing inward toward the centerpole. In the teepee Bonfire, logs were pushing inward, against logs on the opposite side. In the wedding cake, it is possible that a tier of logs may begin pushing in the same direction. Such an imbalance of forces can cause the centerpole to crack and break.

A Leaning Stack

Rogers Engineering Service of College Station helped to dismantle the collapsed Bonfire and to free victims. Upon request of the University, the company's president, Alton G. Rogers reported on the rescue work, and on other observations done through their research, which utilized photographs, interviews, and on-site investigation.

According to the Rogers report, the stack had been leaning in the direction in which it fell long before it actually fell. The first level of the stack, about 19 feet high and 39 feet in diameter, was not plumb, or perpendicular with the Earth and its gravitational pull. The first stack, was however, perpendicular to the ground itself, which, the study found, slopes in the direction of the eventual collapse—the southeast. According to their calculations, the ground was about nine inches higher at the northwestern edge of the first stack than it was on the southeastern edge. The first tier of logs, according to Rogers, was about 870,000 pounds. According to Rogers, the Bonfire stack leaned more and more each day leading up to the November 18 collapse.

The leaning of the first stack produced a bending stress on the centerpole. The centerpole snapped in three places—at or near the top of the first stack, at or near the top of the fourth stack, and about nine inches beneath the ground. The pole itself was ninety-two feet high. It is unknown exactly when the centerpole snapped. The severance of the pole could have caused the collapse, or it could have been an immediate result of the collapse.

The fact that centerpole broke around the top of the first tier lends credence to the leaning log theory.

The Sloping Ground

In the past, Bonfire builders have used surveying equipment to make sure that the stack was plumb. Apparently, they did not do so in 1999, making the sloping ground an even greater factor in its building and collapse. In 1992, the Bonfire site was moved from Duncan field on the south side of campus to the northeast lawn known as the polo fields. In the months leading up to the field, over a hundred thousand dollars was spent in preparing the field for Bonfire construction. A March 1992 newspaper reported then-Bonfire Adviser William Kibler as saying that part of the $100,000 cost of moving Bonfire included leveling the field. In a March 23 memo, Kibler wrote to vice president Malon Southerland that the cost of moving the Bonfire would be $160,000, and the first item listed as part of that cost was leveling the field "to ensure proper drainage."

On a June 23, 1992 memo, Southerland attached a note that said, "This will dramatically reduce the first year costs, so the long term costs may be more carefully evaluated." In the memo itself, he wrote, "We see no reason for the Physical Plant to alter the grade of the field at this point. We want to build Bonfire on the field as it is one year and evaluate any need to change the grade thereafter." In a July 29 memo, Kibler again stressed that "The Redpots need the field cleared and leveled in order to make a final determination regarding the placement of the center pole. Their plan is to determine a place for the centerpole and then begin shoring that site with railroad ties to insure stability of the pole once it is raised." It is unclear whether the field was ever leveled or for what reason leveling was desired. It does seem clear that leveling the field could have prevented the dangerous tilting of the Bonfire, and that administrators like Southerland had both a cost-cutting and a trial-and-error approach (let's try it this way and see what happens) to Bonfire construction.

The Centerpole

The centerpole is the one constant of Bonfire construction that has not varied for decades. It is always two telephone poles spliced together. Apparently the 1999 poles were not treated. Previous centerpoles may or may not have been treated with creosote, which is illegal to burn in Texas.

On the day of the accident, Texas A&M engineering professors, associates, and consultants investigated the collapsed stack. On November 23, they met and discussed possible causes of the collapse. A transcript of their discussion was released to the A&M archives.

Among other things, the A&M engineers were concerned that the centerpole had not been strong enough. Some argued, though, that the centerpole is not erected in order to hold the stack up. David Trejo, an A&M Assistant Professor of Civil Engineering, said that the centerpole "was never intended to be the stabilizing element in that stack." The purpose of the centerpole is not to hold up the million pound-plus stack. In the beginning of construction, it helps to hold up the early trunks tied to it, but it is not meant to hold up logs attached thereafter.

Ray James, an A&M research engineer, wrote in a report to A&M that the centerpole, was brittle and dry. James reported that the 1999 collapse was "very similar" to the 1994 Bonfire leaning, when the Bonfire began to lean to one side and had to be pulled down. The year 1994 was extremely wet, and the fall of 1999 was one of the driest on record. Throughout the fifty-six years of using a centerpole, its strength was never questioned or tested. Attempts to strengthen it and insulate it from heat were aimed at trying to make it stand up longer after Bonfire had been lit.

Cut Guy Ropes

Of the eight guy ropes attaching the centerpole to the perimeter poles, the four lower guy ropes are traditionally cut during the later stages of Bonfire construction. "The stack gets so near those ropes that in order to operate the crane safely and so forth, they are removed," said Bonfire Advisor Rusty Thompson at a January 11 news conference. "Historically there's never been a problem once those ropes have been removed."

After the accident, engineers interviewed by The Dallas Morning News and Associated Press stated that cutting these ropes could have contributed to the snapping of the centerpole by decreasing the stability of centerpole and making it more vulnerable to stresses from any side. The practice had not been seriously questioned or tested in the past.

The fact that the ropes were cut just two or three hours before the collapse adds weight to the argument that the cutting of the ropes contributed to the accident. If the ropes had not been cut, the Bonfire may have stood up longer, or it may have collapsed slower (as in 1994), allowing workers to get off of it safely.

Faulty Construction and Violations of University Policy

The construction of a multi-story structure made almost entirely of logs and baling wire requires, it would seem, the utmost of care and concentration. In order to build a sound structure, workers would have to be even more careful than at a normal construction site. After all, they are not working with rectangular planks and boards. They are not using standardized materials, and the structure is not as stable as a building standing on a foundation.

Despite the increased danger of building the Bonfire, there seemed to have been a lesser degree of seriousness, oversight, and consistency of safety standards applied to its construction. Furthermore, even fundamental policies on safety, alcohol, hazing, and the height of the Bonfire were not enforced. These violations of policy increased yet further the risk of a tragic accident.

The Height of Bonfire

Upon inspection of the center pole, it was discovered by investigator Dr. John A. Weese, an A&M engineer, that the fourth level of the stack had already surpassed the university-imposed Bonfire height limit of fifty-five feet. The fourth tier stood at 59 feet at the time of the accident. The fifth and sixth stacks (nine and four feet in height) would have made its height at burning 72 feet, over 30% higher than the 55-foot limit established in the 1970's. The general public did not know until after the tragedy that the Bonfire was being built beyond its limits.

In reaction to the post-tragedy findings, associate vice-president and former Bonfire adviser Bill Kibler told reporters that the 55-foot limit is "an expectation," and not a hard and fast rule. Kibler had made the impression to the public and the media during the eighties and early nineties that the height limit was a rule and that it was enforced. In 1986, Kibler, wrote in a memo that the Bonfire adviser should enforce the rule. It is unknown whether 1999 Bonfire adviser Rusty Thompson did so. Questions from reporters were not responded to.

When builders are hanging on swings hanging by pulleys from the top of the centerpole, taller bonfires mean greater danger. By not strictly regulating the height of the Bonfire, Texas A&M put the lives of its students at greater risk. Compounding this danger is the fact that students with little or no training were allowed to work on the upper levels of stack. If the University had enforced its height rule, the fourth tier would have stood at forty or forty-four feet. Would fewer students have died had the height of the Bonfire been properly limited?

Loose and Upside-Down Logs

"It seems the key element is how those (logs) are tied together with wire," said civil engineering professor Harry Jones at the engineers' meeting, who was surprised that such a tragic accident had not happened earlier.

Many Bonfire workers have commented that the wiring on the 1999 Bonfire was loose and shoddy. That night, there was an overabundance of loose logs. "They were tightening loose logs all night," one student told the *Statesman*. The crew chief, who asked that his name not be used, blamed the looseness of the logs on the lack of training. Although Bonfire organizers teach a class on cutting and loading trees, there is no wiring class. Crew chiefs are responsible for teaching their own crews, and this sophomore crew chief had learned wiring the year before as he worked on Bonfire.

The engineers also found that several of the logs in the second tier had been placed upside-down, with the "butt" end up. This may have contributed to the imbalance of the stack. Such upside-down logs make the bonfire logs more "vertical," and less inwardly leaning, but make the stack less stable.

Freshman and Sophomores on Stack

One of the reasons why the logs were so loose may have been because of the lack of experience or maturity of the workers doing the wiring. In 1994, Redpots published a safety manual that stated that students must have two years of experience before working on any level of stack above the first. In the past, this rule has been upheld because it was tradition that underclassmen not be allowed to work directly on stack and were limited to carrying logs to stack. This tradition apparently became obsolete as organizers sought more workers.

Dozens of freshmen and sophomores were working on the stack on every level when the accident occurred. In fact, thirty-three of the thirty-nine injured and dead were underclassmen. Derek Woodley, a freshman from Georgetown, Texas, had only one night of experience on stack when he was allowed to work on the fourth stack on the night of the accident. He suffered deep cuts and a broken wrist, ankle and back when the stack collapsed.

Describing the qualifications for working on the upper stacks, Woodley told the *Dallas Morning News,* "Girls can if they want to. It's no big deal. As long as you are physically able to climb up there and you've got a pair of pliers on you, they'll let you up there." From the witness report of Brittny Allison, as quoted in a previous section, we see that not only are freshmen allowed on upper levels of stack, but that first-timers are. In fact, she would have wired in her first log without any direct oversight had the collapse not interrupted her work.

According to the transcript of the November 23 engineers' meeting, either deputy general counsel Jan Faber or Alton Rogers said that in the early seventies, when he helped to build Bonfire, neither sophomores nor freshmen were allowed to work on stack at all. "The only ones that could were Redpots and Brown pots," he said. "And I think that part of this tragedy is that we had freshmen and sophomores out there tying those logs who have absolutely no experience. So I think that this is part of the tradition that has evolved with time that's been lost and it's lost some of the quality that we had in building those."

"One of the younger" crane operators

The safety handbook also states that only professional operators are allowed to operate cranes in Bonfire construction. When the Bonfire fell, there were two people operating cranes rented from H.B. Zachry Company. One was a licensed operator named Eugene Couch (38, of San Antonio), who is an employee of H.B. Zachry. The other was Michael Rusek, a 24-year-old engineering technology major and Aggie Band member.

Rusek's qualifications included two hundred hours of crane operation, apparently mostly or completely from working on the Bonfire. Dr. Bill Kibler, associate vice-president for student affairs and Bonfire adviser from 1983 to 1992, told the press, "The safety handbook calls for a professional operator. It doesn't say 'licensed.'" Kibler told *The Dallas Morning News* that under his tenure as Bonfire adviser he could not recall having any student crane operators.

Federal licensing involves passing skills and written tests, and a drug test. It is mandatory for operating a crane while working for H.B. Zachry, but Zachry had rented the crane to Texas A&M without attaching an operator.

When on November 16 a crane operator hit one of the cross-ties so hard that it knocked a chunk off of it, one of the students blamed it on "one of the younger guys" operating the cranes. How many "younger guys" were there? When the broken centerpole was examined, it was found to have broken where a set of cross-ties had been nailed into it. It is yet to be seen what role being hit by the crane may have played.

Cables, Interlocking Logs, and Log Burial

It was discovered during the Bonfire investigation that some of the methods used to stabilize the Bonfire in the past were not employed at all or may not have been employed to the same degree as in years past. In the past, a steel cable has been wrapped around the stacks after certain intervals in construction. A Bonfire stack could, then, have several cables wrapped around it. This year, the cable was found in the storage area, unused.

In the past, some logs have been allowed to jut out of one tier and extend into the tier above it. These interlocking logs tend to hold the tiers together and create a more solid structure. At least one student reported that many of these interlocking logs may have been inadvertently sawed off so that their head end did not jut out into the tier above it.

In the past, some of the logs on the first stack had been partially buried in the ground to further stabilize the stack. Questions arose as to what extent this was practiced. Some believed that there were not enough partially buried logs.

Alcohol and the Bonfire

Just as the Aggie community was beginning to recover from the accident, it was hit with the embarrassing news that two of the Bonfire workers that were killed were intoxicated with alcohol well beyond the level allowed for operating a motor vehicle. Texas state law prohibits driving for people with a blood-alcohol level of .08. Alcohol tests are typical procedures conducted in examination of the recently deceased; on December 3 officials released information on blood tests done on the first eleven victims of the Bonfire tragedy. Jeremy Frampton at the time of death had a blood alcohol level of .316, and Jerry Don Self's blood alcohol was .161. Frampton was 22, and Self was 20. A third victim, Christopher Breen, 25, had a small amount of alcohol in his blood.

University policy states that drinking at Bonfire work sites is prohibited, and anyone caught drinking or caught drunk must be sent away. It is also illegal in Texas for people under the age of 21 to drink alcohol. Upon release of the blood alcohol tests, the Texas Alcoholic Beverage Commission (TABC) began an investigation to see what laws may have been broken, such as the selling of alcohol to a minor. The chairman of the TABC is Allan Shivers, Jr., also a member of the Bonfire investigative commission.

Some members of the press and the local community protested against publishing such information in the newspaper. One resident reacted to the protest by writing a letter to *The Eagle* saying that if two out of the eleven workers on the stack were drunk, then extrapolating such a ratio for the seventy students estimated to be on stack the night of the accident would produce an estimate of a dozen intoxicated workers. If a dozen drunk students worked on stack on a consistent basis, could the structural integrity of Bonfire 1999 have been compromised?

Bob Wiatt, UPD chief told the *Dallas Morning News* that "a few students drinking could not have caused that accident." He said that only a "massive show of force" could have caused the Bonfire to fall.

On December 20, the TABC reported that hospitals had done only one blood alcohol test on the twenty-seven students injured in the accident. That one test showed that a nineteen year-old student had in the early morning of the 18th traces of alcohol in his bloodstream. Partly because of the lack of alcohol tests, the TABC resorted instead to interviewing students about alcohol use at Bonfire.

Three days before Christmas, results of a second alcohol test on Jeremy Frampton revealed that the man had only a .094 blood alcohol level, slightly above the legal limit. The news, according to his father, Richard Frampton of Turlock, California, clears his son's name. The second test was conducted using liquid from Jeremy Frampton's eye, rather than blood.

Police investigating the Bonfire accident took pictures and wrote up inventories of what they found at the Bonfire site. Police found four beer bottle caps around the Redpot shack. They discovered six empty beer cans in a flatbed truck parked at the site. The truck may have been used to haul logs to the site. They also found a full can of beer in the cushions of a couch within the Bonfire perimeter. One College Station Police photo showed what seemed to be a steel flask used to carry hard liquor. One of the Brown pots who fell to his death had a beer in the pocket of his overalls.

Juan Mendez of the Texas A&M Engineering Extension Service wrote in a Dec 3 report on his participation in rescue efforts, "I did see something that caught my eyes. It was beer cans I saw. It was not just one brand, but many other brands." Mendez reported seeing eight to twelve cans around stack. He said that he picked up trash and beer cans as a courtesy while not involved with rescue operations. Rescue worker Todd Reynolds also found six or seven cans around stack, and wrote in his report, "I started to remove some trash around where we were working and found some more cans. I spent most of the (time) working around the stack and removing trash as we were clearing logs. Some of this trash had beer cans in with other things." Mendez and Reynolds complained to the university that it had distorted the truth by suggesting that alcohol was not involved in the accident. (Ward and Gamboa, *Austin American-Statesman* 2/24/00).

Further evidence of alcohol at the 1999 Bonfire stack may have been lost when students and rescue workers threw away bottles and cans during rescue operations.

One TABC investigator told the *Fort Worth Star-Telegram* that "Bonfire is a 90-year tradition, and drinking at Bonfire is a 90-year tradition." Indeed, the University has long struggled with limiting the amount of alcohol associated with Bonfire. In the 1980's and early 1990's, the University and student Bonfire organizations focused on trying to eliminate alcohol from the Bonfire site on the night of the burning. Drunk students would commit unruly acts in surrounding neighborhoods on Bonfire night, causing church leaders, community members and students to protest loudly. Although the campaign to "Keep alcohol from shattering the tradition" failed to accomplish its lofty goal of eliminating alcohol from Bonfire, it did lower the amount of alcohol taken to Bonfire on the night of the burning.

Because drunken behavior on the night of the Bonfire burning actually threatened the continuation of the tradition, that problem was addressed first and concentrated upon. Meanwhile, the problem of drinking during the erection of Bonfire was relatively ignored. Even as student university incident reports (complaints made by students to dorm managers and other administrators) and police reports piled up, no public campaign was launched to eliminate alcohol at cut and stack. This policy imbalance persisted despite the fact that intoxication at the construction sites is more dangerous than at the burning.

Because A&M has released a great number of emails and memos concerning Bonfire, a picture of recent alcohol violations has become clearer.

In March 1997, a Bonfire performance review subcommittee reported that a Bonfire injury the previous fall was in part due to the intoxication of a Bonfire worker.

During the construction of the 1998 Bonfire, university police found about thirty students (including twenty minors) with a 15.5 gallon keg in a storage shed at the Bonfire construction site. The police had to call an ambulance for an 18 year-old student who was found passed out and vomiting on a sofa in the shed. It is unclear what kind of disciplinary action was taken by the administration in response to this violation of school and Bonfire alcohol policy. When asked about it by reporters, Rusty Thompson could not recall the incident or the university's response.

The following spring, Thompson hired a Buttpot—a former Redpot—to educate and make aware Bonfire workers of hazing and alcohol policies.

On March 9, 1999—about eight months before the tragedy—Vice President of Student Affairs J. Malon Southerland wrote in a memo to other administrators, "I think we are dangerously close to having a serious incident that connects alcohol, residence halls and Bonfire." Because of Southerland's concerns, a committee of administrators was formed to discuss the relationship of bonfire and residence halls, and the use and abuse of alcohol in the residence halls' bonfire activities. In April 1999, Ron Sasse, the director of residence life, recommended "a training effort to assist student leaders ... to motivate others without using alcohol." The committee met a couple of times before the Bonfire accident occurred, but apparently took no tangible actions.

In fall 1999, Texas Aggie Bonfire, as a student organization, was found in violation of hazing and alcohol policy by the Student Organization Hearing Board. Bonfire leaders in Crocker Hall had apparently held a Bonfire-related party in which they provided alcohol to freshmen and forced them to do push-ups. Various acts of hazing have traditionally been committed to get students into the right Bonfire mood and to initiate workers. Rusty Thompson emailed to Southerland on October 14, 1999 that "[Head Stack] Travis Johnson did an outstanding job of providing evidence to the board of all of the proactive and educational efforts that Bonfire has made with all of the Bonfire leadership, but the Board still felt that Texas Aggie Bonfire should be held accountable for the actions of Crocker Hall. Of course, Texas Aggie Bonfire is stunned by this outcome and is filing an appeal."

Hazing and Other Rituals

Hazing may seem like an issue unrelated to the Bonfire collapse of 1999, but when speaking of the atmosphere of safety, or lack thereof, hazing is directly related, in that students focused on, or in the process of, hazing, are less focused on safety. Historically, hazing has been an older and more controversial problem at Texas A&M than drinking, and has been interwoven into most A&M traditions—from military drill teams to the Aggie Band. An A&M student died of hazing in 1984.

As described in previous sections, two residence Halls (Walton and Crocker) had, by the time of the accident, been suspended from Bonfire because members had participated in and been caught at hazing. Hart Hall was on the verge of suspension or other disciplinary action at the time of the collapse. A yellowpot had been removed from participation on November 10. And of course, there had been the attack against Ramiro Reyes, for which there were no punitive actions.

Residence hall Bonfire hazing has involved setting students' backs on fire with lighting fluid and making them smother the flames by rubbing their backs together. Corps Bonfire hazing has included being hit by axe handles. General Bonfire hazing often involves submersion or contact with sticky or yucky substances.

The Brownpots who died in the collapse were conducting an initiation ritual that apparently involved large amounts of alcohol. Some other rituals or activities involved with Bonfire have been urinating from the upper levels of stack, often on those one dislikes. And another ritual described in a student's witness report involves Bonfire leaders collectively filling a bottle with a certain male body fluid and then dropping it into the logs of stack. Love letters and other belongings have also been dropped into the stack to be burned.

Hazing distracts not only students, but administrators too, from safety issues. A good portion of the memoranda and emails released by the University officials dealt with hazing, whereas very few dealt directly with safety, design, construction, or engineering. But the University has never meted out a serious crackdown, and it has dealt with hazing almost exclusively after the fact. These methods have proven useless in preventing hazing, and the University should have understood this after more than a hundred years of dealing with the hazing problem. The fact that the University has not cracked down on hazing, which occurs largely in university-sponsored organizations (the Corps, dorms, and Bonfire), may be evidence that its administration allows it to continue in order to pander support from former students.

Faith, Obsession, and Apathy

Over the years of Bonfire construction, the University, its students, and local and state construction, fire, and air regulators seemed to possess a deep faith and trust in the Aggie Bonfire. It would not fall, it would not cause major fires, and it would not pollute the air with cancer-causing agents. But it has done all three.

Traditionally, A&M has been more of an engineering school than an agriculture school. Only during a short period near the beginning of the century did Aggies major in agriculture in greater numbers than in engineering. Farm boys did not go to college to learn to farm better. Today, A&M is one of the nation's major engineering schools.

Nevertheless, perhaps because Bonfire slowly evolved out of a spontaneous trash pile into a multi-leveled tower of logs, a blueprint was never written and calculations were never made as to what was necessary to make Bonfire safe and stable. Furthermore, testing wasn't necessary because the "testing" happened every year at the burning. Although students often competed against the previous year's Bonfire-builders, it was over the height and how long it stood after it was lit, not over how safe or architecturally sound their respective Bonfires were.

Although state fire and air regulators received complaints and actually observed the Bonfire in the early 1990's, they concluded that the Bonfire did not break any pollution or safety laws. Although construction projects are normally regulated by city inspectors, Texas A&M never applied for building permits, and the city never asked for one.

But even without official state regulation of the Bonfire, many verbal and nonverbal warnings of the dangers of Bonfire were sounded over the last two decades. Furthermore, there is evidence that administrators heard some of these warnings and foreboding signals, and admitted that there were great dangers and legal liabilities to the big fire. But out of dedication to tradition and to tradition-minded students and alumni, and perhaps out of blind faith in Bonfire, the Administration ignored many of the most important heeds for caution and reform.

The Collapse of 1994

On the morning of October 26, 1994, as students "pushed" to finish the Bonfire before the UT game, the Bonfire leaned and logs from the first stack began to fall over to the ground. Because the Bonfire did not quickly collapse, workers were able to get off and away from the stack without injury. The Bonfire stack had to be taken down by pulling the centerpole towards the ground. Because the area had been drenched in rain for weeks, and because two metal cables actually broke in attempts to bring the centerpole down, the structure itself was declared by university officials to be sound, and the collapse was blamed on the sogginess of the ground.

Ray Bowen had been named President of the university in 1994, and Malon Southerland was the vice-president of student affairs. Kevin Jackson was the Bonfire Adviser at the time. No formal investigation of the stack or its design was conducted by the administration, and it decided to allow students to build a second Bonfire with the same logs. As Redpots stayed up for days straight, the second Bonfire was successfully built in one week and lit before the UT game.

Because of the collapse, students wanting to work on the Bonfire in subsequent years were made to sign legal waivers freeing the university from liability for injuries suffered while building Bonfire.

Some time after the collapse of the first 1994 Bonfire, Dr. T. J. Teddy Hirsch, then-head of the structural engineering subdepartment at A&M, warned Vice President Southerland that the "wedding cake" style of Bonfire was unstable. He had observed the construction of Bonfire for 43 years, and he had long been disturbed by the design concept of logs standing on top of logs. "These six layers, the logs are almost vertical," Hirsch told the Austin American Statesman after the 1999 collapse, "That's where they become unstable. They are a stack of logs on top of logs."

Besides the 1994 collapse, Hirsch pointed out that in the years leading up to the 1994 partial collapse, the Bonfire had been falling in on itself very quickly after being lit. The old tee-pee style Bonfires could stand for hours, and the Bonfires of the late eighties and early nineties too often measured their rectitude by the minutes.

When Hirsch warned Southerland of the design flaws, the vice president referred him to then-chairman of the student Bonfire committee, Zach Coapland. Hirsch met with Coapland and a group of Redpots in late 1994 or early 1995 and told them that they should revert to the tee-pee style of Bonfire. He also said that builders should use a concrete or other more fireproof centerpole to prevent early collapse. According to Hirsch, Coapland told him that Bonfire was a student-run project, and that Bonfire leaders would meet and decide what to do. "No decision was made," Hirsch told the *Statesman*, "and because it was a student project, I accepted it."

Coapland, David Zuehlke (chief Redpot in 1994) and Southerland have all stated that they do not remember Hirsch's warnings or the meeting.

After the 1999 tragedy, Texas A&M research engineer Ray James reported to the school that the 1999 stack collapse was "very similar" to the 1994 collapse. One possible difference, according to James, from his limited observations, was that the 1999 pole seemed brittle and dry.

Other engineers also thought that the Bonfire design was at best questionable; Professor Loren Lutes stated his concerns in an email to President Bowen after the 1999 tragedy. In explaining the engineers' silence on the Bonfire's instability, Lutes wrote, "Many structural engineering faculty members are well aware of Teddy's unsuccessful attempt to have the design of the stack altered. I think there has been a widespread feeling that if he couldn't do it, none of the rest of us had a chance of having any effect."

One Texas A&M engineer, on condition of anonymity told the Houston Chronicle that "they should have known there was a problem in 1994. They can blame the rain, but that should have been the wake-up call. It was obvious that the stack can fall, and it did.

"But it's hard to express that opinion when you're fighting religion, and the Bonfire is a religious experience on the Texas A&M campus."

1996 and 1998

Coming on the heels of the 1994 partial collapse were a student death in 1996, and in 1998, the beating of a female student during the construction of Bonfire and the discovery of thirty students drinking in a Bonfire shack. Considering that Bonfire is worked upon only two months each year, a partial collapse, a student death during transport, a major assault, and revelations of keg parties on site all in the space of ten months of work would have prompted most employers to conduct a thorough investigation and a serious review of policy and procedure. The quick pace of dangerous events, however, resulted in no serious re-examinations.

Redpot Reunion

On November 22, four days after the accident, 1977 Redpot Kelly Dewitt emailed V.P. of Student Affairs Malon Southerland, saying that "many months ago," he had emailed the Bonfire endowment about the quickness with which the Bonfire would fall after being lit in recent years. He had met with other Redpots at a Redpot reunion and discussed the matter. They came to the conclusion that the current Redpots were not using as many core logs, "logs used in the early construction of the stack which give (stack) stability." These "core logs" are usually thinner in diameter and bound tightly to the centerpole.

Dewitt wrote to Southerland that back in the seventies, they "would go out pretty far with these type logs on every stack except the very top ones." Reduction in the diameter of such a core could result in a reduction in the Bonfire sturdiness and a quicker collapse after lighting. "Even a 3 inch reduction each year can be significant when measured over a long period of time," Dewitt wrote. "In retrospect I see many ways we could have improved the stability of the structure, and the safety of the project, but it was not seen as necessary at the time."

1986 Health Warning

In 1986, Robert Stiteler, the university's safety and health officer, wrote a memo that suggested that the size of the Bonfire be decreased by one-half. He proposed to do this by reducing the height by ten feet—to 45 feet—and reducing the width by ten feet—to 35 feet. Stiteler claimed that such a size reduction would reduce "cutting time and stacking time thereby reducing time for potential injuries and also allowing more time for studies."

Stiteler received a response from then-Bonfire Adviser William Kibler, reasoning, among other things that a reduction in the size of Bonfire "would almost assuredly result in extremely negative reaction and protest from a significant portion of the student body and a significant population of former students." Also "bulleted" as a reason for keeping Bonfire big was that "community relations may be improved by announcing a 50 percent reduction in Bonfire size, but that would clearly be more than off set by worsening relations with students and former students."

Revealing Memos

Two interesting and conflicting memos were sent to William Kibler in the years following Stiteler's warning. In a September 1987 memo to Kibler, then-Vice President for Student Services John Koldus wrote, "It is well-established fact that bonfire constitutes by far the single most liability-laden student activity on this campus."

Six years later, when Kibler was promoted to Associate Vice-President for Student Affairs, V.P. for Student Affairs Southerland wrote a commendatory letter to Kibler for his service as Bonfire adviser; "Bill, please accept my thanks and gratitude for your ten years of service as Advisor to Bonfire and Chair of the Bonfire Committee. This is one of the more important tasks that we ask any staff member to take on as an extra assignment."

One Vice President calls Bonfire "the single most liability laden student activity on this campus," while the vice president in charge of building the Bonfire calls it a "task" and an "extra assignment." Unfortunately, it was an extremely dangerous project, but the university did treat it as an extra assignment for a single bureaucrat. The "task" of building a six-story, all-log structure could have been the central duty of several bureaucrats and technical experts, but it was the extra assignment of one administrator.

Why?

How could the warnings of respected engineers have been ignored? How could administrators and builders ignore the warning signals of a deadly traffic accident, hazing suspensions, alcohol arrests, assaults on women and men, and a collapse in 1994? Any one of these warnings should have jolted administrators and builders into reforming and overhauling the Bonfire construction process and possibly the design itself. Through my research on the Bonfire hierarchy and building process, I have discovered six central themes to A&M's standard operations that make up an organizational culture which allowed the A&M administration as normal practice to ignore signs of imminent catastrophe.

Student-Run Project

Since the Corps of Cadets relinquished total control of the Bonfire tradition, the construction of Bonfire became more and more independent of direct university control. Apparently, the idea that the Bonfire is a student-run project eventually became the official tradition. After the 1999 tragedy, the University pronounced repeatedly that the Bonfire is run by students. If it doesn't hold up in court, at least it seems to carry some weight in public opinion.

Laissez Faire

Texas A&M is one of the most politically conservative campuses in the nation. And conservatives do prefer laissez-faire policies. But as we may see in a future chapter, the university is not so laissez-faire with those who oppose tradition. Of course, if the Bonfire is indeed supposed to be a student-run project, a laissez faire attitude seems justified. Or did the university justify its laissez faire attitude by saying that Bonfire was a student-run project?

Crisis Management and Incremental Policy Adjustment

When students got in trouble with the law, or when someone died building Bonfire, or when the public was in an uproar about some unseemly aspect of Bonfire, then the University seemed to go into action. When a crisis occurred, the university managed it by sending the injured to the hospital and the dead to the morgue, and by settling civil suits out of court. If there was a loophole in policy or regulation not enforced, then the university closed up that loophole or enforced that rule, after the fact, and sometimes only temporarily. If a dorm was hazing or students drinking, those students were punished, even though they could often sneak back into cut or stack. How could they do that? Because the university never decided to become proactive in its management. The pattern that emerges out of decades of Bonfire history is that of a crisis management style which attempts to minimize damage after a crisis occurs rather than a pro-active style that seeks to prevent crises. The university never even sought to make its management on-site. When a crisis occurred as a result of the lack of supervision, they patched it with an incremental band-aid and never overhauled their overall policy. Now they have to.

Obsession

The fact that one of the Redpots could ask a policeman when students could start rebuilding Bonfire as people lay dying beneath the stack indicates at least on this one Redpot's part a seemingly pathological obsession with building the Bonfire. Other Redpots, especially the Junior Redpots, show signs of obsession as they must, as seen in their DAN books, eat, sleep, and live Bonfire. This pre-occupation with building the Bonfire is compounded with the need and desire to get it built on time. Such a compounding of effects must produce a sort of frantic attitude in which a slightly leaning Bonfire is okay, as long as it is pretty symmetrical (see witness report cited previously). Ignoring the lopsidedness of Bonfire is evidence that getting Bonfire built was more important than the safety of students. Such an attitude may not be pathological, but it is dangerous.

But the obsession with or overvaluing of Tradition is not limited to the Redpots. The lobbying efforts, which began immediately after the collapse, to burn a post-tragedy Bonfire for 1999; the fact that it took three months for the university to suspend Bonfire 2000 in lieu of the ongoing investigation; and the hastily organized memorial service as two students teetered on the brink of death are all evidence that Aggieland may have allowed itself to become consumed with its own glorification of Tradition.

Unquestioned Faith

Most people who opposed the Bonfire—many faculty, students, and community members—never knew the details of its construction, design, and lack of supervision. But they had faith, for some reason, that the A&M administration had everything under control. After all, if there's one thing that Texas A&M is good at, it is tradition. And Bonfire was the ultimate tradition.

Those close to the Bonfire knew how the design was passed down from pot to pot, how there was little university or engineering supervision, and knew that student shenanigans were embedded as traditions into the umbrella Bonfire tradition. But they seemed to have faith in tradition itself, as if history were on their side, as if being faithful and being decisive (whether right or wrong), and doing so for Tradition, would produce results similar to those of the past. And in the past, no one had been killed by a falling stack.

The Iron Triangle

Does the administration fear possible student and alumni reaction or does it use its specter to maintain desired policies?

University culture and policy to a large extent are controlled by two elements: former students and red-ass current students. This is no accident. Administrators support these spirited "traditionalists" and the "traditionalists" support the administrators. Such an "iron triangle" is both an armor and a trap. The one thing that all three can agree upon is tradition, so policies on such traditions as Bonfire rarely change, even though, on the ground, procedures change every year.

Why were warnings not heeded? Was it an overzealous dedication to tradition? Was it the tradition that Bonfire be left up to the Redpots, and that outsiders not interfere? Or was it a fear of backlash from Red-ass traditionalists who would punish those who attempt to change what is already perfect? Was it an unquestioning faith in the sturdiness of each year's Bonfire, a sense that the strength and safety of Bonfire had developed its own momentum that would roll down through the years? Or was it simply the apathetic assumption that the Bonfire would be safe—especially if we don't think about it too much?

The answer is probably yes to a degree, to all those questions. And, yes, tradition itself has something to do with all those yes's. With twelve deaths on its hands, Texas A&M must now question whether a university's organizational philosophy should be founded upon tradition, and whether those traditions themselves must now be re-evaluated and re-interpreted.

Responsibility

The deaths of twelve students as a result of a university-sponsored activity is unprecedented. The Bonfire tragedy may have been an accident, but it was not a natural disaster. As far as can be ascertained, an earthquake did not cause centerpole to break. All of the factors that caused this accident—the design, structure, materials, personnel, training, height of centerpole, role of alcohol, and so forth—could have been controlled by the organizers and builders of Bonfire 1999. Only the weather is uncontrollable, and the weather was not a factor. Nevertheless many Aggies believe that no one should be held accountable for the mistakes that led to the accident. They believe either that it was "purely" an accident (implying that humans could neither foresee nor prevent it) or that we should not lay blame and simply try to prevent future mistakes.

It is ironic that at a university as conservative as Texas A&M, many would like to set aside the concept of "personal responsibility" in the preventable deaths of twelve students. If the organizers and overseers of Bonfire 1999 are not held accountable and responsible for their incompetence and/or apathy, then they or future position-holders will more likely reproduce the organizational culture that resulted in tragedy. If those who are responsible for the accident do not accept their responsibility, then it must be assigned to them, and they must be encouraged, if not forced, to accept the appropriate consequences.

The Students or the University?

The University's first line of defense seems to be that the Bonfire was a student-run operation. The implication here is that the students should take responsibility for the preventable accident. But the Bonfire could have never been built without the University "running" a great deal of the operation, including administrative oversight, preparation of the field, regulating student behavior, providing public relations services, covering tens of thousands of dollars in costs, and soliciting donations.

Futhermore, Texas A&M uses the tradition to promote the university to prospective students, and also to foster the connection to former students. Aggie alumni contribute twice as much money to their alma mater than Longhorns despite being outnumbered by one third. The tremendous bond felt by Aggies owes much to the ever-burning flame of Bonfire.

The following is an excerpt from a 1992 memo from then-Bonfire adviser William Kibler to Vice-President for Student Services John J. Koldus concerning the Department of Recreational Sports' complaints that the polo fields will be unavailable for certain sports (like polo) when the Bonfire site is moved there. The Bonfire site was moved from Duncan Field to the polo fields in 1992.

> Regarding the questions of liability, it is now and always has been the responsibility of the university to ensure that our campus is as safe as possible. It would not be the personal responsibility of the student leadership of Bonfire if a student trips on a wire on the polo field any more than it has been at Duncan Field. The University must decide if any activity is too risky to be allowed to take place on the campus, whether it is Bonfire, polo, rugby, or any other activity. All these activities involve elements of risk and it is our collective responsibility to minimize these risks to the greatest extent possible. This is essentially why we have the problem we have—I cannot see a way that we can safely build Bonfire and hold polo matches on this same field at the same time.

Although Texas A&M has lately stressed that Bonfire is a student-run activity, at least in its internal communications, liability for Bonfire still lies squarely with the university itself.

Redpots

One could say that the Redpots are responsible. They are like the architects and foremen of Bonfire. They take the handed-down designs from previous Bonfire-builders, they train workers, they make sure that the plans are executed. They make sure that workers aren't drunk. In many respects, the Redpots failed. Drunk and untrained students were allowed on the stack. The centerpole was taller than it was supposed to be. Inexperienced students were allowed to work on the upper levels of stack. Hazing and horseplay contributed to an atmosphere not conducive to safety and serious construction; although some noticed the leaning of the first stack, no one acted on the observations. Finally, Redpots may have strayed from the designs of previous Bonfires, and thus built a faulty one.

But it must be said that the Redpots are college students. They are young. Some of them may not even be old enough to drink. They are mesmerized by the traditions of Aggieland. This means in part that they may be pre-occupied with activities other than building a strong Bonfire. Nobody told the Redpots that they are not trained in the field of constructing a multi-storied edifice. Previous Redpots had built strong Bonfires, and they learned from the previous Redpots. Furthermore, some of these Deadpots were on hand to give advice, if not also to lend to hazing activities. Finally, there are eighteen Redpots and thousands of students involved in Bonfire. Much of the training of stack workers was delegated to crew chiefs and lower pots, and they (such as the drunk Brown Pots) may not have been as responsible or skilled as the Redpots themselves.

The Bonfire Adviser

The administration knew that the Redpots cannot build a Bonfire on their own. Some construction workers help with the building of it, and the Bonfire Adviser is assigned to oversee the entire project. Rusty Thompson was the Bonfire Adviser in 1999. Before he became Bonfire Adviser in 1998, Thompson had served on the Bonfire Committee for several years, and worked also as a residence life adviser. He is not an engineer. On a morning TV news program days after the collapse, Thompson stated that although he is not an engineer, "it is not really an expectation of my job that I am. It is my job to make sure students have all the resources they need." (Stutz, *Dallas Morning News*, 11/23/99)

Thompson works in the Student Affairs office, and he is responsible for making sure that the Bonfire is built properly, safely, and within University regulations. In this, he failed.

What University regulation was not broken in the name of Bonfire? What University regulation has not been broken in the name of Bonfire for the past decade? Every major area of University regulation—alcohol, hazing, safety, harassment, intimidation, and violence—has been broken and ignored in the building of Bonfire, and done so more times than can be estimated. Thompson is only responsible for the violations and mistakes of the last two years.

A female student riding in the bed of a truck on the way back from cut in 1996 died when the driver of the speeding truck lost control of the vehicle, and it flipped over more than once. After that incident, riding in the beds of trucks was officially prohibited. By 1999, it was again practiced on Bonfire trips. In 1998, thirty students (including twenty minors) were caught by University police with alcohol in a Bonfire shack. The next year, drinking and stacking was once again a common practice. Hazing was widespread in 1998, and then again in 1999. A woman was beat up in 1998 by Bonfire builders, and a man was roughed up in 1999. Finally, it was established in the 1980's that the Bonfire adviser would ensure that Bonfire would not exceed fifty-five feet. Thompson apparently forgot or ignored this rule. How many lives would have been saved if Thompson had simply done what he was paid to do?

But an examination of Thompson's emails reveals that perhaps Thompson's job is not to actively regulate and oversee the safe and sane construction of Bonfire. It seems that he is more like a crisis manager/ public relations emergency response administrator. When a problem arises, then the Bonfire Adviser goes in action. The Adviser knows (we hope he knows) that there are many violations going on, but perhaps it is not the responsibility of the Adviser to do anything until an incident report, a police report, or a plain old complaint is filed. When residents complain of loud music; when a mother complains that his son had his foot chopped at cut; when racist, sexist, or anti-gay remarks are made by Bonfire organizers; when a television station wants to broadcast Bonfire; when Pots making "wake-up calls" end up ruining dorm doors; or when a fellow bureaucrat becomes concerned that a student might break his neck as a result of "groding" and sue the University; then the Adviser flies into action, often consulting and advising with other bureaucrats.

Vice-President of Student Affairs

Who oversees the Bonfire Adviser? Who writes his job description? Who decides whether the Bonfire Adviser should be a crisis manager or a pro-active enforcer who prevents crises and accidents from happening in the first place? This job belongs to the Vice-President of Student Affairs, J. Malon Southerland.

As the 1994 Bonfire was being pulled down because it had begun to lean dangerously, Southerland marveled at the strength of the centerpole, which did not break or collapse easily. Such amazement apparently renders an evaluation of Bonfire design unnecessary. The vice-presidential office of student affairs then proceeded to push off T. J. Hirsch's warnings about the design of Bonfire onto the student Bonfire organizers.

A review of Bonfire design could have been conducted just in case. But apparently, "just in case" and "pro-active" were not in the administration's vocabulary; they deal with Bonfire issues only after they have exploded in their faces. It is no wonder that the office could not enforce fundamental university regulations in the building of Bonfire.

There is evidence that Southerland was insulated from the actual affairs of the students. He was shocked that racist remarks had been written on Bonfire head gear in the late 1990's, and in 1986 he called an incident of male cadets assaulting a female cadet while building Bonfire an "isolated incident," and said that "male-female relations in the corps are not a problem." His warning in his March 9, 1999 letter that a "serious incident" involving dorm life, alcohol, and Bonfire could be imminent was too little too late.

The Texas A&M University President

In January, A&M President Ray Bowen told *The Eagle*, "At the end of the day, the buck stops here."

"How can I say to someone, 'I want you out of this job,' when I'm at the top of that command? I have to set the standard."

He wonders if he should have noticed anything wrong with the stack, having passed it every evening in the fall of 1999. "I ask myself, 'Did I see anything that should have registered?' . . . Was there anything I should have seen? Was there anything I missed?"

Upon arriving at the scene of the tragedy, Bowen said that he felt useless, and that he "wanted to climb on top of that stack and lift those logs one by one."

Bowen graduated from Texas A&M in 1958. This means he was a student at A&M when a student was killed by a truck while guarding Bonfire in 1955, and also when the Bonfire stack suddenly collapsed during lunch in 1957. Bowen became president of Texas A&M in 1994. He witnessed the partial collapse of Bonfire 1994, and he also presided over the university when a student died in a Bonfire-related traffic accident in 1996.

Bowen knew of the dangers of Bonfire. He knew that it could collapse. He knew that students can die in the massive, unsupervised operation. Having been a student, he also knew how things operated at Texas A&M. He knew that student-run operations can and will involve violations of school regulations, some of which can and will jeopardize the lives of students.

Bowen is an engineer by training. He asks himself "Was there anything I missed?" Apparently he missed the 1994 Bonfire leaning even though he was president at the time. After the 1994 leaning, administrators such as Southerland claimed that the wet ground had caused it and that the Bonfire structure itself was sound. Bowen, as an engineer, could have foreseen that a number of different factors could cause the Bonfire to lean dangerously. He could have decided not to simply take the word of laymen, and he could have ordered a serious investigation into Bonfire design, construction, and overall safety. Instead, he allowed the students to rush and build another Bonfire on the same ground in time for the big game.

"Was there anything I should have seen?" Bowen saw students die while building Bonfire. He saw alcohol, hazing, and violence in the building of Bonfire. He saw how students break rules and buck precautions in the name of tradition. As an engineer, he saw a massive construction project grossly undersupervised, under-regulated, and underplanned. It is not Bowen's sight that is in question; it is his lack of action. No matter how embarrassing or sobering were the various Bonfire crises Bowen saw, he never ordered a thorough evaluation and overhauling of any part of the Bonfire building process or stack design.

There is great evidence that Aggie culture was the number one contributing factor to the collapse of the Bonfire. The President is supposed to stand above Aggie culture, rein it in, regulate it. Perhaps his office was too busy monitoring Bonfire dissidents to transcend university culture. Perhaps Bowen was too much of an Aggie. He had too much faith in the safety of traditions. Indeed, there may be safety in tradition—political safety—but not physical safety. Perhaps one was compromised for the other.

"I take responsibility for everything that happens at A&M." Taking responsibility for the Bonfire tragedy and resigning from the presidency would defy Texas A&M lawyers but would manifest the honor of the Aggie Spirit.

The Aggie Spirit

The Aggie Spirit

What is the Aggie Spirit, and how best can Aggies manifest the Aggie Spirit through its traditions and rituals?

The rest of the book examines the Bonfire, Texas A&M culture, and the dialectic between them. The following sections include a brief, selective history of Texas A&M, a history of the Texas Aggie Bonfire, six interviews with seven current and former Texas A&M students and faculty, and a section simply entitled, "Conclusion."

There are three main purposes to the rest of the book. First, we will try to understand the deeper cultural roots of the 1999 Bonfire tragedy. The practices that led to the Bonfire collapse have their roots in the history and traditional culture of Texas A&M, and in order to prevent another such tragedy, we must understand the deeper roots from which those practices and the current student and organizational cultures sprung.

Second, the Bonfire itself must be understood in the context of Texas A&M culture and history. The Bonfire is an evolving symbol of an evolving culture and an ongoing history. Conversely (and thirdly), we can better understand the Aggie Spirit and culture by studying their manifestations in Bonfire culture and history.

In understanding the fascinating dynamic between Aggie culture and Bonfire culture, four areas call for special attention. First, Bonfire is supposed to unite all Aggies, and yet two-percenters and minority groups tend to feel alienated from the tradition. Second, aspects of Bonfire culture like student independence and bucking authority, misogyny and sexual discrimination, secrecy, and hazing emerged from Corps of Cadets culture. Third, the culture of suppressing dissent at Texas A&M applies doubly to Bonfire. Fourth, although Texas A&M has sought to transform itself into a "world-class university" for over three decades, some believe that Bonfire and certain other traditions are holding it back.

All this hullabaloo about Texas A&M history and culture and Bonfire history and culture is aimed at trying to get a better feel for that mysterious force known as the Aggie Spirit. When we get a handle on that, and upon understanding the Aggie culture, we can ask ourselves whether the Aggie Spirit is truly manifested through our culture and rituals. If the Spirit is not truly represented through such, then we must ask ourselves how we must transform our traditions and culture to honor the Aggie Spirit.

A Selective History
of Texas A&M

This chapter presents a history of Texas A&M and its surrounding community with a concentration on social and institutional factors that contributed to the Aggie culture. Aggie history both demonstrates and molds Aggie attitudes about gender, manhood, race, camaraderie, politics, the Confederacy and Old South, human progress and technology, and the natural environment.

Possibly the most important factor in the evolution of Aggie culture is the relative barrenness in which it evolved. For much of the over six-score years of its existence, Texas A&M was located a 100-mile train's ride away from any medium or large city. And because it was an all-male college in which all students were required to train for the military, no major population of females was to be found in or around the university.

Although recent political movements on American campuses have stressed over and over again the domination of American culture and society by white males, it cannot be overly stressed that the Texas A&M student body consisted almost completely of white male Texans up until the 1970's. Furthermore, these white males were all willing and able to join the Texas A&M Corps of Cadets. The Corps of Cadets, through most of Aggie history, transformed Texas farm boys into Aggie men. They did so through a culture of military discipline, university education, and hazing.

Plantations and a Railroad

Texas A&M is located in the city of College Station, situated in the west-central part of East Texas, north of the halfway mark between Houston and Austin, Texas. College Station and the adjacent Bryan together make up the largest metropolitan area in Brazos County. Before there was a college or a College Station, Brazos County was home to Indians, then a part of the Spanish empire, then part of northern Mexico, then part of the Republic of Texas, which joined the United States, only to secede as a member of the Confederacy.

Before the civil war, "the value of property in slaves exceeded that for all other forms of property including land," according to Mary Clare Fabishak in one of the few histories of the area (*Single Industry Boomtown: The Rise and Decline of a Dependency Relationship – College Station*). Brazos County was dotted with dozens of plantations growing almost solely the crop of King Cotton. Shortly after the Civil War, the Houston and Texas Railway connected Bryan to the rest of the railed world and most directly to Millican, Hempstead, Cypress, and Houston. The connection spurred a sudden growth of Bryan. In one instance, four houses sprung up literally overnight, as residents of Millican broke down their houses and rebuilt them further up the rail in Bryan.

In 1866, Texas accepted the terms of the Morrill Act of 1862. The state was granted 180,000 acres of federal land, which could be sold to create a permanent university fund for "the endowment, support and maintenance of at least one college where the leading object shall be, without excluding other scientific and classical studies, and including military tactics, to teach such branches of learning as are related to agriculture and the mechanic arts . . . in order to promote the liberal and practical education of the industrial classes in the several pursuits and professions of life."

Bryan, Texas offered the lowest bid for the university, but made a great effort. Three citizens offered a total of 2,416 acres of land to the university; about two thousand of it was prairie and the rest of it forest, consisting mostly of post oak trees. The state legislature decided to place the first public college of Texas on the donated land, about five miles southeast of Bryan. Much of the land was raw wilderness. In the early years of the university, students and residents had to watch out for attacks by wolves. It was in these years, ironically, when there were plenty of trees to make huge bonfires, but it never occurred to people to do so.

Because of political and bureaucratic troubles, it took ten years for the Agricultural and Mechanical College of Texas to open its doors, and when it did, on September 17, 1876, six students showed up for class. Classes were delayed until Governor Richard Coke showed up for the dedication speech on October 4; by then forty students had shown up. Coke's dedication speech has long been studied by Cadets earning their A's in campusology: "Let your watchword be duty, and know no other talisman of success than labor. Let honor be your guiding star in your dealings with your superiors, your fellows, with all. Be true to a trust reposed as the needle to the pole, stand the right even to the sacrifice of life itself, and learn that death is preferable to dishonor."

Aggie History Before 1963

Corps of Cadets

Through Governor Coke's speech, the college was christened with a bow to Honor itself, and a to-the-death devotion to Right. All students were also in training for the military, so the high-minded words of Coke must have reverberated over the years with a particular tone, one that spoke of honor and righteousness in military combat.

A Rules and Regulations book was given to each military cadet upon entering the University. He was expected to carry himself in the most upright of manners and live with honor and appropriate responsibility. The cadets' entire week was regimented, including daily chapel, mandatory classes, study time, meals, sleep, and inspections by military superiors. The rulebook also required cadets to own "two pairs of shoes, seven shirts, seven pairs of socks, four handkerchiefs, six towels, one clothes brush, one comb, two pillowcases, two pair of sheets, one pair of blankets, one comfort, four pairs of drawers, four undershirts and seven collars." Long hair, moustaches, drinking, gambling, guns, private parties, and visiting places of public amusement (such as the dozens of saloons in Bryan) were not tolerated. A famous saying came out of Corps discipline: "Aggies don't lie, steal, or cheat."

For its first forty-three years, the Corps wore Confederate gray uniforms and were sometimes trained by Confederate veterans. In 1916, amidst World War I, the federal government implemented the National Defense Act, which established Reserve Officer Training Corps (ROTC) programs throughout the nation. The Corps of Cadets became an ROTC, and half of all A&M graduates during World War I served in it. Fifty-three Aggies died in World War I, and they were honored by the planting of fifty-three oaks around the main drill field. The Bonfire was burned on this field for years, sometimes scorching these trees.

The A&MC trained and educated even more officers and soldiers for World War II. All of the senior classes of 1941 and 1942 were commissioned at graduation. Twenty thousand Aggies served, fourteen thousand of whom were officers. A&M contributed twenty-nine generals, more than Westpoint, and over 900 A&M graduates died. Aggies have earned eight Congressional Medals of Honor.

Hazing, Practical Jokes, and Antics

One could say that the stringent rules and regulations were placed on A&M cadets because the military commanders and administrators of the school understood how rowdy some of the Texas boys could get if they were not tightly controlled.

Cadet antics included stealing chickens, stealing the President's Thanksgiving turkey, gambling, burning outhouses, drinking and throwing keg parties in the woods, soliciting prostitutes, and snow-balling teachers. Some pranks involved weapons, such as shooting the light at the top of the Academic building, blowing up the local trolley tracks with dynamite, and firing the cannons in front of old Ross Hall. Throwing together a pile of trash and burning it was one such antic that eventually transformed into Bonfire.

Not only did the Aggies kidnap and brand the University of Texas mascot – an ornery longhorn bull – they even kidnapped Rice University students attempting to re-capture their own giant stuffed owl mascot. The students were paraded around campus, abused, and retained for days until the Rice President called and demanded their return. Even as the various antics came and went, one thing remained: hazing. Although freshman cadets – fish – suffered the most hazing, the culture spread even among the civilian students when they began attending A&M. Freshmen cadets must do push-ups on command, whip-out (say howdy and introduce himself) to every upperclassman and remember their names, get paddled, perform midnight drills or runs across campus, and take regular browbeatings and humiliations from sophomores and others above them. Throughout Aggie history, some of the more serious forms of hazing have included beatings, strappings and burnings. Hazing rituals have long been associated with Bonfire, and the Bonfire itself may have at one point been seen as a form of hazing. Freshmen were required to work under the command of their superiors for long hours and under grueling and dangerous circumstances. Nevertheless, if the hazed survive without permanent damage, they more often than not appreciate their experiences and the male bonding established through it, and go on to haze others.

A&M has fought hazing, at least on paper, from the very earliest days of the institution. The legendary President Sul Ross (who saved A&M from obscurity), presiding during the late nineteenth century, warned that he would expel those students who hazed. Twenty-seven cadets were dismissed in January 1913 after a years-long rash of often-violent hazing. When over four hundred students petitioned to have the expelled cadets reinstated, the faculty refused, and the students refused to go to class. Those who signed the petition were expelled as well. The entire state government became involved and a state anti-hazing law was passed. The petition-signers were allowed back into school after signing a pledge never to haze again. Two were subsequently caught and expelled (Dethloff, 237-241).

The hazing did not stop, and statewide furors over hazing at Texas A&M besmirched its name in 1921 and 1924. When state investigators probed the Corps of Cadets, the freshmen and sophomores refused to speak about the organization's "private life" (305-306). This "conspiracy of silence" has for most of A&M history concealed violations of university policy and state law. The Board of Directors tried to ban the "more serious forms of hazing" in 1929 and after World War II. Such a task was especially difficult after World War II because the Cadets began to ritualize many of the practices of former days which had been, at best, customs. Thus, yell practice, muster, the bonfire, and observance of memorials were increasingly codified and ritualized, and while the form was retained the earlier meaning was often lost. Hazing became more of a ritualistic practice in the postwar years than *the bon-vivant*, fraternal initiation of earlier years. Because it had become more of a ritual, it was more sacrosanct to the Corps of Cadets. An attack upon hazing by the administration after World War II created a profound reaction among cadets, who believed they were doing what was right, as well as among former students, who were in effect being memorialized by the rituals (Dethloff 476).

President Gibb Gilchrest carried forth perhaps the strongest effort ever in A&M history to rid the campus of hazing. As a result, all 2100 students of the Corps of Cadets protested in front of his home. A movement of Corps members and veterans eventually prompted the state to hold hearings on Gilchrist's presidency. He was accused of mismanagement by students, alumni, and faculty. The state legislature decided that the charges against Gilchrist resulted from his anti-hazing policies, and the 1947 hearings were adjourned without any action against him. The next year, he was assigned to be the first chancellor of the Texas A&M System.

Women and Texas A&M

In the early years of the University, only a small number of women were allowed to attend the university, and these women were almost invariably the daughters and wives of faculty and administrators. According to a 1975 *Houston Chronicle* article, these early women were given military uniforms but "scrapped them for buttons and bows because the cadets liked it that way."

In 1915, the A&M administration made it official policy that women were not allowed to attend regular sessions of university classes. This prohibition didn't stop some women. In 1925, Mary Evelyn Crawford, a sister of a professor of mechanical engineering, became the first woman to graduate from A&MC. In 1933, some local women who had no blood relations with A&M faculty were refused admission. The reason the local judge gave was that A&M was a military school, and that the state legislature had not specified which sexes could enter the school, as it had for the other Texas public colleges. Although A&M was founded for the industrial classes, as far as women were concerned, only the relatives of faculty could attend.

Blacks and Texas A&M

In the decades starting from the inception of A&M to the Great Depression, blacks regularly made up one-third to over one-half of the population of the Brazos County. They worked as mostly sharecroppers, tenant farmers, or servants. One famous Texas A&M servant was "Uncle Dan" Jackson, who worked at Texas A&M as a janitor in the early decades of the twentieth century. He was quite popular among the cadets and was often elected class president. Blacks were not allowed to attend Texas A&M before 1963.

Although unauthorized blacks and Hispanics were not allowed on campus in the early part of the twentieth century, Aggies may have visited the property of blacks uninvited, and at night. One of several locally auctioned Ku Klux Klan robes dated from the late 1910's or early 1920's donated to Texas A&M has embroidered into its cloth the name "D X Bible." If the legendary A&M football coach Dana X. Bible was a member of the Klan, it may mean that other members of the A&M faculty and student body too were not accepting of nonwhite peoples. Even after blacks were allowed to attend A&M, the first black starter on the football team, Hugh McElroy '71, reported that a cross was burned on the lawn of the athletic dormitory for his viewing.

1963 to the present

The year 1963 was a wild one for Texas A&M. On April 27, 1963, the Board of Directors announced that daughters and wives of faculty were formally allowed to enroll in the college. Women were also allowed to enroll in courses of study or to use facilities that were not available elsewhere in the state, and all graduate studies were available to women.

When President James Earl Rudder met with the entire Corps of Cadets in G. Rollie White Coliseum, many chanted, "We don't want to integrate," meaning, integrate with women. Most Aggies present and past were shocked and angry. Some found consolation in that the presence of women might improve football recruiting (Dethloff 569). The movement to keep Texas A&M all-male penetrated the state legislature but only resulted in a resolution to maintain one majority male and one majority female university in Texas.

In the summer of 1963, black students were allowed to attend the University for the first time in its history.

On August 23, 1963, the Texas Legislature changed the name of the college from Agricultural and Mechanical College of Texas to Texas A&M University. Again an uproar ensued. They had tampered with the "good name" of Texas A&M College.

In November of 1963, President John F. Kennedy was assassinated in Dallas, and the Bonfire was cancelled and dismantled in his honor.

In November of the following year, the reform-minded President Rudder was named chancellor in addition to his duties as President. In September 1965, Rudder and his Board of Directors made membership in the ROTC and Corps of Cadets noncompulsory. Throughout the rest of the sixties, the number of women at A&M increased exponentially, and in 1971, the University formalized what already existed on the ground: full coeducation.

In his definitive history of A&M, Henry C. Dethloff writes that Texas A&M is not simply a university, but that it is "a way of life and an attitude toward life." In conventional Aggie thought, this way of life is centered around traditions. With the Corps being purely voluntary, this group of young men and eventually women became an elite organization enforcing these traditions. Dethloff claims that the "better" traditions "live on," including Bonfire, Muster, and Silver Taps. Such traditions express Aggie "fraternity" and make it a student body with a "difference."

Since the writing of Dethloff's history, which ends in 1976, Texas A&M has continued its traditions, and its football-centered rituals. But the student body has changed immensely. It is one now of many "differences." Aggie Bonfire is a manifestation of the Aggie Spirit for some of these "different" groups, but not all.

A large number of the 42,000 students still look toward the Corps of Cadets, and the Corps-dominated Yell Leaders and Red Pots for cultural signals. In the 1970's, the Corps went co-educational. By the late nineties, the size of the Corps was about 2,200, and included about 80 or 100 women.

In 1984, hazing practices of the Corps drew widespread attention as a 20-year old sophomore died of heatstroke, after he was forced to do exercises in the middle of the night.

In August 1997, the spotlight again was shined, this time on the renowned Aggie Fish Drill Team, which had regularly won national championships in military drills. Freshman Travis Alton reported to the Corps Commandant that he had been punched, kicked, and forced to cut himself by Corps upperclassmen. Three other freshmen also came forward with reports of being physically abused. One had his hands crushed with a gun, and another had his face scraped with a scouring pad. The Fish Drill Team was suspended by President Ray Bowen.

In its plan for the future, *Vision 2020: Creating a Culture of Excellence for the 21st Century,* as outlined by current President Ray Bowen, Texas A&M aims to be one of the top ten public universities in the nation by the year 2020. As Texas A&M becomes more and more of a rigorous academic institution rather than a military-styled cultural-educational fraternity, it is yet to be seen how traditional ways at Texas A&M will evolve, and what new traditions might transpire.

Before a Living Tree was Killed 1909-1941

It began as a joke. In the fall of 1909 or thereabouts, two Texas A&M students decided that they needed to do something to get people excited about Texas A&M's upcoming football game against the University of Texas. They gathered some trash in the middle of campus and then set it on fire. Students left their classes to watch the pile burn.

The year of the first bonfire has always been in question. According to long-time pep-raiser and decades-long official "Greeter," P.L. "Pinkie" Downs, Jr., there were no bonfires during his undergraduate years, 1902-1906, and according to Ernest Langford, former director of the University Archives, there was a Bonfire in his freshman year of 1909. The first bonfire was a "pile of scrap wood" about twelve feet high.

"We made the rounds of all the buildings and anything loose was deposited in a pile on the parade ground. We burned it the night before we went to Austin," Langford reported to the Texas A&M *Battalion*. In the same article, he said that in 1912, students "confiscated" lumber that was supposed to be used to build Leggett and Milner Halls and threw it on the Bonfire pile. This made for a substantially larger Bonfire (DeFrank, Tommy, *Batt* 11/10/64).

Frank G. Anderson, Aggie coach and Commandant, wrote a much-referenced letter to the *Battalion* in 1972, long after he had retired. In it, he described the 1920 Bonfire and other early Bonfires as being made up of "community trash, boxes, etc. that the merchants stored for the pick-up week preceding the bonfire, the woodpiles of all the professors and every piece of loose wood and much that was not loose which was on or near the campus." He has also been quoted as writing that some of the early favorites for burning were "untended, unwatched, and hopefully, unoccupied outhouses." (*Batt* 8/27/84).

Students would turn the burning of the bonfire into a pep meeting, as they were called back then, where speeches were made and spirit yells shouted out. Further in the letter, Anderson wrote that, "All of these materials were quickly combustible, even though the pile might be quite large, the fire seldom outlasted the speechmaking. The students had a big time."

In 1915, the Aggies built a bonfire *after* the game against University of Texas. After the now legendary 13-0 victory over UT, the Aggies went back to A&M and celebrated in downtown Bryan. According to the Bryan Fire Chief of 1927 to 1954, C.E. Griesser, "The people who lived on Old College Road (north of the University) thought there was a cattle stampede. There must have been 1,500 to 2,000 of them. They picked up all the old trash boxes and dry goods boxes behind the stores and piled them in the middle of the street at 26th and Bryan. That stack was up there 15 feet high, I guess. I witnessed the whole thing from the corner where James drug store was.

"That street hadn't been down a year I believe. It exploded and left a hole eight to ten feet in diameter. I mean, it came up with a bang. It scattered Aggies and bonfire from hell to breakfast."

According to Griesser, the Aggies went beyond pyro-antics. "After the game, they painted '13-0' on every cow and every horse and every dog and every boxcar they could find around here."

The Bryan Eagle's report on the students' celebration seemed to sum up its playful nature: "They seemed to know where every bell, whistle and everything that would make noise was located and proceeded to make use of this knowledge, and mingled with their yells and the yells of their friends, they made things merry for several hours. A big bonfire was built on the pavement near the Smith Drug company corner on West Anderson street and was kept burning for some time to furnish sufficient light for antics of every description. When the fire had soldered out and an examination was made the pavement was found to have cracked and broken into small pieces under the fire. This, however, can be easily remedied." (11/25/15)

An interesting sidenote: In 1916, after UT beat A&M 21-7, some apparently sore Aggies confiscated UT's mascot, a Longhorn steer, and branded it, "13-0." Upon re-acquisition of their mascot, the UT students were able to change the brand to say "Bevo." All subsequent Longhorn mascots have been named Bevo.

The 1915 bonfire was the last one built after a game, and by the 1920's the bonfire was held always on the campus of Texas A&M. The first bonfires were burned in front of the Memorial Student Center. Since the bonfire needed trash, locals saved their old boxes and papers for months in order to contribute to the bonfire (*Battalion* 11/19/71).

The first thirty or so bonfires were really nothing to write home about. In fact, the first known photograph of Bonfire was taken nearly twenty years after the 1909 bonfire. Ironically, the Texas A&M yearbook until 1949 was named The Longhorn, and the 1928 Longhorn shows a picture of a heap of junk which was the first photographed Aggie Bonfire. Even after this first photographed Bonfire, future Bonfires were not necessarily taken as seriously. Yearbook photos were not taken in 1929, 1937, and 1939-1941. These of course included depression and war years, when Bonfire may have been the last thing on Aggies' minds.

In the 1930's, private companies began contributing substantially to the bonfire effort. The Missouri Pacific Railroad let some of their cars bring in "boards and boxes from throughout the state, some from as far away as the Texas Panhandle." (*Batt 11/19/71*)

In 1933, the playful nature of Bonfire was again revealed in a serious fire. In a story entitled, "College Radicals Start Bonfire Three Weeks Early, Fire Quenched After Student Body Is Aroused," a *Battalion* writer implied (perhaps with tongue in cheek) that Aggie left-wingers may have been to blame for the Bonfire being set ablaze three weeks earlier than scheduled. But, he wrote,

> The almost tragic incident was not without its humor; put five hundred thinly-clad, yelling maniacs on a drill field at two o'clock in the morning trying all conceivable methods of putting out a fire and humor is the only possible result. The world's largest volunteer fire department went into action with intense enthusiasm and no cooperation. Spontaneous commands of "Put that hose here!" "Point that thing on the other side!" "The middle! That's where she needs it!" all contributed to the combined effect that the stream usually missed the fire and drenched the volunteers. Numerous drenchings had their effect; the would-be helpers finally retired to the sides to allow the regulars to quench the fire in a methodical manner.

According to the story, the then-Corps Commandant John E. Mitchell said that the next blaze would have to be handled by the students alone, because the fire department was not coming out again.

The year 1935 was an important one for the Bonfire. To quote Coach and Commandant Anderson's famous letter again: "The morning following the 1935 bonfire, a very irate farmer came to my office to say that the boys had carried off his log barn, lock, stock and barrel." Anderson, who had that year been appointed Commandant, charged every company and battery a fee so that the farmer would be paid in full for his barn.

In 1936, Anderson, issued an order that "no one would be allowed to collect bonfire materials or place them on the bonfire other than authorized personnel, and that the manner of building a legal bonfire would be under the direction of the commandant." According to Anderson, "This made the student body very unhappy, but being boys of an earlier generation, they figured that those in position of responsibility should call the shots."

Back then, there were a great number of dead trees between the railroad on the west side of campus and what was then Easterwood Airport. Commandant Anderson got permission to remove these dead trees and burn them in the bonfire. In his letter he calls this the "first log and legal bonfire." It was only about twelve feet high, but according to Anderson, it got the job done. Over the years, there had been some dispute among Bonfire historians about the first log bonfire. The first log bonfire was in 1936, and it was built using logs despite the desires of students to simply use trash along with some stolen outhouses.

We've Never Been Licked
1942-1959

The building, or rather, throwing together of the pre-1942 bonfires often resembled the bonfires themselves—characterized by explosions of activity, spontaneous actions and like the flames of the bonfire itself, a sort of improvised dance.

Although the military commander of the cadet-students took control of the bonfire in 1936, it was in 1942 that the Bonfire began to transform into a military activity, and in more than superficial ways. The very nature of the Bonfire became military and martial. With this transformation came the drive to build bigger and bigger Bonfires, culminating with the 1969 monster fire, which stood at 110 feet.

In 1942, *We've Never Been Licked*, a war movie set at Texas A&M was filmed on campus. In order to build a bonfire for the movie, living trees for the first time were cut and placed in a pile on campus. This was the first fresh log Bonfire. This Bonfire stood only about twenty-five feet tall, but it was still twice as tall as its 1936 ancestor. Until 1967, *We've Never Been Licked* was shown by the Corps in order to get cadets enthusiastic about Bonfire, and to challenge civilians to work on the fire. It must have been an ironic reminder to students that one of the most vaunted Aggie traditions was in essence re-created by Hollywood movie-makers.

Whatever the origin of the log Bonfire, the war was on. The initial enemy was UT Austin. Both universities held annual bonfires, one built by military boys and other built by those UT "tea-sippers," including fraternity and sorority members. Each year, Aggies and Longhorns would try to light each other's bonfires ahead of schedule. Eventually, the University of Texas quit building bonfires, as Aggie legend puts it, because they could compete no more with the burgeoning A&M Bonfire.

The year 1945 marked the first documented time when UT students tried to light the Aggie Bonfire. In another playful yet somewhat sadistic article in the November 29, 1945 *Battalion*, Ed Brandt tells the story:

> Equipped with Molotov Cocktails, gasoline ignitors, the latest Zippo lighter, and a gallon of that nasty orange paint, three of the wavy-hair boys from the forty acres visited the A&MC campus Tuesday night with the intention of setting off the annual bonfire and smearing a little paint here and there. But alas, alas, their little scheme went up in smoke of its own when they were caught by the bonfire guards.
>
> There were three of the little men in the visiting party—three of the scrawniest looking specifmens of human life anyone can imagine. On the top their heads was that beautiful t. u. wavy hair that you hear so much about, and dangling from their belts were those ever present keychains....
>
> Arriving on campus around 6:30, the adventurous sons drove around the grounds "getting the lay of the place" until shortly before 9:30. In their minds was the idea of crawling onto the parade grounds from the Grove, heaving their cocktails, and taking out for the tall timbers, where the car had been hidden earlier. But upon seeing the strength of the bonfire guards, it was decided the best thing to do would be to go into Bryan and go to the show, coming back about 3 in the morning, when the shift should be changing. There was only one small matter the lads hadn't counted on, and that was the fact that they were caught.
>
> When asked what they had to say about the whole thing, one of them came up with the remark "We was robbed," which is certainly the truth, as they are now minus that lovely wavy hair they were so proud of. Another said that they would probably be laughed at when they got back to Austin, and that they would most likely have to hide out for about a week. The third was so weak from trembling all night he didn't have the strength to speak....
>
> The total extent of their damage was painting out the words "College Station" on two city limits signs, and replacing them with "Texas u." in sickening orange paint. When this was discovered, the tea sipping boys gladly obliged in removing the paint when they were "asked" to do so by their captors.
>
> After adorning their car with little verses to let all know where the boys had been, the three bald-headed rascals were sent on their

"merry" way back to Austin, the home of the Longfaced Longhorns and the Disgraced Dogies.

Ironically, the three t.u. freshmen looked much like crew-cut Aggie cadets when they returned to Austin.

In 1945, Bonfire was forever changed. A center pole was added to the first post-War Bonfire. The center pole is just what it says, a pole stuck into the ground at the center of the Bonfire. Today's center poles are buried about ten feet in the ground. The first center pole was simply one pole in the middle of a tee-pee styled pile of tree trunks and limbs, with the usual outhouse (known as the t.u. tower or t.u. frat-house, or t.u. tea-house) on top. One picture of the 1945 Bonfire also shows an old tire hanging from the pile, and a skirt of tree limbs and branches on the ground surrounding the pile.

Junior yell leaders lit this first center-poled Bonfire, as opposed to the head yell leader doing the honors as would occur at future bonfires. And in contrast to the alcohol-drenched parties of later Bonfires, this one was followed by a formal ball at which the Aggieland Orchestra played.

The year 1946, marked the first "tall center pole." This center pole consisted of two poles spliced together, end to end, with some degree of overlap. This first tall center pole raised the bonfire from twenty-five to fifty feet. All future Bonfires would utilize this innovation.

In 1948 one of the greatest Bonfire legends played itself out. Again them wavy-headed UT boys tried to light the Bonfire, this time by bombing it from an airplane. Two UT students flew a single engine airplane 100 miles northeast to College Station. They made six passes at the Bonfire, coming within 25 feet of the ground. They dropped three homemade incendiary bombs. The first two were duds. The third one started a fire on the Bonfire! The fire was put out, however, and the Aggies guarding the Bonfire kept their cool enough to take down the serial number of the airplane, written on its underbelly. Legend has it that at least one Aggie had his rifle trained on the plane. The UT students were reprimanded once they touched down back in Austin.

A 1951 Bryan News article describes how these early timber bonfires were lit:

> A thousand gallons of oil were used to saturate the timber. Armor units used 100 one gallon buckets in "bucket brigade" fashion to transfer the petrol from trucks to the crown of the woodpile. The oil was donated by local filling stations.

The article also describes the Bonfire pep rally, now called a yell practice. It stated that "official Aggie greeter" P.L. "Pinky" Downs told the crowd how the Aggies were "gonna beat the hell out of Texas." In the 1950's, the phrase, "Beat the hell outta Texas" or "Beat the hell out of t.u." began appearing more and more in Bonfire literature and in Bonfire speeches. Eventually, the wording would evolve into an oft-used explanation of the Bonfire's symbolism: "Bonfire represents every Aggie's love of his university and his burning desire to beat the hell out of t.u."

The 1951 Bonfire once again broke the previous size record. Besides UT, the other enemy seemed to become the previous Bonfires. From the late Forties to the late sixties, one aim of each year's Bonfire was to make it bigger. If it wasn't bigger than the previous one, then it wasn't a failure; it just wasn't a complete success.

As noted previously, according to A&M historian Henry Dethloff, during the post-war period, "many of Texas A&M's traditions became more codified and ritualized," and this included the A&M Bonfire.

Because the Bonfire was now organized by the military commanders of the Corps of Cadets rather than students, the fifties saw written flow charts and instructions as to the organization and chain of command of Bonfire workers and leaders. The Assistant Commandant became the school administrative official in charge of the Bonfire. Beneath him was the Head yell leader (Bonfire Chief), and beneath him was a Senior yell leader (Coordinator of Committee Chairman). Beneath him were various Chairmen—of Wood Cutting, Center Pole, Transportation, Communications, Emergency, and so forth.

As ordered by the Commandant, the Bonfire was to be guarded day and night. There were to be eighteen guard posts. Each guard post would be supplied with firewood to keep warm, and guards could wear either their full military uniform or wear casual clothes. There were to be three rings created by the guard posts. There was the outer periphery, which consisted of eight guard posts. There were four guard posts in the middle ground. And there were six guard posts that created the inner ring. Orders from Corps of Cadets Headquarters state specifically that "No One will be allowed inside the inner ring of the bonfire under any circumstances at any time."

Oftentimes, students guarding the bonfire have become a little overzealous in their protection. Perhaps the explanation for this lies in the fact that Bonfire in the 1950's became a military operation with clear goals. One of the goals was to keep people away. This is a pretty simple command, and failure to do so would be either insubordination or incompetence, and in a military context. Either way, it's a soldier's rear end on the line. The implication is to use violence if necessary, but never to disobey orders and let unauthorized people within the perimeter.

A sign of the more military nature of the Bonfire was a sign itself. The C Armor unit painted up an elaborate sign decorated with sabers dripping blood, that said, "With Logs & Trees we have built this Fire/A Burning Example of our Desire—So watch it Sips—But don't go Near . . . for Hell's a lot Cooler . . . from what we hear . . . And Friday morning a Grave there'll be with this epitaph for all to see . . . 'Now Six Feet Under/ Beneath this Sod/Lies All That's Left/of the T-Sip Squad' Died No 29, 1951." Before this sign was a mock grave on which sat five cow skulls and a pile of bones. Of course this was (supposedly) all in good fun, but the nature of the Bonfire was taking perhaps a more violent tone.

In November 1951, Aggies discovered oats growing in the middle of Kyle Field,the Texas A&M football field. The oats spelled out TU. There was some controversy over whether UT students or locals did it, since UT students prefer "UT" over "TU."

In 1953, yet another perimeter of guards was established—the Outpost Guards. These guards stood around the gates to the university and were required to wear military fatigues. Communicating by radio, they relayed details of any "suspicious cars" to the radio operator. No more than ten people were to guard any one gate, and no cars were to be stopped.

In 1954, no one had as of yet died while working on the Bonfire. At this time, Aggie student John Sullivan wrote a hilarious satire entitled "Death of a Tradition," which was published in a collection of student writing entitled MSS.ONE. The satire is written from the point of view of himself twenty or so years in the future. In the light of the tragedy, the following excerpts from this satirical essay make an important point:

> Each year at Thanksgiving I wonder what the present students at Texas A. and M. think, if they consider this matter at all, of the bonfires we used to build. I remember when every freshman class always tried to build a bonfire bigger than that of the preceding freshman class. It was this spirit of competition, I guess, that caused the eventual termination of Aggie Bonfires.
>
> When I was a freshman, our bonfire had a larger diameter than any bonfire ever built. During the next three hectic years I noticed that the bonfires seemed to be growing gradually larger, but I never realized what consequences this desire for bigger bonfires would bring.
>
> In 1963, six years after I graduated, I read of fifteen freshmen being killed during bonfire construction. I began to wonder how much farther this competitive spirit would be allowed to go . . .
>
> Of course as the bonfires grew larger students at the University of Texas had more desire than ever to set fire to their rival's huge pile of logs. In 1964 armed guards had to be stationed in an airtight perimeter around A. and M. campus to ward off the torchbearers from

Austin. A few university students were killed when they broke through the perimeter and made a dash for the bonfire in a car loaded with barrels of gasoline. The governor gave both schools a harsh reprimand, but since it was an election year no serious action was taken.

The climax to the bonfire problem came in 1975 when a center pole of the desired length could not be found, and the water tower was selected as the main support. School authorities protested against this willful destruction of school property, but an insane frenzy had gripped the student body and nothing could stop them.

Huge trees imported from the Redwood Forests of California were shipped across country and heaved onto the stack by frenzied freshmen. Bagley hall and the Mechanical Engineering building had to be razed to make room for the stack. Freshmen died by the hundreds as the monstrous logs were pushed into place . . .

Once again the (Texas) University students tried to burn the tremendous pile of wood. Four hundred of them marched on College Station carrying torches and singing "Texas Fight," but they were shot down like flies as they came onto the campus. Thirty who were taken alive were tied to the water tower to add to the blaze.

The 1975 bonfire was ignited by forcing a freshman to drive a gasoline truck into the stack. The flames immediately burned two hundred to death, and approximately five hundred were overcome by smoke . . .

Perhaps some day Aggies will build bonfires again, but I am certain that restrictions will be placed on the size of the stack.

The 1954 Bonfire, still a teepee-styled pile, was 73 feet tall, ten feet taller than the 1953 Bonfire. These early log Bonfires were built apparently from incredible tall trees from East Texas, where magnificent straight pines and other trees could be found. In later decades, shorter oak logs from north, south, and west of Texas A&M were used, perhaps prompting the tier-system of construction.

In 1955, the first Aggie died while doing Bonfire work. James Edward Sarran was eighteen years old and a member of Squadron 13 in the Air Force ROTC. He was a sophomore production marketing major, born in San Antonio but raised in Brownsville, Texas. Sarran and Robert Long had been on all-night guard duty at the west entrance of the campus. They were standing behind a parked truck that had brought them coffee when another truck rushed toward them.

Sarran pushed Long out of the way of the oncoming truck but was mortally wounded in the process. Sarran suffered multiple fractures and head injuries. His right leg had to be amputated beneath the knee. But Sarran never regained consciousness and died on November 24, 1999. He was the first Bonfire hero.

Why did James Sarran have to die? It was a war. People die in wars.

But was his guard post, at the western entrance of the University, even necessary? If it took whole armor units of soldiers-in-training to carry and dump 1000 buckets of gasoline on the Bonfire in order for it to light up and burn, how could UT students ever light the bonfire and have any part of it burn for a substantial length of time? They couldn't burn the whole thing down. They could perhaps start a small blaze using some of the smaller twigs and branches lying around the stack, but to light even one of the logs would be nearly impossible without large amounts of inflammatory liquids. The logs, after all, had recently been chopped down, and had probably been rained on; this is November in East Texas, after all.

With this in mind, it is hard to understand why the Assistant Commandant and the student bonfire leaders would not only allow for, but order, the stationing of over twenty guard posts around the university, when maybe six men with a fire extinguisher would have sufficed. First, we must understand that the tradition of guarding the Bonfire, as all Bonfire traditions have done, evolved. It evolved out of the building of smaller more fragile Bonfires that truly did need protection from being completely burned up.

Second, it was simply what the two universities did. UT students also set up guards around their bonfire.

Third, the fact that the manpower devoted to the Bonfire seemed to be a bit extreme points to the nature of the Bonfire as being immersed in the military training program in which all the students participated. Why do cadets do push-ups on demand? It's part of the training and part of the tradition. When looked at this way, having over twenty guard stations with perhaps several men at each station makes sense. It can be seen as a military exercise, perhaps a very toned-down war game.

In 1955, the Bonfire was burned on schedule, this time on Duncan Field, on the south side of campus. The Bonfire was moved because it had endangered nearby buildings and scorched the trees dedicated to World War I veterans.

One Texas Parade writer characterized the Texas A&M-UT bonfire competition as "Battle of the Bonfires." In this battle, UT students didn't let the death of Sarran give pause to their dangerous exploits designed to light the Aggie Bonfire prematurely. One year after Sarran's death, two UT boys built a bomb. This one was not to dropped from a plane. This one was connected to a detonator. They drove to Texas A&M at 7:45 on a Sunday morning and took or threw their bomb out of their car. But the wire to the detonator was only thirty-five feet long and the detonator was kept in the car. As a result, the bomb wasn't even close to the Bonfire when it was detonated. It created a harmless explosion, after which the two UT students drove off in their nearly brand new Pontiac. They were chased down and caught by a couple of Aggies in another car.

With permission, the Aggies looked in the UT students' trunk. They found "a can half full of gun powder and some gasoline stains."

In 1956, *The Battalion* began reporting Bonfire injuries. With the Bonfire still incomplete on November 27, the newspaper reported 92 injuries: 60 from poison ivy, 13 abrasions, 7 sprains, 7 problems with ashes in the eyes, and 5 cuts. Safety reports of annual Bonfires also became regularized in the 1950's. Cadets organizing the Bonfire had to make an annual safety report to the Commandant.

By this time, cadets were regularly excused from at least one day of class in the fall semester in order for the Bonfire to be completed. In 1956, the cadet chaplain wrote a memo to ensure that cadets were excused from the Bonfire on Sunday for church services. Also by 1956, the Aggie Bonfire had become known as the "world's largest bonfire," and was garnering interest from national magazines like The Saturday Evening Post.

1957

Luckily, Texas A&M has some of the largest mess halls in the world, and Aggie cadets ate lunch all at the same time. On Saturday November 24, a few days before the scheduled burning, the bonfire stack fell as the Aggies ate lunch. An uncredited report in *The Battalion* entitled "Spirit Falls, Rises in Bonfire Shakeup" told the story well:

> The stack began leaning Saturday morning. The center pole was loosened by the strain of the guy ropes on it and by the weak foundation of soggy ground, made so by the unceasing rain that fell all last week.
>
> Since the stack fell during the lunch hour, no one was injured.
>
> When the Ags discovered the heap of logs strewn on the drill field, they quietly walked through the mud and stood in amazement. As Ted Lowe, head yell leader said: "Everything has happened to us now."
>
> For several moments, no one knew what to do or where to begin. Then a cry spread over the area made muddy by thousands of feet: "Okay you freshman, sophomores, and juniors, don't just stand there. We've got a bonfire to build.

By sundown, the center pole had been raised again, this time on the western end of the drill field. The cadets began stacking again, and more logs were to be hauled out of the muddy forest. Because trucks could not be driven through the heavy mud, logs were being hauled by hand for as much as half a mile. In the final paragraph of the Batt story, head yell leader Lowe was quoted as saying, "We've still got a chance to make this one the biggest yet."

In the aftermath of the 1999 tragedy, many blamed the tiered wedding cake style of the 1990's design of Bonfire on the instability of the stack. The collapse of the 1957 Bonfire shows that even the teepee-styled Bonfires could be unstable. There was no investigation of the design of Bonfire after the 1957 collapse, presumably because no one had died. But injuries and deaths had been avoided only by sheer dumb luck. If the stack had fallen earlier or later, Aggies may have been on or near it. This first collapse occurred only eleven years after the first use of the modern centerpole. It should have been the first sign that logs standing or leaning on soil are inherently unstable.

1958

As Bonfire had gotten bigger, more time had to be spent on its construction. The Bonfire by 1958 was still a teepee of logs leaning against a center pole, but the logs piled against it were as tall as 75 feet. Time taken away from academic work became an issue. Commandant Joe E. Davis and administrator Bennie A. Zinn wrote in an undated letter to Vice President Earl Rudder that "reports from the academic people indicate that very little effective class work has been done in the ten or eleven days (of Bonfire construction)."

They suggested that Bonfire be constructed in four days, and that the students be allowed off on the Monday and Tuesday of the four-day construction period. They recommended that the two days be made up at the end of the semester.

In perhaps a show of academic one-upmanship, the university administration decided that academic education was even more important than suggested and decreed that the Bonfire must be built in *three* days: the Saturday, Sunday, and Monday before its burning. All the trees had to be cut, hauled and stacked in those three days.

Cadets worked on "Operation Bonfire – Rush" for three days from dawn 'til dusk. Food was brought to them at their work sites, and church services were held in the forest at their cut site. In three grueling days, the cadets finished a job that usually took ten.

The stringent time limit was loosened slightly in 1959 and eventually expanded to the two-month period now utilized.

Progress
1960-1969

By 1960, Sputnik had gone up, and Americans could see the Russian eye in the sky looking down on them. In the early 60's, President Kennedy challenged Americans to do a myriad of things—to ask what we could do for our country, and to put a man on the moon. When the Berlin Wall was erected, and Krushchev informed us that they would bury us, it simply added another gauntlet at the feet of Americans. In the nuclear age, we had to get better, smarter, faster, bigger, and just plain badder.

The Aggies, who had already met the challenges of two world wars and had come out smelling heroic, met the challenging early 60's with bigger and bigger bonfires. The Bonfire of 1960 topped 100 feet. The other early sixties Bonfires regularly topped eighty feet, and each year's builders from the mid-fifties to late 60's set out to top the previous year's. The "progress" being made each year on Bonfire fit in with the prevailing American culture perfectly.

1960

By 1960, Bonfire safety had also become an issue on which campus leaders desired progress. The Bonfire at this point was not being covered with gasoline by a bucket brigade in case it caught on fire as an Aggie was standing on it pouring gasoline.

In February 1960, Frank S. Vaden, Jr., Assistant to the Commandant, wrote a four page memo to James P. Hannigan, Dean of Students, on the subject of the Bonfire. Upon observation of the erection of the 1959 Bonfire, Vaden wrote that the Bonfire required a budget of approximately five hundred dollars plus an unspecified amount for a "contingent emergency fund."

Vaden bragged that there were "no serious casualties" and only one wreck during the building of the 1959 Bonfire, but complained that the method of removing logs by human muscle from the forest was extremely time-consuming and would require tremendous amounts of time if there were a spell of rainy days.

On the second page of his memo, and without apology, Vaden writes:

> Some of the hurry, hurry, hurry, which has existed among the leaders of the bonfire construction each year has been due to the desire to construct a larger bonfire, using larger logs, than that of the class preceding them. As a result the center pole this year was, in my opinion, 25 or 30 feet longer than necessary and at least 2 logs on the drill field were too large, because of their great weight, to place on the stack without cutting them into smaller sections. I believe that a safety control should be exerted on the size of the total stack, and also on the size of the individual logs used, by a directive (probably from the Executive Committee) limiting the height of the center pole above the ground and on the circumference and length of the logs to be used. Since the available timber may vary from year to year and certainly the size of trees will vary, I know of no practical way to limit the over-all amount of wood which goes into the bonfire but certainly if the height of the center pole is regulated and the outrageously large logs not permitted to be used on the stack this will, in effect, limit the size of the bonfire so that each class will not be attempting to better last year's record.
>
> [...]
>
> It seems to me that one of the most dangerous parts of the operation is the actual stacking of the logs on the bonfire itself. The man in charge of this part of the operation must be on their toes at all times, should not only keep an eye out for the men working but should constantly check the equipment being used . . .

Near the end of his memo, Vaden writes that safety lectures for freshmen should be expanded to include a safety film and that a "qualified safety man" should give the talks.

In some ways, Vaden was a visionary of his times. As the students were caught up in the bonfire "craze," Vaden was the first to seriously suggest a limitation on size. He foresaw the dangers in the stacking process itself even as most other people, up until the 1999 tragedy, thought that the great dangers occurred during cutting and burning.

Head Yell Leader Joe Leeper made another suggestion for the 1960-61 Bonfire. It was fourth on a list of four recommendations, and was entitled, "Miscellaneous":

> For obvious reasons, I am suggesting that No women be allowed in the cutting area. First, because there are various songs which cadets sing in the cutting area which, if heard by women, could prove embarrassing. Second, because women tend to interfere with the men and their work. By No women I am including college officials wives [sic].

Judgmental readers should not jump to the conclusion here that Texas A&M and Bryan-College Station were redneck backwaters stuck in a time-freeze. In 1960, the feminist movement was more of a concept, not a reality. The type of thinking represented above, perhaps reprehensible, was representative of middle America.

Vaden's size limitation suggestion went nowhere, as the 1960 Bonfire was bigger than ever, this time standing over 100 feet tall, according to one source. But the 1960 Bonfire, under Vaden's instruction as Assistant to Commandant, did produce more stringent safety practices, as described in detail in a three page report by Robert Jerry Brown, President of an organization called the Student Safety Society, and also Chairman of the Bonfire Safety Committee. He reported that injuries went down from 106 in 1959 to 92 in 1960. Twenty-eight of the injured had to go to the College Hospital, but none of these injuries could be considered serious, according to Brown.

The 1961 and 1962 Bonfires could not match the 1960 feat in height. The 1962 Bonfire saw injuries go down to 89, which included ten "one-of-a-kind injuries" and two "horseplay" injuries. Of the 89 injuries, 46 were suffered by freshmen.

1963

The 1963 school year started, with women and blacks officially allowed to enroll.

On November 22 1963, President John F. Kennedy was assassinated. In honor of the President, the Bonfire was canceled for the first time since 1909. In a statement to the students, a proud President General James Earl Rudder wrote:

> I would like to express my appreciation to the student body for its exhibition of true Aggie Spirit in the recent days of crisis.
>
> Upon hearing the tragic news of President Kennedy's death, student leaders, meeting with members of the staff of the University chose to sacrifice the traditional Thanksgiving bonfire as an expression of deep sorrow. This feeling permeated the entire student body and will be long remembered as a tribute to the President of the United States.

President Rudder could not resist commenting on the Thanksgiving Day football game, however, as he stated that "the nation watched the inspired and magnificent Aggies come within inches of upsetting the number one football team in the nation."

1964

In 1964, the tradition resumed, and with it, students revived another old tradition. Members of the Aggie Band, who at this time, had the right to mount the "t.u. Frat House" on the very top of the Bonfire, tried one early November evening to steal an outhouse from the Christ's Holy Sanctified Church. "A colored man," as it was put in a memo, caught them and called the police. But the students returned later that night and successfully stole one and a half of the church's two outhouses.

Also in this year, embers blown from the Bonfire started several small fires and one major house fire.

1965

This year's Bonfire was ninety feet tall, and was once again guarded by three concentric rings of guards carrying short-wave radios, and now developing their protection system to include a series of passwords and signals. All this to prevent "pre-ignition."

The tradition of rowdiness also continued, as one Junior High teacher wrote a letter complaining about Bonfire workers riding in a convertible. As an artist, she wrote, she had painted "the undraped male figure for perhaps 15 years; but nothing is as revolting as exhibitionism."

1966

During the mid-'60s, America escalated its war in Vietnam. Race riots broke out in Watts and Harlem. College students returned from Freedom Summer to radicalize campuses around the nation. Texas A&M could hardly have been considered radicalized, although a chapter of the Students For a Democratic Society did form. It is during this period which Texas

A&M seemed to remain relatively unmoving as other major universities became more and more politically active.

The 1966 Bonfire did indirectly acknowledge the war in Vietnam, although what statement it made is up for interpretation. Two to three thousand gallons of napalm and diesel fuel were poured onto the Bonfire in order to light it.

And as America's war against Vietnam became more technologically advanced, so did the building of the Bonfire. During this time, cranes became a regular vehicle on the stack field, helping to prop up the center pole and lifting logs to upper levels of the Bonfire, which, in this year, stood eighty-five feet above the ground. Furthermore, the first proto-tiered Bonfires developed in the mid- and late sixties. Although the stack retained a pyramidal style, the pyramid seemed to have two or three vaguely differentiated levels, all of which leaned inward.

1967

The "layered" Bonfire design was documented in a November 1967 *Eagle* article, which described the process as "placing logs end-on-end for a layered effect." Previous Bonfires had been triple stacked. The 1967 Bonfire was quadruple stacked.

The center pole was 105 feet in length, making this Bonfire one of the tallest ever, but the 1967 Bonfire was also one of the widest bonfires of all time. The diameter of the first stack was one hundred feet, making the area covered by the base larger than that of a professional basketball court. Over three thousand logs were used to build the bonfire. The entire stacking process took about eight days, and stacking chief Bill Bellomy claimed that 1100 logs could be stacked in six hours, with the help of cranes.

1968

The year 1968 was one of the most tumultuous of post-war American history. Martin Luther King and Bobby Kennedy were both assassinated. Police and activists clashed outside of the Democratic Convention in Chicago. The Aggie Bonfire was built and burned shortly after Richard Nixon was elected to office on a conservative platform calling for more order in American society.

In building the 1968 Bonfire, Corps leaders decided to add civilians to the top leadership ranks. They allowed one civilian in 1968, and he wore a red helmet to help identify himself to others more clearly. Later, all top positions of leadership were signified by the wearing of red "pots" whether or not the student was a "non-reg" (civilian) or not. The top position of power would no longer be the Head Yell Leader (always a Corps member); it would eventually be the Head Stack, one of eight senior Redpots. Eight junior Redpots would do most of the logistical work.

1969

Amidst the tumult of the late sixties, Aggies built the largest Aggie Bonfire of all time, possibly the largest bonfire ever, anywhere.

They began by finding a cut area only seven miles from campus. Next, they put together a center pole over one hundred feet tall. They were aiming at a stack of one-hundred and five feet, four feet higher than the previous record.

All Aggies were enlisted in the effort. The substantial numbers of civilian students were organized by future Texas Land Commissioner Garry Mauro. Even women helped by serving in the first aid tent.

The final product, with t.u. frat-house atop, stood 109 feet and ten inches above the ground. That year, the Ags really built the hell outta Bonfire.

Students watch a pile of trash and scraps burn in the middle of the field during a pep rally. The Texas A&M Cushing Library dates this picture at 1924-1928.

1930's Bonfire.

Cushing Memorial Library, Texas A&M University

An early 1940's Bonfire.

Cushing Memorial Library, Texas A&M University

This photograph from the filming of the World War II film, "We've Never Been Licked" shows two cadets fighting on the ground. Behind them stands the first Bonfire constructed with freshly chopped trees. This Bonfire was specially built for the film.

*The 1948 Bonfire sprays
big flames and small
sparks into the sky.*

Cushing Memorial Library, Texas A&M University

*An early spliced centerpole
stood within this 1940's
Bonfire.*

Cushing Memorial Library, Texas A&M University

At the 1953 Bonfire yell practice, the Aggie Band brings down its instruments and runs toward the stack as all Aggies raise their arms in jubilation.

Cadets working in army gear pull the guy rope taut on the ill-fated 1957 stack. Luckily, the cadets were out to lunch when the stack collapsed; as you see here, few wore pots in those days.

Cushing Memorial Library, Texas A&M University

The 1968 Bonfire consisted of multiple tiers of logs leaning inward toward the centerpole The civilian and cadet in the foreground mirror the new reg/non-reg leadership of the Bonfire.

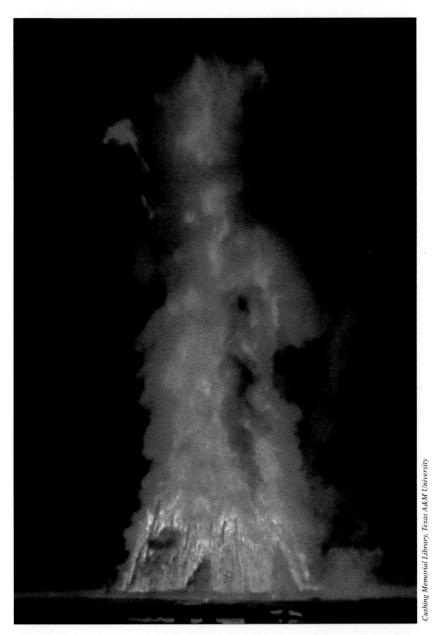

Cushing Memorial Library, Texas A&M University

The biggest Bonfire ever stood at 109 feet and 10 inches. Compare the Bonfire to the people in the foreground and the pole to the left. Ironically, very few pictures of the 1969 Bonfire exist.

Cushing Memorial Library, Texas A&M University

During the lighting ceremony, students march to the Bonfire and throw torches on it.

Cushing Memorial Library, Texas A&M University

By 1975, students had begun constructing the neatly tiered Bonfires. The logs stand on end, perpendicular to the ground, and the tops of the tiers form right angles with the center pole. Notice the cross ties utilized with this style of construction.

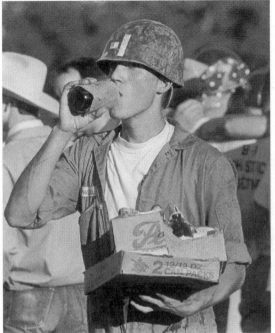

A Bonfire "tradition" (1988).

Cushing Memorial Library, Texas A&M University

In the 1990's, more and more women swung axes.

Cushing Memorial Library, Texas A&M University

125

The Trees Strike Back
1970-1974

On April 30, 1970, a Texas A&M professor of Wildlife Science named Dr. Donald Clark proposed at a Student Senate meeting that Bonfire be abolished. Because he thought it wrong to destroy large areas of forests for the purpose of building a bonfire, he proposed that the Bonfire be replaced by an environmental clean-up campaign.

Although the proposal went nowhere, it signaled a pro-environment backlash against the Bonfire just months after Aggies had built the largest bonfire of all time.

That year, Texas A&M had its traditional Monday-before-Bonfire holiday, so that students could work on the Bonfire. A group of architecture and environmental design students utilized the holiday to repaint Travis Elementary School in Bryan, refurbish the Brazos County Girls Club, and to plant trees. Speaking to the press, the group's spokesperson, freshman David Dacus said, "We are not attacking the Bonfire. We are offering an alternative. We just don't think the Bonfire is a representation of the student Community."

The group was quite media-conscious, and wore T-shirts with "Good Guys" stenciled on the backs so that they could make "things look good for TV people who are supposed to be there."

Well, the erectors of Bonfire, and the University administration were not exactly clueless to media manipulation either. The counterattack came first through the Redpots themselves. Head Yell Leader Keith Chapman explained in a Battalion article, "We can only use the large straight trees in the area. We leave the crooked trees, which provide most of the shade, and make more room for grass to grow, thus aiding the larger wildlife in the area.

"We don't use all the trees. Actually we use a lot of the little ones that are getting crowded out." He also went on to explain that no underbrush is destroyed during cut, so no small animals' habitats are put in danger.

That year, the Texas International Speedway had requested the Aggies' service in cutting down trees in the area of the Speedway race track. Chapman explained that the Speedway would dispose of tree limbs and other pieces of vegetation, and that this would allow future vegetation to grow. Furthermore, enough trees would be allowed to remain standing that "there is absolutely no threat of erosion or nature un-balance."

A local environmental organization called the Brazos County Environmental Action Council suggested that instead of cutting down and burning trees, the Bonfire could consist once again of trash.

Chapman's counter to this was that the nature of the fire would make such a fire dangerous. Chapman may have assumed that the group's suggestion was to burn a one hundred-foot tall pile of trash, which indeed, would have been dangerous.

And as for the trees, George Boyett, general manager of the Speedway, told the Battalion that if the students did not remove the trees, the Speedway would have done so. The trees would have been cut down anyway. This counter-argument to environmental objections was used effectively from the early seventies up through the late eighties. Interestingly, no one has ever publicly wondered whether these landowners would have had their land cleared away, or as much land cleared away, if it weren't a free service provided by Texas A&M, and if it didn't bring them local prestige and recognition.

The University bolstered their position with a secret weapon in 1971. In a letter dated December 2, 1971, and addressed to W.A. Smith, Extension Forest Specialist, Texas Agricultural Extension Service (a Texas A&M agency), Edwin H. Cooper, the Assistant to the President, writes:

> Dear Bill:
> President Williams has asked me to once again tell you how very much he appreciated the splendid paper, Ecological Benefits of Using Post Oak Trees for Annual Texas A&M Bonfire. As it developed, we

did not need to use the paper since resistance to the event was rather insignificant.

We are carefully preserving the paper, however, for possible use next year, or thereafter.

Please accept our sincere thanks.

Although "resistance" had been "insignificant," some could not shake the ill feelings that 1971 Bonfire had instilled in them. Out of the woodwork came Frank G. Anderson, former A&M coach and Corps Commandant. On January 18, 1972, he published a lengthy letter in the Battalion. Entitled, "The bonfire as it was," the letter begins with "Someone planted a tree in the ashes of the recent bonfire." (There is no documentation as to who planted the tree or why.) The letter goes on to explain the history of the bonfire, and how when he became Corps Commandant, he presided over the first "legal" bonfire (as opposed to a Bonfire consisting of stolen materials), and that it consisted of dead trees collected from the west side of the university. He explains that for this very first "tree" bonfire, he:

> personally marched the 'bull ring' to the spot and took my turn at the saw. The sophomores and freshmen had a good time and thought it was 'good bull.' In a manner an old tradition was ended and another was begun. I have mixed emotions about the present bonfire situation. The first log bonfire was not large but was large enough to get the job done. I think it is silly to strive each year to make it bigger than ever before. The work group has increased in size from the small disciplinary bull ring of the past to an annual bonfire which seems to breed a wide degree of for or against opinion, with great numbers involved.
>
> As a coach, I thought most of A&M's traditions were good. As Commandant, I thought many of them were bad, and managed to get rid of a few of those that kept the enrollment down.
>
> As an oldtimer, I'll line up with my side of the generation gap. Many aspects of building the bonfire contribute to making a closer knit association among the students. I can't like a bonfire which destroys trees. Thanks to those who planted the tree.

The tree either died or was cut down, as Bonfire was burned at the same site in 1972.

The Pro-Bonfire counterattack continued in 1973, as another Battalion article allowed yell leaders to explain that the industrial wastes donated by the local Fireman Training School "burn faster and hopefully cleaner" when it ignites Bonfire.

Another benefit was explained thusly by senior yell leader Mark McClean: "Clearing land is normally expensive but we do it free." Mike

Phillips, combined band commander, further explained that "the thick brush that grows in the lowland chokes the grass and we clear it out to get to the trees." Phillips said that removing the brush allows the land to become grazing pasture for "domestic and wild animals." Three years previous, the Pots had stated that no underbrush was destroyed.

The effort to put a pleasant environment-friendly face on Bonfire was somewhat betrayed by eight male Aggies on the night of November 26, as they drove two trucks and a black Grand Am onto the campus of Rice University in Houston and chopped down their 104 year-old "Victory Tree."

"The students, equipped with axes and saws, had the ancient oak lying on its side in a matter of minutes and were back in College Station by 3 A.M. to throw a branch of the tree into the fading bonfire," reported the Battalion.

The old tree had been used by the Rice football team as a site for pre-game talks. Rice Head Football Coach Al Conover said he was appalled, but some Ags would say he had it coming. The previous week, Rice's band, during the half-time to the Rice-A&M game, parodied Texas A&M traditions. A&M President Jack Williams, when asked if Texas A&M was going to investigate this act of retaliation, replied, "What? Investigate the cutting down of a tree? Of course not."

That year, the Bonfire ignition was prepared for by Training School firemen, each one wearing an asbestos suit. The bonfire stood at a mere 77 feet. Administration concerns had begun limiting the size of the Bonfire since the record 110 foot Bonfire.

The Bonfire's popularity among students plummeted in the early 1970's. In 1971, in a poll of 7,000 students, thirty-five percent said that "bonfire efforts should be used in a more constructive manner," and fifteen percent were undecided. Less than fifty percent of the students thought that the time and effort used to build the Bonfire should continue to be focused on it.

Vice-President of Student Services, John Koldus, took advantage of the lull in Bonfire support to make a few amendments to the tradition. Citing "serious and tragic" accidents of the past, Koldus established three reforms. First, he assigned the responsibility of Bonfire to the Assistant Director of Student Affairs. This position would evolve into the "Bonfire Advisor" in later years.

Second, he stated that classes would not be dismissed on the Monday prior to Bonfire, as had been tradition for decades. Finally, he said that the height of Bonfire would be "controlled." He minimized the psychological effect of such a directive (especially on alumni) by acknowledging that the tradition "unifies A&M Former Students throughout the world in a spirit of loyalty."

The 1974 Bonfire stack was limited to seventy feet tall. With the outhouse on top, it stood 78 feet above the ground. Despite the limited size, the entire College Station fire department as a precaution stationed itself downwind of the Bonfire.

Although anti-Bonfire elements may have been slightly appeased by Vice-President Koldus's efforts, the pro-Bonfire forces continued their public education campaign. A 1975 Battalion article interviewed Jeremy Schuster, head of the Range Science Department, which was converting University-owned forests back to their prehistoric state, as a savanna. This meant that students would be needed to cut down the trees, which could be used for Bonfire.

Schuster explained that "at one time this area was grassland that was maintained by periodic natural grass fires. When man intervened and stopped the fires, the range was invaded by the brush and scrub trees that are now on it." After the land was cleared, range science classes were to use the newly created grasslands (range-land) as a laboratory for study and experimentation.

It is hard to say whether Texas A&M students believed their own university's unusual environmental beliefs. It may not have mattered whether they did or not. Bonfire to many students had nothing to do with the environment; to them it was not a matter of how many or few trees were cut and burned. Head Yell Leader Steve Taylor explained it best in a 1974 Eagle article: "The bonfire to me is important because it instills a respect for some important principles. They are old-fashioned, but I think they are still important in today's society. I'm talking about things like school spirit, respect, and tradition . . . the tradition not so much of seeing the bonfire burn but of getting a whole university working together."

With the whole country fissured over Vietnam, Watergate, women's liberation, and civil rights, Bonfire provided a counterpoint symbol of unity and traditional values. Although the entire university was not united through Bonfire, at least the Bonfire represented a united university. Of course, it also represented the university united on the whole foundation of bonfire traditions and values. And that is precisely why the university could not and cannot unite over Bonfire—because it represents to some the "good old (white) boy" system of power and political, social, and cultural dominance.

Nevertheless, the need for such a symbol in times like the late sixties and early seventies is sincere and completely understandable. Besides, many of those traditional values are of importance to all Aggies, good old boy or bad new girl. Unfortunately, the task of sorting through the morass of values globbed together in the Bonfire is rarely undertaken, and the question comes down to a simple yes or no Bonfire. Bonfire is supposed to represent the Aggie Spirit, but rather than questioning what the Aggie Spirit is, students mostly answer with a simple thumbs up or down on the question of the Bonfire's continued existence. A corollary question rarely asked is "Can we express our 'traditional' values through something other than Bonfire?"

Women and the Bonfire
1973-1988

Women first began working as part of the Bonfire effort in the late sixties and early seventies, when they served in first aid tents and handed out cookies and coffee with the Student "Y" Association. Women were encouraged to do so by the University Women Bonfire committee. By 1972, three hundred women participated in first aid and cookie crews.

In later years women began participating as "Bonfire Buddies." These women exchange gifts, often handmade, with a male student who works on the Bonfire. As *The Battalion* once explained it, "individuals exchange gifts in hopes of motivating the workers."

As far as actually helping to build the Bonfire, women first pushed their way into the work areas in 1973. Winnie Jackson, Class of 1977, tells the story in her 1978 letter to *The Battalion*:

> In the fall of 1973, 10 women freshmen talked about wanting to work, really work, on Bonfire. When we questioned the people in charge we were told there was no written rule that said women could not work, and that if we could get a crew we could work in the cutting area.
>
> We got a crew up and at 5:30 the following Saturday morning we were at the cutting area. We were to help clear out brush so that the trucks could get into the area to load, and then we were to carry felled logs out of the woods to the trucks.

Our shift went quickly and uneventfully. We did our work seriously and received a lot of encouragement from the other crews of men. Later we found out, after we had gone home, the head of safety came out to the cutting area with the intention of "running those women off."

The following night we volunteered for and were put on a pulley crew in the stack area. Once again we did our job realizing we were participating in and contributing to the one of the greatest Aggie traditions.

It was after that year that the stack area was closed to women, and women crews were not allowed in the cutting areas, except to bring in food and first aid . . .

As for me, I'll never forget what I felt inside when I saw that Bonfire burn and I was able to say:

"That's my Bonfire!"

1976

As Jackson's letter stated, women were essentially banned from Bonfire in 1973. In 1976, women began creeping back into the Bonfire. Women from Fowler Hall served guard duty in the days leading up to the burning. "If the people who come to try to start the fire early, see a lot of people out there, they might get discouraged," said Susan Hufsman, Fowler bonfire chief, "The girls will be right out there next to the guys . . . some girls going out there at 4 A.M."

1977

The 1977 Bonfire was in need of laborers. A letter from Pam Bielefeld, '78, stated, "Everyday there are just enough men out there for one crew and that is pretty bad turnout for our student body." She concluded, "Every man is needed. Now."

As if in response to this November 18 letter, a female student around the night of the 19th snuck into the perimeter around stack dressed as a man. She wore heavy clothing and put her hair into the back of her shirt. She was able to carry a few logs to the stack before a male worker tried to strike up a conversation with her. She didn't sound like she belonged. She was escorted out of the perimeter by upset pots.

1979

The first official pink pot was given to the head women's bonfire coordinator. Pinkpots lead women in making lunches for Bonfire workers and working at the Bonfire concession stands. Pinkpots have, throughout the years, sometimes made and served thousands of lunches in a day and kept concessions stands open twenty-four hours a day during Push.

On October 8, 1979 around five or seven female members of the Corps of Cadets attended their mandatory Corps tree-cutting class. Whereas the men who went to the class received cutting cards, allowing them to work on the Bonfire, none of the women were issued cards. They were told by those who conducted the class that University policy prohibits women from entering the cutting area.

The cadets were eager to begin cutting and dragging out trees for Bonfire. One of the women, senior Georgia Hughes of Squadron 14, told *The Battalion*, "If we have cutting cards, hell, yeah, we'll be out there in force."

Another female cadet filed a sex discrimination lawsuit. It was this that prompted the University to change its policy that same month. On October 18, the Texas A&M Bonfire and Yell Leader Committee held a meeting at which around thirty-five visitors (mostly Red- and Yellowpots) were present. Chairman Colonel Thomas R. Parsons opened the debate on women working on Bonfire by allowing visitors to make comments. According to a memo by Parsons, most of the objections were raised by Redpots. As reported by *The Battalion*, they stated that:

> Safety would be jeopardized since most women have not had much experience in that type of work . . . the women had no trained super-visors within their ranks, they would not be physically able to per-form the work, women in the cutting area would lead to more "horse-play," and not enough red pots were available to supervise large groups of women workers.

All but two of the committee members voted to recommend that women be given the same opportunities to work on Bonfire, provided they went through the same training. The recommendation was made policy when vice president for student services John Koldus signed off on it. Koldus told *The Battalion*, "I think it's fine. My daughters have been helping me for a long time with things like that, and I don't see anything wrong with it."

Co-Bonfire Adviser Ron Hilton said that some committee members voted for the recommendation simply because it was a legal inevitability, not because they actually supported it. The other co-Bonfire Adviser, Tom Murray, worried that women working on the Bonfire might cause a serious accident, thereby causing the Texas Municipal Power Authority to discontinue allowing students to cut from their land.

Although there had been no explicit written rule stating that women were not allowed to work on Bonfire, they had not been allowed to do so by the Redpots. By the time the rest of the nation was debating the Equal Rights Amendment (and had passed it in nearly two-thirds of state legislatures) women at Texas A&M were still excluded from a state-sponsored function. Now that the doors were open, only women members of the Corps were prepared. Because of the previous ban on women, no civilian women had showed up at any of the cutting classes and could not cut trees for Bonfire.

On October 20, the first cutting day of the first cutting weekend, women for the first time officially (that is, with Committee and Pot approval) participated in cutting down trees for Bonfire. Twenty-five women from Squadron 14 cut that weekend, right alongside the men. Redpot Sterling Price reported to *The Battalion* that "there were no accidents and no problems" during the five- and seven-hour mandatory Corps cutting shifts that weekend.

Georgia Hughes concurred, "They've been really good to us. We haven't tried to pick a fight and neither have they."

But there are always dissenters. Senior coordinator Mark Rhea told the Batt that "for the amount of work they did, it wasn't worth the trouble to set them up a separate area and keep a supervisor with them the whole time. They didn't cut more than 10 logs."

1980

Although the Bonfire stack had been lowered to sixty-five feet, Redpots had a hard time finding enough people to cut and stack the trees. Only the Corps of Cadets can force its members to work on the Bonfire. Dormitory yellow pots can only pressure their residents to work on it by waking them up early and using incentives like awarding kegs of beer to the dorms with the most workers. And the Redpots can only do so much of the 125,000 man-hours of work required to build the Bonfire. One legendary Redpot received a grade point average of 0.00 after working on Bonfire one fall semester.

One senior explained it this way: "There are different people going to A&M now. The University used to let people out of class to build the bonfire. Students now look at grades and are also getting lazier . . . The school is getting more impersonal. People come out here with their buddies. If I didn't know anybody, I probably wouldn't come out either."

1981

Much of the shortage was due to the decrease in Corps membership, and the decrease in the portion of the University that is associated with the Corps. Furthermore, the University and Bonfire organizers had been discouraging a huge portion of the campus from participating: civilian women.

Things changed in 1981. Micki Dunham, a female member of a student organization called Off-Campus Aggies and former Cadet, was put in charge of *recruiting* civilian women to work on Bonfire. Forty women were recruited.

Dunham set the women up to cut only trees of less than twelve inches in diameter. "We're not going for the big logs. The women in the Corps will sometimes take down some pretty good-sized logs, but we're going to keep them relatively small until we have enough people out there to cover it . . . The most important thing is safety . . . not to worry about speed—it's just to control the ax so that . . . no one will get hurt."

Women were placed in separate areas to cut so that they might "feel comfortable with themselves without the pressure of somebody watching them."

Some men responded to the presence of women with quite revelatory comments about the nature of Bonfire itself. Head Redpot Art Free said that "Bonfire is mostly a man's game—kind of a macho deal where the guys can go and get away and have a good time. But we'll find them an area to cut in, if they want to cut."

Others, like James Birdwell, Senior Redpot, were either chivalrous or safety-minded (it's hard to tell), "As a safety precaution to the women and everyone out there, we prefer they don't work. We're not doing it to pick on anybody or make anybody mad. We're just trying to be careful."

Most Bonfire men favored women's opportunity to work, especially if they didn't hurt anyone. After all, as some said, it's not a male Bonfire or a female Bonfire. It's an Aggie Bonfire for Aggies.

As more civilian women cut trees week after week, some of the Redpots began coming around to the idea. Several of them claimed that although women don't help Bonfire much, they don't harm the efforts to build it either. They also had a good safety record.

Redpot Karl Burgin said that women do not cut as much as men but only because boys are raised to know how to use an axe and girls aren't. Head Redpot Art Free conceded that "this bonfire belongs to every Aggie, female as well as male."

Senior Jenny L. Pickett of El Paso didn't appreciate the Pots' seemingly charitable remarks and stated, "I don't feel we cut any less wood than any other organization, and if we do cut any less, it's because there are more men than women and not because we don't cut as much per person." She added, "It's a matter of opinion anyway."

A More Well-Rounded Bonfire

Just one year before, the Bonfire suffered its worst worker-shortage ever, and it happened just a couple of years after another publicized shortage. And then came the women. Perhaps they do not cut as many trees down as men, but they make up half of the campus. When hundreds or thousands of women work on Bonfire, there is less likely to be a shortage of workers. Furthermore, the publicity of the controversy was a great boost for Bonfire awareness. And finally, the presence of women no doubt attracted some men to cut trees, and let their macho selves be free even, or especially, around the women.

How many cookies does the Bonfire need? By taking women from the cookie crews and putting them behind the ax handles, Texas A&M may have saved Bonfire itself. But it only did so by destroying Bonfire, or to put it more mildly, by letting it evolve—from a male secret treehouse gang operation with military procedures, to a slightly more open testosterone-driven funfest. Even women have testosterone.

Interestingly, throughout the seventies, the Bonfire became less protrusive in shape, shorter, and more rotund - more feminine. This resulted from the full transformation of Bonfire into a wedding cake-styled structure with distinctive tiers, each leveled off evenly at the top. The Bonfire evolved into a six-leveled, neat-looking structure that did not top seventy feet. Over the years, it had grown from an amorphous trash pile into a conical teepee into a well-defined sculpture with six concentric stacks forming distinctive right angles.

The Second Bonfire Fatality

On November 6, 1981, Wiley Keith Jopling was riding a tractor to the cutting site at Granada Ranch, northeast of Bryan. Jopling was sitting on the tractor's left rear fender when the tractor hit a bump. The bump knocked him forward, off the fender, and he was crushed beneath the tractor's wheels. He was pronounced dead twenty minutes later at St. Joseph Hospital in Bryan.

According to *The Eagle*, "One redpot arrived at the hospital an hour after Jopling died. When he was told of Jopling's death, he slammed his helmet down and broke into tears."

As a result of the accident, Head Redpot Art Free and the Bonfire Committee instated a new policy that no one was allowed to sit on the fenders of tractors, only on the rear bumpers. Furthermore, there was to be no riding in flatbed trucks, and all tractors were to be towed by trailers.

Jopling was a rare true Aggie. He came from an agricultural family, had been a member of Future Farmers of America, had worked in ranching, and planned to advise financial institutions on loaning money to farmers. According to his dorm's head resident, Jopling "loved bonfire." He was honored at Texas A&M by raising the flags at half-mast, by his dorm fellows wearing black arm bands, and by a moment of silence at Corps supper.

The Director of Student Affairs absolved the Bonfire Committee of responsibility over the accident.

1983

The 1983 Bonfire stood at only fifty-four feet above ground and is featured on the cover of this book. The Bonfire would officially remain at fifty-five feet or less throughout the eighties and nineties; of course, as learned after the 1999 tragedy, this official height limit was not always honored.

1984

Just because male Bonfire-builders let women kill trees and load them, doesn't mean that women could simply walk up to the stack itself and do anything. Excerpts from the following Kathy Wiespape column for the Batt tells what happens when she entered the sacred "perimeter" in the fall of 1984:

> Back in October, when the center pole was raised, I went out to Duncan field to shoot some pictures for my photojournalism class. My plan was to try to capture the expressions on the workers faces as they pushed the center pole into place . . .
>
> About a hundred people stood around the edges of the field. The redpots and brownpots were standing next to the pole. I figured they were the people to check with about how close I could stand to shoot.
>
> I walked out to where they were standing . . . Just as I opened my mouth, someone grabbed me from behind.
>
> "Get outside the perimeter!" the cadet screamed, dragging me from the center pole. "No women inside the perimeter!"

After Weisepape tried to explain what she wanted to do, she asked what the perimeter was.

> He pointed to the four poles forming a square around the middle of the field. I looked around. Sure enough, there were no women inside the square.

"And that's as close as I can get to shoot?" I asked. But he had already rejoined his friends inside the perimeter.

So there I was, twenty yards from the center pole, with no tele-photo lens. Meanwhile, a male Battalion staff photographer and three male students in my class stood about 15 feet from the redpots, snap-ping away.

Since then, I've learned that women have never been allowed in-side the perimeter. Until a couple of years ago, the cutting site was off limits. Now women are allowed to cut, but I've been told by both male and female friends that they're subject to a great deal of verbal abuse if they do . . .

"Boys will be boys," one cadet told me when I complained about the way I'd been dragged away from the bonfire.

This column shows that things had improved immensely for women wanting to get close to the stack. Some Aggies say that in the old days, women had to have sex with a Redpot to get into the inner ring around the stack.

1986

By now, the conservative resurgence of the eighties had legitimized itself as an economic expansion and had begun making up for the setbacks of the recession of the early eighties. Furthermore, Ronald Reagan had made America strong again. The U.S. missile stockpile was at an all-time high and America had proven its might by invading Granada and bombing Tripoli. This atmosphere may have helped to embolden the erectors and would-be erectors of Bonfire.

On the night of November 18, Simone Weaver, a cadet first lieutenant of Company W-1, had been told that she could not work on stack itself. So she asked the "scarecrow" if he needed a break. He did, so she stood on the 55-gallon oil drum and began directing trucks carrying logs to the stack.

After scarecrowing for about five minutes, five men knocked her off of the oil drum, causing her to flip in the air and land on her back. Putting together some of Weaver's quotations from an *Eagle* news story, we get a good picture of what happened next:

> I was a little winded, but I was OK. I looked at them, and at least two of them were wearing hard hats with the letters 'DG' on them. I got up and got back on the barrel, and I think it surprised them that I didn't get up crying . . . After I got back on the barrel, I told them to go do something useful, and they told me they were doing something useful by getting rid of me . . . While I didn't appreciate what they had

139

said to me, I wanted to be as unantagonistic as I could be. A brown pot came over to me and asked me if I was all right and the guys left . . . About five minutes later, the same guys came back and this time they grabbed me . . . They dragged me off the barrel and knocked my hard hat off my head. They carried me to the perimeter and threw me outside of it . . . I fought back (as they dragged me). I know I gouged some of them because every nail I had is gone. I'm used to being carried off because in the course of Corps life, it happens . . . But this time I was furious, especially when I heard the 'whoops' and the cheers behind me from everybody on stack. Not one person came to help me. No one . . . In fact they thought it was 'good bull' that I was abused . . . I'm not condemning bonfire because I think it's a great tradition. But the attitude of 'We're gonna build this great bonfire for Aggie spirit, but we're gonna beat Aggies while we do it' has to go.

Asked why she didn't work on the cookie crew instead, Weaver responded, "I don't know how to bake cookies."

Weaver reported the incident to University police. After the attack, William Kibler, then-Bonfire advisor, followed a familiar pattern of making a public statement about women's freedom to work on the Bonfire, but doing so only after women had been beaten or filed a law suit against the university. Kibler stated, "There is absolutely nothing keeping women from working on stack. Working on stack is regarded as a kind of privilege by the people who work on the bonfire. Bonfire requires a lot of very physical work, and if a woman is willing to do the same work as a male, then she should be allowed to work on the stack."

About a month after the assault, Simone Weaver filed charges of Class C misdemeanor assault against six freshmen male Cadets. All of the freshmen were eighteen or nineteen years old. Weaver insisted that the freshmen were ordered to assault her by a higher-up. "They're not talking; they're not saying who sent them to do it. Freshmen don't do things like that on their own . . . I wish I knew who sent them on the detail. Things would be a lot different for those freshmen if I knew."

Upon filing charges, Weaver again mentioned that "there were non-regs there that did nothing. There were females not five feet away who didn't even blink."

In February, five of the charged cadets pleaded guilty in exchange for six months deferred adjudication, and the sixth cadet had his case dismissed. The six months deferred adjudication sentence meant that if the cadets did not break any state laws and did fifteen hours of community service, the judge would not find the cadets guilty and would take the offenses off their records.

In a February 5 article in *The Battalion*, Curtis Culberson reported that J. Malon Southerland, who was serving as the interim Corps Commandant at the time, would not speak on disciplinary action within the Corps of Cadets. Furthermore, "Southerland said that male-female relations in the Corps are not a problem and that the case was an isolated incident." (See the interview with Wendy Stock for an alternative view of Corps gender relations during this period.)

1987

October 30. Those rascally female photographers were at it again, and again wanting close-ups of the center pole being raised. This time, the photographers—Marie McLeod and Jennifer Friend—were taking photos for the A&M yearbook, *The Aggieland*. Upon approaching the perimeter, Bonfire workers began yelling, "Females on the perimeter! Get the females off the perimeter!"

McLeod and Friend ignored their alarm calls, and walked up to the hole that was being dug for the center pole, and began taking pictures. After they took some pictures, a Redpot asked them to leave the perimeter so that they could raise the center pole. The two women did so, but male photographer Eric Swellander was still in the perimeter taking pictures. So the women went back in, and were again escorted out, this time by a Corps member.

Somehow, McLeod was able to get back in the perimeter and take pictures of the center pole being raised. But conditions were not ideal, as she described, "I was squatting taking pictures of the pole as it was going up with a wide angle lens so I could get it all in. I could hear them back there chuckling and I kept feeling dirt being thrown all over my back."

Again, after the center pole had been raised and was being coated with oil, McLeod entered the perimeter and took pictures near the pole. She describes what happened next: "I hear this comment while I'm in the perimeter taking pictures. 'We'll f— her brains out if she doesn't get her ass out of the perimeter.' They were just totally crude."

Friend, while guarding photographic equipment outside of the perimeter, was harassed by revelers who acted like they were going to throw a bucket of oil at each other, and then at her.

An article on the incident was published in the Batt on November 4. What followed was one of the most entertaining and revealing exchanges of letters to the editor that I can remember reading in our school newspaper. These letters are included in this volume so that readers may better understand the continuing evolution of Aggie male-female relations.

Conflicts between the sexes continue to make the Bonfire building process more dangerous than it should be, especially for women.

A letter published on November 9:

> EDITOR:
>
> I am infuriated at the conduct that *some* of you Ags showed toward *Aggieland* photographers Marie McLeod and Jennifer Friend. It seems to me that you would rather waste your time harassing females in the perimeter than work on centerpole.
>
> I really don't know why you think you have a right to tell these women that they are not allowed in the perimeter. They were there to photograph an event for our yearbook. Apparently you are unable to handle their presence, and you proved it by yelling obscenities at them. Well, let me tell you, you can yell anything you damn well please because that is not going to stop women from entering the perimeter. Someday, whether you like it or not, women will be helping to raise the centerpole. Face the facts. Women already have been making progress by helping cut down trees at the cutting site.
>
> Jane Landry '88

Jane Landry's tone and word choice brings to mind the image of an adolescent girl shaking her finger at a grown man. It was immediately pounced upon in a November 11 letter:

> EDITOR:
>
> After reading Miss Landry's letter, I got the feeling that she was implying that men who work on bonfire are just male chauvinists. According to my handy dictionary, she is correct. It states that chauvinism is the prejudiced belief in the superiority of one's own group. However, my handy dictionary also defines chauvinism as a fanatical patriotism. Hence, the men who work on bonfire are bonfire chauvinists—ones who love and defend the spirit and tradition of bonfire.
>
> But hey, can you blame us? Women cannot produce the amount of labor that is needed to build bonfire. I have seen the women that Miss Landry wrote about, the ones "helping" cut down trees at cutting site. Women come out for half a day and spend the whole time cutting down their "dorm log" that the men have to go in and carry out. Granted there are women out there almost every weekend—riding around in the back of a truck. Gee, thanks for the help.
>
> Since this is the type of help we get from women and since they want to help us even more, we had better make bonfire a year-round project. That might give women enough time to produce the amount of wood required to build bonfire. So you face the facts, Miss Landry—women are not wanted in the perimeter. You are of no use to us in there.
>
> Paul Schwarz '88

Schwarz's last sentence, "You are of no use to us in there," implies that women are of use, but only outside of the perimeter, perhaps in particular parts of the family or individual domicile. Excerpts from a November 11 missive:

> EDITOR:
>
> Women and men must understand that they are not on the opposite side of the perimeter called life.
>
> In order to fully live it must be understood and felt, by these men out there, that they cannot expect true happiness without a deeper and fuller understanding of women. From my experience, as a man, it seems women hardly have been treated like true human beings . . .
>
> If not for the good of all women but their own, it is time that each man took a deep breath and thought about how a woman truly feels, thinks, and is. But they too, must realize the fault is not all theirs. The society, whatever the word means, has programmed us in these insanely insane ways. Beyond the immediate ugliness, which the perimeter incident is symbolic of, lies great beauty in us all . . . And apologies to all if and when I have been one of "those men out there."
>
> Dharam V. Ahluwalia
> Grad student

This all-encompassing, life-redeeming letter surely drew groans from the frontlines of the battle of the sexes. November 18 saw a more to-the-point set of letters. The following response to Paul Schwarz's letter expresses hope that he may be relieved of at least one of his burdens:

> You [Paul Schwarz] close by saying, "Women are not wanted in the perimeter; you are of no use to us there." I hope that when you get married, your wife buys a vibrator and tells you, "You are of no use to me in the bedroom anymore." That is one less thing you will have to do.
>
> Michelle Herren '90

An excerpt from a November 18 letter by a woman Aggie:

> To the guys I cut with, loaded with, yelled with, and carried logs with, I was just another worker, no different from anyone else. They respected me at cut not because I told them they must or else I'd scream discrimination; they respected me because I went out there expecting no respect until I proved to them I was worthy of it.
>
> On Nov. 7, I went out to stack to work. At least three redpots told me to let them know if any of the guys gave me a rough time, but there was no problem. I was there for more than three hours, and in that time I carried logs from point A to point B, worked the tag line, wired logs on the ground, and wired logs up on stack. I worked on stack because the pots out there have worked with me. I've earned

143

their respect and their trust. If I hadn't worked for it, they would never have allowed me up on stack—and very rightfully so.

The CT's and the non-regs don't discriminate; they abuse and verbally harass everyone, regardless of who he or she is. They give me a rough time, but if they didn't then I would feel like an outsider, not part of the unit. I give them a rough time right back, too. Then we all laugh and continue working. We're not male and female, we're Ags. We work together and there is unity. That's what bonfire is all about.

Laura Gilliland '89

Gilliland's was one of the first written accounts of a woman working on the Bonfire stack itself. It seemed women who "earned" the right to enter and work in the perimeter were able to. Women who had not "earned" such a right would be subject to harassment, as some men are harassed.

November 18, an excerpt of a letter in response to Paul Schwarz's:

Why should a freshman who can barely swing an ax get inside perimeter? I can probably swing an ax better than a lot of them . . .

For every tree we "help" cut down, that's one less you have to tire yourself out on. Besides, if women weren't out there helping, whether riding in a truck or working cookie crews, who would feed the male chauvinists who think they run the world? Obviously no one's informed you that women have been running things for a long time; we just let you pretend so you won't pout.

Lisel Lochridge '89

A November 18 letter from two women:

EDITOR:

Girls, girls—can we talk? It seems that the fuss being raised about bonfire and the fact that women are not allowed to work inside the perimeter is, well, wrong. A&M is one of the last schools where chivalry may still be found.

The point is this: The men who build bonfire do much more than just stack logs. They smoke cigars, dip snuff, and—rumor has it—converse in normal, intelligible patterns of speech using common but profane words. Not that any of this is particularly admirable—it's not—but it does serve to promote a profound sense of camaraderie.

And I don't see anything wrong with that. The fact that they don't want us out there is not because we're incapable of wiring logs together, and they know that. It's because the boys don't feel comfortable being "bonfire-ish" around girls and quite frankly, I don't mind letting them have their fun. It's not hurting me any. Call it chauvinism; call it anything you like. But what goes on in the boys' locker room is none of our business. Let the boys be boys.

Nancy Haire '89
Kim Spessard '89

A November 18 letter of gratitude:

EDITOR:

To all the ladies who work for bonfire:

We are writing this letter to extend our thanks for what you have done for us at bonfire cut site. The steady supply of ice water, the lunches delivered, and the Cokes, candy and tobacco that are made available are most sincerely appreciated. Cut site would be much less productive if it weren't for the help you give us. Considering some of the recent publicity concerning women at bonfire, we felt it necessary to show our gratitude.

Robert Hefner '88
Bonfire officer, Company P-2
Accompanied by 185 signatures

This sincere show of appreciation may have been lost on women sick of being relegated to serving cookies to the men. And then there was this unapologetic November 18 correspondence:

EDITOR:

In the Nov. 9 issue of the *Battalion*, Jane Landry wrote an interesting letter. Too bad that she's living in a dream world or a Utopia if you will. In her letter she said, " . . . you can yell anything you damn well please, because that is not going to stop women from entering the perimeter . . ."

Well, maybe if that doesn't work, a well-placed backhand would. Get a clue, woman! Why is it necessary that women always have to cause trouble. Women are supposed to be the sweet, cute people; their place should not be the perimeter, where they might injure themselves. Women are willing to accept equal rights with men in some cases, but when it comes to more important subjects the woman jumps behind her gender, insisting they can't handle the pressure.

If you want to play with the boys, you got to play with their rules. If you can't play by the rules, then don't play the game.

Steve Carrera '91

Just like the extremely specific divisions of labor in Bonfire-building, some of which has inspired the re-application of old words to new meanings (swamping, scarecrowing), Carerra desires a specific division of the sexes, one in which each sex carries with it not just responsibilities but corresponding attributes. Interestingly, women are supposed to bake cookies and be sweet and cute, but apparently when they enter the perimeter they transform into monsters that need to be fought off with "well-placed backhands."

Women on Stack NOW

While the letters page was burning up, this year's Bonfire stack witnessed some of the most surreal scenes that any Bonfire stack ever has (and that's saying something!).

Three members of the President's Office's Sexual Harassment Committee visited the stack on November 9. Committee Chair, Grace Chisholm, Dr. Linda Parrish, an associate professor of educational psychology, and Dr. Virgie Nolte, counseling psychologist for the student counseling service talked with five Redpots at the stack.

These Redpots learned the meaning of sexual harassment years before the rest of the nation was educated through the public battle between Anita Hill and Clarence Thomas. Parrish and crew had been working on adding to the University's policy of sexual harassment. "A lot of the time, people don't know what sexual harassment is," she told the Batt, "So it is going to take a lot of education to tell people.

"All I ever wanted to do is show the females in the student body that because they're students here they can be a part of everything that happens here and that the female faculty will support them.

"There are a few or at least some women on campus that might feel a little bolder if they had some support."

Parrish added that women would be harassed if they ever became Redpots, but that a woman would probably not achieve this honor in her lifetime. None of the sexual harassment committee members actually entered the perimeter.

Two days later, members of the University National Organization for Women (NOW) got their hands dirty, within the perimeter. Led by President Sammy Samfield and Vice-President Dede Whitley, the group of five women and one man helped to move logs, sometimes pots and feminists together carrying a common log.

After working for a while, the NOW members talked with Redpots about what one NOW member referred to as the "last remaining bastion of male dominance on campus." The Redpots stressed that the Bonfire was misunderstood and that anyone can work on the Bonfire, as long as they are properly trained and are willing to work hard.

The two groups agreed to conduct a forum on the bonfire, at which both pots and feminists would speak. Laura Gillilard, a woman who had been working on stack and was to write a pro-Bonfire letter to the Batt (see above), commented after the meeting with NOW, "It was great. They (NOW members) were more open-minded than we thought."

The Redpots did not show up at the scheduled forum, nor at the rescheduled forum. At a press conference, they explained that there was a Bonfire accident that they had to attend to. An exchange between NOW faculty adviser Wendy Stock and Redpot Ned Murphy sums up the press conference.

> Stock: Do we have your guarantee that from now on, and the guarantee of whoever is organizing the bonfire that from now on there will not be any further incidents as occurred in the past, to the best of your ability?
>
> Murphy: Anybody—male, female, non-reg, corps—who wants to work on this fire and know when it burns that they put work in it, can come out.
>
> Stock: What are you going to do to protect women's rights to do that?
>
> Murphy: ... The best way to protect women's rights in this is have the women work. The women that are out here have respect because of their ability to work.

In subsequent years, as civilian and Corps women became a larger part of the Bonfire workforce, they became more and more accepted. But they still suffer from sexism and the occasional assault (see later chapters and interviews).

Resistance, Reform, and Recalcitrance 1987-1992

The late eighties and early nineties were marked by the greatest wave of campus activism since the early 1970's. The anti-apartheid movement, the environmental movement, ethnic studies movements, revitalized feminist movements, and the anti-war movements combined to radicalize the very atmosphere of college campuses around the nation.

Texas A&M is one of the most conservative universities in the nation. Nevertheless, Texas A&M was drenched under this wave of campus activism, that is, relative to its extreme dryness in the years before. Campus organizations like Students Against Apartheid and NOW had already existed, but between 1988 and 1992, added to these were Amnesty International, The Medicine Tribe, Texas Environmental Action Coalition, Earth First!, Rainforest Action Network, an anti-Persian Gulf War coalition, and, yes, even an organization called Aggies Against Bonfire.

Rallies and protests by left-wing and environmental organizations occurred seemingly on a weekly or monthly basis. Issues as wide-ranging as Chinese democracy, renovation of the student center, to the L.A. riots became topics of public discussion and activism. The A&M recycling program was established, and students, faculty and community members began publishing an alternative news and opinion journal called *The Touchstone.*

The largest environmental organization on campus (and there were several) was Texas Environmental Action Coalition (TEAC). This organization included hundreds of members and several individual committees, some of which would meet for six hours or more, deciding plans of action. The most interesting non-environmental activist organization was The Medicine Tribe, which would do everything from raise money for the United Nations Children's Fund to conducting a die-in before the CIA recruiting table to dramatize CIA murders.

It was in this atmosphere—one that included a wide variety of organizations and ways of thought—that Bonfire was looked at from a more holistic point of view. It wasn't simply a feminist issue, nor an environmental issue. Nor was it simply a matter of waste. It was all those things and more—Bonfire as a symbol, as a cultural icon, as an incarnation of the Aggie Spirit was being questioned, challenged, and openly resisted.

Alcohol and the Christian Ethic

For all of Bonfire history up through 1999, no public controversy was ever made about bonfire workers being drunk or that this might cause accidents while cutting, stacking, or driving. Locals often complained about the unruliness of bonfire workers, such as when the cry went out to "stack naked" and many Aggies did so, literally. But for the most part, alcohol was perceived as a problem only during the actual burning of Bonfire.

Although alcohol is supposed to be regulated on campus grounds, the University traditionally ignored alcohol at Bonfire events. At the Bonfire burning, revelers were allowed to bring alcohol onto school grounds, drink, get drunk, vomit, and do and say just about whatever came to mind.

In 1987, the University Police and Texas Alcohol Beverage Commission began patrolling the Bonfire grounds on the nights of its burning. In 1987, plainclothes officers issued citations for minors in possession of alcohol, as well as for supplying minors with alcohol. Although Director of University Police Bob Wiatt admitted that alcohol was not authorized for Duncan Field, his force would not cite anyone over 21 unless they were acting unruly.

"We need to cut out the rowdyism that has been here in recent years," Wiatt told *The Battalion*, "The last two bonfires turned into drunken orgies." Complaints had been made of obscene language, fights, and people running into others, according to Wiatt, who announced that "We want to keep bonfire as a family event."

That first year of police monitoring resulted in six arrests and seventy-five citations for offenses relating to minors and alcohol. "Everything was very peaceful," said Wiatt.

In 1988, nine arrests were made, 115 citations passed out, and three patrol cars made "stinky" from reveler vomit. Some Aggies were sent to the hospital from injuries due to drunkenness, cars were driven on residential lawns, and many Aggies were guilty of what Wiatt calls the "rampant discourtesy" of public urination. Wiatt characterized this night as an "active evening."

The Reverend Steve Sellers ran the Episcopal Student Center on what was then known as Jersey Street (now George Bush Drive). Duncan Field, where the Bonfire was burned, is directly on the opposite side of George Bush Drive. Excerpted here is a letter Sellers wrote to *The Eagle* in response to an editorial that characterized the 1988 Bonfire as a "success."

> As a priest in this community whose chapel is right across Jersey from the bonfire site, I witnessed far more than your news accounts revealed. Here is a sampling: A man being crushed between two parked cars when an "overexuberant" driver collided with cars parked in front of my building; no fewer than a dozen "over-exuberant" youngsters insulting the man when he was unable to get up because the cars had him pinned to the ground; a crowd of other "over-exuberant" youngsters refusing to make way for the ambulance and other emergency vehicles; a half dozen youngsters trying to push the paramedics away from the man; hundreds of "over-excited" people using every tree and bush on church property for toilets; hundreds of others who used church grounds to dispose of the beer cans and bottles; and several others who decided to walk away with various "souvenirs" from the church.
>
> In addition, my building, which was opened as a public service that night, was trashed inside and out. My home—a half a mile away—and dozens of others in our neighborhood south of Jersey were littered with cans and bottles from this "successful" evening.
>
> I am told by others in our community who have been here longer than I (this is my second bonfire) that the night is meant to symbolize every Aggie's "burning desire" to defeat the University of texas [sic] in the yearly football game. It is meant to bring out the best in school spirit. At least that's the official story. From my vantage point, the main pupose of bonfire—officially and unofficially—is to provide an opportunity for thousands of young people to become drunk and disorderly in public.
>
> It is most perplexing that you view this sort of affair as a "success."

Sellers later noted to a reporter that activities more lewd than public urination had occurred in the bushes about his church. About a year earlier,

Professor B.E. Aguirre, had written a letter to *The Eagle* entitled, "Bonfire tradition counter to Christian ethics."

> Every morning in the late fall I walk beside desecrated forests. I see the best of our young men ordering my fallen comrades in neat piles, stacking them up one by one eventually to burn them in an obscene act of atavistic madness; all of this is done in public, with the acquiescence of others, myself included, who should know better. These are acts within a magic circle of cultural traditions impervious to reason.
>
> I write to protest this destruction, to say that it is wrong to waste the resources of our land in this way. Thousands of elderly, poor, disadvantaged people in our town could use the wood to heat their homes in the winter, and the energy and enthusiasm of our students could be redirected to help rebuild homes in bad need of repair, to bring charity and love and hope to their fellow human beings in want. What is needed is a rethinking of the meanings of our traditions, abandoning those which, in light of our present understandings, do not conform to our ideals; we could create others which would correspond more closely to our hopes. Is it too much to ask of ourselves to live the Christian ethic?

In 1988, Aguirre recommended in another letter that Aggies get back to the roots of the Bonfire—to return to the traditional, smaller Bonfire. Through the eighties and nineties, Aguirre could be counted on to consistently state his mind on the Bonfire issue.

Aggies Against Bonfire

The origins of Aggies Against Bonfire lie in the brain of Aggie student Bryan Skipworth. In the spring of 1988 and the fall of 1989, Skipworth began talking to people about Bonfire. It may have been difficult to take Skipworth seriously because he had a reputation of carrying out pranks rather than conducting "serious" activism. He had once put a home-made Nazi arm-band around the Sul Ross statue because Ross had been a "slave-owner, Confederate general, and Indian killer," as Skipworth put it. Of course, a member of the Corps quickly took the armband off of the statue and explained to Skipworth that Sul Ross was not a Communist.

The first meeting of Aggies Against Bonfire was organized by students Bryan Skipworth, Alex Jordan and Kelly Harper. The November 1, 1989 meeting convened behind the Sul Ross statue in front of the Academic Building, and at least twice as many pro-Bonfire students showed up as anti-Bonfire students.

Jordan started out the meeting by saying that the group wanted to advance, not hinder, Texas A&M, but that Bonfire was "wasteful, both of

151

resources and manpower, and that it exhibits ignorance to the rest of the world. We believe that it goes contrary to the values an institute of higher learning should have."

Skipworth spoke up, "The people that work on bonfire are working to waste. They are good people, and they are working very hard. I just feel it would be better if they worked towards something else. I think some questions need to be raised about why we are doing this."

The pro-Bonfire students said that Bonfire provides stress-release, teaches students how to work in a group, and was also a great way of meeting people.

Both the pro-Bonfire and anti-Bonfire groups stressed that alternatives need to be found to the current Bonfire, rather than simply calling for its elimination. Some of the anti-Bonfire students said that the trees cut down could be used as firewood to warm homeless people in the winter. Another idea was a campus-wide multicultural party.

Skipworth felt that the meeting was useful despite the clash with the pro-Bonfire group. "I just think bonfire is ignorant, wasteful, and hazardous to the environment. This is part of higher education, to question things around you."

One week later, United Campus Ministry, which consists of a group of ministers representing seventeen Christian mostly-student congregations, passed a resolution addressed to the "student body, faculty and staff of Texas A&M University." The resolution read

> Because this university loves tradition and because we are, by definition, conservators of tradition, we have concluded—after a study of the land grant act establishing Texas A&M—that it is time for the university to end the bonfire as it now exists. In the context of a world despoiled and deforested, it is no longer morally right for so many human and natural resources to be wasted. Instead, we suggest a more positive use of the energy and human resources to benefit the community.

That same week, the Texas A&M Faculty Senate decided to form a committee to "explore alternatives to bonfire." Senator Richard Shumway, referring to Wylie Keith Jopling, said during Senate discussion, "As the adviser of a student who was killed in a bonfire accident . . . I have a hard time not supporting this resolution."

Health and physical education lecturer Max Stratton defended the tradition, "Though [Bonfire] was not an academic experience, it was a tremendous education. There is a lot of participation in it and there are a lot of leadership abilities that are put into it."

Merwyn Kothmann, a range science professor, said, "I had a young man who came in and told me as a freshman his number one goal was to become a redpot." According to Kothmann, Bonfire results in many "academic casualties."

A week later, after receiving more support from local churches, Sellers spoke to the Bryan-College Station Minesterial Association, "Bonfire is no longer justifiable from a moral standpoint. We think its gotten way out of hand, and enough is enough."

Sellers said that students could re-apply their energies in ways that serve people, such as when "in the 1960's, the Corps of Cadets went to Mexico and built an entire water system for a poor community."

Sellers touched on the silent agreement among students and administrators to prevent negative publicity about Bonfire and Texas A&M. "There is a terrible conspiracy of silence about anything negative that happens during bonfire cut." He said that when a student had lost two fingers when a log was dropped on top of them, the information had to travel through the grapevine to him, and then he had to inform *The Eagle* himself, so that the information could be publicized.

"That student will have to go through the rest of his life with eight fingers," said Sellers. "How many more young bodies are we going to sacrifice on that altar?"

Keep Alcohol from Shattering the Tradition

The builders and supporters of Bonfire did not sit on their hands and allow criticism to reach critical mass. Under the student body presidency of Kevin Buchman, the student government formed the Task Force for Safety and Elimination of Alcohol at Bonfire. This group, along with the Bonfire Alcohol Awareness Committee, and other Bonfire organizations launched a public information campaign that has lasted to this day to "Keep alcohol from shattering the tradition," as its catchy slogans states.

T-shirts were made, posters printed, fliers posted, and people urged not to drink at Bonfire. Buchman himself was incredibly ambitious near the beginning of the campaign. He told *The Battalion* that "We're going to make a big push to end alcohol at bonfire." He continued, "There is a strong movement to do away with bonfire and we have to do everything we can to make sure bonfire has a positive impact on the school . . . I don't think a lot of students realize how important it is to eliminate alcohol at bonfire."

It is a matter of opinion or "spin" how well the anti-alcohol campaign worked, but the media campaign was a stunning success. Seventy-nine tickets were given out by UPD for alcohol offenses concerning minors, down from the previous year's one hundred and forty; the numbers cited by College Station police were unavailable. Sixteen people were arrested by University and College Station police, up ten from the year before. The increase in arrests was attributed to the availability of a paddy wagon.

Although CSPD Lt. Mason Newton said, "It didn't work . . . It was a typical bonfire crowd," UPD chief Bob Wiatt, student government leaders, the Bonfire Alcohol Awareness Committee, and *The Battalion* all characterized the anti-alcohol efforts as a success. "Bonfire crowd sober, subdued," read the *Battalion* headline. "Bonfire was a tremendous improvement over last year and the years before," said Buchman. "We turned the negative aspects of bonfire into a positive experience for everyone." Bob Wiatt was "exceptionally pleased."

The 1989 Bonfire was not a fluke. The drunken orgies were less drunken and less orgiastic in the nineties than in the eighties. The Bonfire forces had reformed the Bonfire to a certain degree. People continued to complain about rowdy behavior, lewd language, and drunken behavior, just not as loudly.

Spring 1990—Spring 1992—Debates, Studies, Reports, Letters, and Reform

Students, the student senate, the faculty, and the faculty senate all continued to debate the merits of Bonfire. The Board of Regents had established a committee to study Bonfire at the end of the 1989 fall semester. The debate over Bonfire was unusual because it had extended and had remained intense through the spring, whereas discussion about Bonfire is usually centered around October and November.

The Student Senate Ad Hoc Committee on Bonfire issued a report on the Bonfire in April, after thirteen weeks of study. The report recommended a reduction in the size of Bonfire and minimum academic requirements for Bonfire workers. The committee also wrote that if a site could not be found where the owners had not already scheduled the trees to be cleared, then Bonfire should be cancelled for that year.

The faculty senate issued its report in May. It was compiled by student leaders and faculty, with consultation from University and community representatives. The report recommended a fifty percent reduction of Bonfire over four years. The height of Bonfire would be reduced by 2.75 feet and the circumference reduced by 7.5 feet each year until the goals were reached.

The reduction in size would decrease the likelihood of injuries and the amount of time students must spend building Bonfire. The report repeated the student senate committee's recommendation that Bonfire be built only if land were already scheduled to be cleared, but the faculty report added that two trees should be planted for every tree burned.

The report recommended the elimination of alcohol at Bonfire and the selling of extra wood, the proceeds going to humanitarian charities. The report also said that a minimum grade point average should be set for Bonfire workers, and that a clean-up crew should clean up local neighborhoods after Bonfire.

In June, a poll was conducted by *The Battalion*. Four hundred summer school students were asked whether they favored or opposed the plan to reduce Bonfire size by fifty percent. Sixty-three percent said that they opposed it, and thirty-one percent said that they favor it. A majority of students opposed such a plan, but not an overwhelming majority. Almost one-third supported a fifty-percent reduction, a figure that seemed high compared to what the general campus atmosphere and the administration's attitude about Bonfire reform would indicate.

In October, 1990, a petition signed by 87 Texas A&M faculty from 9 departments in 4 colleges was sent to Texas A&M President William Mobley and the Speaker of the Texas A&M Faculty Senate, Dr. Bill Stout.

> Given current critical problems associated with impacts of human activity on the biosphere, the Texas A&M University faculty listed below believe that the annual campus bonfire is a needless waste of natural resources, a symbol of a lack of concern for the environment and a very conspicuous source of embarrassment for this institution within the international community. This "tradition" should not be supported by state funds and should not be conducted on state property. It should not be associated with Texas A&M University.

The petition had been organized by, among others, Dr. Hugh Wilson, a professor of biology specializing in botany. He told *The Battalion* that it was important that faculty members make their concerns public. Faculty Senate Speaker Bill Stout reacted by saying, "This is nothing new. The number of signatures, however, is quite substantial."

In November 1990, the Texas Air Control Board had received three complaints about Bonfire. By law, the Board had to investigate, but also by law, the investigators must catch the nuisance in progress. The board's definition of a nuisance is: One or more contaminants, or a combination thereof, in such a concentration and of such duration as are or may tend to be injurious to or to adversely affect human health or welfare, animal life, vegetation or property, or as to interfere with the normal use and enjoyment of animal life, vegetation or property.

Bryan Skipworth commented that, "It almost sounds like they're writing this for bonfire . . . If there's a north wind, and they don't declare it a nuisance, then somebody is doing some underhanded thing." Skipworth was referring to the fire and smoke hazards caused by Bonfire when a wind from the north blew embers, ashes, and smoke into the neighborhood south of Duncan Field. By 1990, the College Station Fire Department had for years deployed all or a substantial portion of their firemen in that neighborhood during Bonfire.

The media campaign to eliminate alcohol from Bonfire was perhaps at its most intense in the fall of 1990. Student government and Bonfire-related organizations had realized from the previous year that it may take some time to rid Bonfire of alcohol and were now talking about a "phasing out" of alcohol over a period of years. Furthermore, they stressed that they were not advocating abstinence; they simply advised students to drink in moderation and not to bring alcohol to Bonfire itself.

The University Police finally decided to enforce the law against drinking on school property, and Bob Wiatt announced that people carrying alcohol at the bonfire site would be issued citations.

In the hour or so before the 1990 Bonfire activities began, Aggies Against Bonfire was allowed to hold a protest behind Duncan Dining Hall. Police were on hand to prevent violent clashes between protestors and Bonfire supporters. Protestors held up signs that said, "Keep this tradition from shattering the environment," "Build Homes, Not Bonfire," and "Farmers Think," in reference to the Aggie spirit yell that goes, "Farmers Fight."

By Bonfire 1990, thousands of U.S. troops had been stationed in Saudi Arabia in preparation to fight a war against Iraq, led by President Saddam Hussein. That August, Iraq had invaded and taken over Kuwait. Although U.S. President George Bush insisted that the involvement of the United States was motivated by a desire to liberate Kuwait and defend freedom and national sovereignty, many Americans, including hundreds of Texas A&M students, believed that the military build-up had more to do with the United States protecting its access to the vast amounts of oil in the Middle East. But most Texas A&M students supported the military build-up against Iraq, and a yellow ribbon was tied around the 1990 Bonfire by Senior Redpots.

As usual, tens of thousands of onlookers came to the Bonfire. Cadet Dax Soule pointed out about the crowd that "They have 50 people against [Bonfire] and 70,000 for it. It's obvious how A&M feels about it."

That year, perhaps to limit the amount of fuel that seeped into the ground, as well as the amount burned into the air, the Redpots reduced the volume of fuel used to light the bonfire from four hundred to three hundred gallons. Nevertheless, the Bonfire burned, and perhaps burned a bit too hotly. A whole six minutes passed before the lit Bonfire collapsed to the ground. The next day, UT Austin beat Texas A&M 28-27, ending six years of Texas A&M dominance.

Local police arrested 89 people, mostly for alcohol-related misdemeanors. Police blocked off both campus streets and George Bush Drive to prevent accidents between motorists and pedestrians.

That winter and spring, as American forces bombed Iraq and liberated Kuwait, hundreds of Texas A&M students protested the war. Others quietly felt the angst of being a citizen of a nation that was killing thousands of troops and civilians in order to preserve access to Middle Eastern oil. Whatever their political stripe, most students admitted that the war had something to do with oil, and many stated publicly that since Americans were dying for oil, perhaps we should all stop wasting so much energy in our country. Some stated publicly that perhaps they should drive a smaller pick-up truck, while others brought up the Bonfire as the most glaring example of waste that our campus produces each year.

But most students and residents understand that when they disparage Bonfire publicly, they are putting something at risk - if not their health, then their standing in the community, perhaps something as intangible as their image or as real as the number of customers that walk into their store. Even at the historical height of Bonfire opposition, the pressure to preserve the "conspiracy of silence" as Rev. Sellers put it, was felt, as demonstrated by a July 1991 letter to *The Eagle* from Mark Fletcher.

> From going door to door and talking to residents in the community affected by the bonfire, I dispute the statement that only a small fraction of residents want the bonfire stopped. Many of the residents support what our group, Aggies Against Bonfire, is trying to do— stop the bonfire—but they will not publicly state it for fear of losing their jobs at Texas A&M University. Many of the residents wanted to help our group but said they could not because they worked at A&M and did not want to be harassed.
>
> I can understand their concern about harassment because I have received many heckling phone calls due to my opposition to bonfire. A member of our group received a written threat on the member's life.
>
> If you were to eliminate the intimidation by some A&M students and the university, you would find that many residents want the bonfire abolished for many reasons.

During the fall of 1991, the Bonfire debate heated up again, as hot as it had ever been. In September of 1991, Cadet Carolyn Muckley made public her complaints about sexual harassment in the Corps of Cadets; three other female Corps members soon joined her in their public airing of their being sexually harassed by male Corps members. Carolyn Muckley is half-Vietnamese. In October 1991, another Asian American female member of the Corps of Cadets quit, the last straw being a Bonfire-related paddling she received from her male commander. In her letter of withdrawal from the Corps of Cadets she wrote that "The Corps is unprofessional, corrupted, racist, sexist and so powerful that such violent and illegal acts are swept under the rug."

Among other things, she had been forced to sing "Jingle Bells" with a Chinese accent. She had also received a phone call from a male cadet who said that he was going to "rape your Viet Cong c— until it bleeds." When her commander, the leader of the elite Ross Volunteers and of Air Force Squadron 15, paddled her and everyone else in the squadron on the rear end with an axe handle, she had apparently had enough. She quit the Corps and had her ROTC scholarship transferred to the Univeristy of Texas at Austin. Her commander was temporarily suspended and investigated.

The commander's supporters argued that he was one of the most avid supporters of women in the Corps and that her complaints had been taken out of context. After all, this is military training, and everyone is treated badly, even by their friends.

That year, allegations of everything from sexist verbal abuse to assault and rape were made by female corps members against their male counterparts. Some charges, including the rape charges, were recanted without explanation. If the Bonfire can be seen at least in part as an institution of the Corps of Cadets, and if the Corps of Cadets contains within itself an ongoing battle of the sexes, won exclusively by the men, then the origins of Bonfire's seemingly steady stream of sexual harassment is glaringly obvious.

The Asian American cadet's charges of racism also hints at why very few minorities work on Bonfire.

In the fall of 1991, the Bonfire committee and Aggies Against Bonfire filed charges against each other through the University judicial system. The Bonfire committee charged that AAB had, among other things, defaced its property by stamping its flyers with slogans like "Stop Bonfire" and "Bonfire promotes waste." The group was placed on thirty days' probation.

Aggies Against Bonfire, perhaps in retaliation, filed charges that the Bonfire committee had violated state hazing laws, knowingly allowed violations of university rules and local, state and federal laws, defaced university property, interfered with the legitimate activities of another student organization, used public areas of campus without reservations, and violated alcohol policies. One of AAB's charges stemmed from a several years' old tradition of Moses Hall to pour lighting fluid on fellow dorm residents and light them while at Bonfire cut. When the University learned of the burnings (because some students had gone to the university health clinic with burns), it disciplined two students by expelling them.

The 1991 Bonfire was marked again by forty or so protestors holding signs saying, "What is the difference between bonfire and a Klan cross burning?" and "Stop the fuelishness." They were met by heckles of "Damn hippies! Get a haircut!" and "Go join Greenpeace." Bryan Skipworth told the press that his organization thought the Bonfire was an "educational disaster."

The Bonfire fell after only twenty-five minutes despite the center pole having been insulated by a steel culvert packed with sand. The culvert was designed to insulate from heat the splice of the center pole, where the two telephone poles were connected, so that the Bonfire might burn longer. Apparently the strong breeze and dry weather burned the Bonfire hotter than expected.

Replant

In March of 1991, the Bonfire Committee, Texas Environmental Action Coalition, A&M Forestry Club, and the Texas Municipal Power Agency (TMPA) initiated a brand new Bonfire tradition. They planted trees in the spring following Bonfire. Bonfire builders had been cutting from TMPA land since 1983, helping the power company clear the land before it was strip-mined. On March 2, 1991, Bonfire builders, student environmentalists, future forresters, and TMPA employees joined together to plant 365 young trees, including red oak, burr oak, dwarf walnut, and laurel trees.

Although the environmentalists still insisted that Bonfire was bad for the environment, and some pro-Bonfire students still clung to the belief that Bonfire was good for the environment, they planted trees that, with any luck, will outlive the entire argument.

After the 1991 Bonfire, in the late winter of 1992, the Bonfire committee and the student government Environmental Issues Committee organized what they called Replant. Six hundred Aggies planted 10,000 seedlings (as opposed to young trees) on land near Carlos, Texas, where Bonfire builders had cleared the land five years previously. The land had since been strip mined for lignite. At this first official replant, there weren't enough trees to accommodate the hundreds of people, and some went home without planting a single tree.

Environmental Issues Chairman Scott Hantman said that Replant has "come to represent our 'growing' desire to beat the hell out of t.u." as opposed to Bonfire, which is our "burning" desire to do so. In the ongoing effort to be the biggest and best, Hantman claimed that Replant "may very well be the biggest campus tree-planting project in the nation." He added, "Of course, we have more incentive."

Another Aggie tradition was continued as well: according to rumor, some Aggies stole some trees from UT Austin and planted them at replant. But the traditional roughneck atmosphere of Bonfire did not impose itself at Replant, and many Aggies who would not participate in Bonfire felt comfortable at Replant.

Replant continues to this day.

Moving the Bonfire

How do you move the world's largest bonfire? Very slowly.

Residents south of George Bush Drive had been complaining for decades about the dangers of flying embers and drunken Aggies. In response to formal complaints, the State Fire Marshal Office had to observe Bonfire in 1990. Although neither the Texas Air Control Board nor the Fire Marshal's office ordered A&M to move Bonfire, Deputy State Fire Marshal Joseph D. Porter did report that "although there is little history of fires related to the Bonfire, the potential for a fire exists." Porter also advised that A&M find a better site for it. Furthermore, three formal university studies between 1987 and 1992 had suggested better places for the Bonfire.

In March 1992, Texas A&M decided to move the Bonfire from Duncan Field to the 9.2 acre rectangular field at the northeast corner of the University. This field was used for playing polo and various other sports. It is on the right side of the main entrance driveway, while a full golf course sits on the left side.

Texas A&M spent over $100,000 on the move, according to Bonfire adviser William Kibler, in order to make accessible to the field electricity, water, lighting, and telephone services. According to Kibler, the University was also going to level the field.

Although there was concern in the beginning about the three gas stations several hundred feet from the site, none of them have blown up or caught fire. In fact, there have been no major fire problems since the move, and the location of Bonfire has become a non-issue, except for questions concerning the slope of the field after the Bonfire collapse of 1999.

Revolt and Reform

By Bonfire 1992, the faculty senate, the 87 faculty that signed a letter to the President, dozens of local churches, the student senate, the Board of Regents, local residents, the *Eagle* newspaper, environmentalists, left-wingers, feminists, two-percenters, and a brave group of rabble-rousers oxymoronically entitled Aggies Against Bonfire had made pronouncements, suggestions, demands, and pleas to change and/or abolish Bonfire, and they had done so all within a few years. Although scores of suggestions had been made—from reduction of size to enforcement of academic requirements—most of these were ignored by the University and Bonfire Committee.

Students did, however, implement two major reforms. In the late eighties and early nineties women were fully integrated into the Bonfire building process. And in 1991, Replant was ordained a new Aggie tradition.

The University moved the Bonfire site from one side of the University to the other. They did so partially to prevent lawsuits, which, in A&M history, has traditionally been one of its greatest motivators.

Despite the kicking and screaming, the conservators of the tradition did act; they did reform themselves, with pride, and sometimes with pomp. Bonfirists changed just enough to prevent the greatest revolt against Bonfire from becoming a revolution against the octogenarian tradition.

Calm Before the Storm
1992-1998

Serendipity (for Bonfire) is the only way to explain the simultaneous exit of the majority of the most dedicated campus activists from Texas A&M. The core of Aggies Against Bonfire as well as the core of most of the other activist organizations had disappeared from College Station by fall 1992. This allowed for an eventful but quiet period for Bonfire, leading up to the tragedy of 1999.

1992

Discussion and debate about the worth and necessity of Bonfire continued into the fall of 1992, and Dr. Hugh Wilson emerged as the one remaining stalwart and outspoken dissenter to the Bonfire majority. It was around this time that Wilson established a Web page called "Dumb as Dirt," which still exists and is completely dedicated to opposing the Bonfire.

The only other item of interest about the 1992 Bonfire is the capture of Aggie tree-stealers at UT Austin. After many successful thefts of trees over many years, five Brownpots were caught at 3 A.M. in the morning with trees in the back of their pick-up truck. Their brownpots were taken from them, but they were not prohibited from working on Bonfire.

1993

This year, several students complained about the way dorm residents were often awakened involuntarily to work on the Bonfire. Freshman Chad White made the mistake of writing a letter to the Battalion complaining about the yelling, banging on doors, loud music, and flagpole clanging used to wake residents of his dormitory, Aston Hall. Soon after publication of his letter, he began receiving screaming prank calls; he opened his dorm door to see a shaving cream pentagram sprayed upon it; and he stepped over a cup of urine placed before his door. Bonfire organizers made public statements reciting policies that prohibited disorderly wake-up calls. In later years, wake-up calls became so violent that some doors had to be replaced.

1994

In October 1994, Steven Sims, Class of 1992, was sitting in his car near the Bonfire site as an unsupervised student crew worked on it. Sims is an African-American, and apparently the Bonfire workers were not. Sims said he heard racist songs coming from the workers' blaring stereo. According to Sims, one of the songs said something like, "If they don't like our southern ways, move them niggers north."

Sims wrote a letter to the Battalion concerning the music, and senior Redpot Ryan Gehrig and head Civilian Pot Michael Owens responded by publishing two letters of apology. Owens' letter stated that "The leadership of Aggie Bonfire does not condone discrimination in any form. This was an incident that never should have occurred." The Bonfire Committee said that music would be screened from then on, to ensure that no more racist lyrics would be played.

When asked about the apology by the Battalion, Sims said, "I never really liked Bonfire in the past. Now, because of those two letters, I can appreciate it a lot more, and I'm encouraged to go out and help and be a part of Bonfire." Sims added that he wrote the letter to the Batt so that others would not be afraid to speak out.

The 1994 Leaning Bonfire

As the music controversy played itself out, the Brazos Valley received 16.5 inches of rain in four days—October 16-19. At 9 A.M. on October 26, Bonfire builders noticed that the stack had started to lean towards one side. Some of the logs had also begun to fall off of the first tier of stack. The university's explanation was that the heavy rains the week before had caused the ground beneath the stack to shift and slope, making one side of the Bonfire heavier than the other. Redpots cleared the area and, after consultation with A&M officials, it was decided that the stack would have to come down.

Cables were attached to the center pole to pull it down. Two cables snapped in the process and as the Bonfire leaned parallel to the ground, a third one slipped off. It took two hours to pull the Bonfire down, impressing onlookers with its strength. Nevertheless, there was much speculation that the centerpole had cracked or broken. The University Bonfire Advisor Bill Kibler dismissed the talk, saying, "There was nothing wrong with the centerpole. The centerpole is obviously cracked now, but that's because the shifting took place with other logs." So the centerpole *did* crack. Kibler simply tried to make the break seem irrelevant by saying that it was caused by the shifting of the stack. Of course no one mentioned that the stack could shift again. It did in 1999.

Malon Southerland, vice-president for student affairs, gave no credence to doubters saying that the Bonfire was "extraordinarily well-built," evidenced by the fact that it took four attempts to bring it down.

As soon as "Bonfire I" was brought down, the yell was out to "Rebuild the hell outta Bonfire!" The city of Bryan donated an 80-foot creosote-coated telephone pole, as all telephones poles are. It is illegal to burn creosote in Texas, except for "ceremonial purposes." Next, three thousand students showed up that day to clear the logs from the building site. Two or three times the normal number of students who work on Bonfire came out to help each night. One thousand hot dogs were donated each night, along with sandwiches and barbecue.

The band, after playing at a football game in San Antonio, drove back to College Station immediately that night to make their Bonfire shifts. The Redpots stayed on site for nearly twenty-four hours a day for a week. With seemingly every Ag from past and present pitching in a bit, a full fifty-five foot Bonfire II was built in eight days.

This year, firemen poured on the wood 650 to 700 gallons of diesel fuel and gasoline, substantially more than the anemically-burning bonfire of the previous year. As it was lit, the closest onlookers fled the extreme heat. A&M President Ray Bowen told the crowd, "Only the Fightin' Texas Aggie Spirit could do the impossible and put that bonfire back up in one week." After burning for forty minutes, Bonfire II crashed to the ground on its own accord.

Possible design flaws in Bonfire I were never investigated.

1995

1995 was an amazing year for Bonfire. There were no major controversies or calamities.

1996

In the early nineties, it was suggested that trees be cut for Bonfire only if a landowner had already planned to clear his land. Fortunately for the Bonfire, this suggestion was never accepted. Perhaps the previous year's lack of excitement had scared away drama-seeking landowners, but for whatever reason, no local landowners had by June 1996 donated a plot of land. So the university advertised. In two separate news stories, they made public their need for a 200-250 acre plot of forested land, easily accessible by highway, and within one hour's drive of Texas A&M. Plus, the trees have to be hardwood and between eight and twenty-four inches in diameter. In return, of course, the landowner would have his land cleared for free.

A plot of land in Milam County was subsequently donated to Bonfire, and cut began as scheduled.

Returning from the cut site on September 22, a Ford Ranger truck carrying ten students - eight in its bed - was heading south on Highway 6. A witness reported that the vehicle was travelling at an "extremely high rate of speed" according to the police report. The driver, Sarah Marie Fullen, lost control of the vehicle as it ran off the left side of the road, crossed back over the highway, and rolled over at least twice before smashing into a highway sign. Nineteen year-old Greg White, a civil engineering major from Austin, was killed. Several others were seriously injured, including two who were in critical condition before recovering.

After the accident, students were not allowed to ride in truck beds on the way to or from the cut site. Students were also encouraged to get plenty of rest and not to drink the night before going to cut. No mention was made of remaining sober during and directly after cut. A rest stop was also set up two miles south of Hearne by the Women's Bonfire Committee to provide snacks and drinks and an opportunity to revive tired eyes.

The daughter of Dr. Richard Strickland, a former A&M professor, was injured in the accident. Strickland said that the Bonfire organizers, students, and the administration had all demonstrated the Aggie Spirit after the accident by showing their genuine and deep concern. "You don't see that kind of attitude across the United States, that level of family that manifests at A&M." Aggies' show of support for the grieving and injured is admirable. But the pattern after nine decades of Bonfire makes one wonder if Aggies should take some of their concern from after a tragedy and place it before the tragedy, in order to prevent it from happening in the first place.

Strickland also put his vote in to "continue the tradition of Bonfire, absolutely."

1997

"Girls with big tits do it better"
"68, I'll owe you one"
"Don't want no short dick man"
"Give me your panties, bitch."

These are all sweet nothings that have been written on helmets worn at Bonfire stack. No one knows exactly how this Bonfire tradition got started, but by 1997, even women had nasty messages scrawled across their pots. In October 1997, the profane phrases came to the attention of VP for student affairs J. Malon Southerland and Bonfire advisor Kevin Jackson. Questioning the validity of this tradition, Jackson said, "We've got three goals at Bonfire: safety, unity, and spirit. My question is: How does this relate to accomplishing those goals?"

Traditions Council chair Jill Newman brushed off the pot decorations by saying, "Boys will be boys."

Mandy Cater, a Battalion columnist, wrote in a column, "The real message these lewd pots are sending is that Bonfire and sexual promiscuity go hand in hand, that sexual harassment is okay." After reading this column, some Bonfire workers wore shirts and helmets decorated with profane sexual messages involving Mandy Cater. Some of the Redpots enjoyed these shenanigans, but Head Stack John Gallemore said that if he saw these shirts or pots, he would ensure that they would not work at Bonfire "ever again as long as I am in charge of it."

By this time, three people had died, dozens seriously injured for Bonfire, but the *Eagle* editorial board came down the hardest on the issue of lewd pot scrawlings.

> Every year it seems that Bonfire is associated with a controversy—racism, sexism, or environmental destruction.
>
> However, the obscenities seen on the pots of Bonfire participants this year are among the worst violations of decency on campus . . .
>
> By sponsoring Bonfire, the University is sanctioning the sexist and vulgar messages implied by the words so proudly displayed on these helmets.

In this editorial, the *Eagle* made some general remarks about Bonfire that cut to some of the hypocrisies and contradictions associated with it.

> The inappropriate atmosphere encouraged at Bonfire would not be accepted at any other forum . . .
>
> Generally, this campus prides itself in its conservative values, yet overlooks the negative behavior associated with Bonfire.

Those who choose to take the moral high ground on issues such as homosexuality and abortion are conspicuously absent from opposing this activity.

Bonfire was founded almost 90 years ago, and aspects of it have evolved into destructive activities. Students of all backgrounds are present at A&M now, and traditions must accommodate the unique perspectives they represent . . .

The University claims to recruit the best students, only to encourage them to participate in morally degrading functions . . .

Traditions are sacred at A&M, and students need to address the insensitive activities perpetuated by some Bonfire participants. A tradition that offends students is not one worth keeping.

Redpots, ostensibly in order to make all students feel comfortable at Bonfire, gave Bonfire participants one week to remove all profane and lewd messages from their pots.

1998

In the fall of 1998, Andice Leigh Seltzer was a member of the Corps of Cadets' Squadron 12. On Halloween night, she was holding the centerpole line at the Bonfire stack when several freshmen from Squadron 17 began pushing and pulling her, trying to make her lose her grip on the line.

They pulled her belt and broke it off, grabbed her by the ankle, sending her to the ground, and then picked her up and carried her a few feet only to drop her. Then they picked her up again, but were stopped by a Red Pot. A few minutes later, however, as she was standing alone, two Squadron 17 freshmen tackled her and began punching her in the face. They were pulled away by a Butt Pot and a cadet from her squadron.

In an interview with the Battalion, Paul Hess, also a member of Squadron 12 made sure that people understood that the attack had nothing to do with Bonfire or Seltzer's sex. "Her buddies didn't like her . . . When your buddies don't like you, it says something about you. There is another girl in the outfit that everyone likes."

Seltzer subsequently quit the Corps and filed a complaint with the University Police. The freshmen assailants were identified, and it was discovered that they had acted under the orders of a sophomore. The assailants and the sophomore wrote letters of apology explaining that they did not mean to harm her when they attempted to take away her pot. Seltzer, for reasons unknown, signed a non-prosecutive affidavit form stating that she did not wish to press criminal charges against the men.

During the 1998 Bonfire yell practice Texas A&M senior football player Dan Campbell announced to the crowd that he was glad he attended a university "where men like women and women like men." This offended many in the crowd, especially gays and lesbians (ironically Campbell himself proudly played the position of "tight end").

Anti-gay and sexist remarks at yell practices have never been shockers at Texas A&M. Nevertheless, President Ray Bowen made the unprecedented move of publicly apologizing for a Bonfire-related incident, saying that "the implied criticism of gays and lesbian people was a personal view and not one condoned by Texas A&M University. Our university is one where criticism—real, implied or unintended—of people for their differences is unacceptable."

Bowen said, "I call on all members of the University community to make real the often-stated goal of the University to welcome all people."

Introduction to the Interviews

Aggieland is made up of people. The Aggie Spirit is what the Aggie community makes it out to be. I interviewed seven former and current members of Aggieland on their views of the Aggie Spirit, the Aggie culture, and Bonfire. Among the interviewed, there are three that support the continuation of the Bonfire, and three who state outright that they support a new tradition. Three are current or former faculty, and three are current students. The final and perhaps most incisive interview is with Matt Carroll '71, a former Corps of Cadets commander.

Karen Kortum and Kim Ryle
Class of 2001

Karen Kortum and Kim Ryle are roommates in Mosher Hall at Texas A&M. They are both juniors and members of the Class of 2001. They met through Bonfire and have both worked on it since their freshman years. Karen is a genetics major from Arlington, Texas, and Kim is a wildlife and fisheries major from Kansas City, Missouri. In 1999, they worked on Bonfire under co-chair of Mosher Hall, Miranda Adams, who was killed in the collapse.

Irwin Tang: How did you know Miranda Adams?

Karen Kortum: I wasn't really good friends with her. We did Bonfire stuff together. We knew each other through Bonfire and also because I was Hall Council president when they passed down the pot to her. The Bonfire leadership is technically part of the Hall Council, which is part of RHA, Residence Hall Association. She was another officer in the Hall Council.

IT: What was she like? The Former Students Association memorial magazine said that she was called the Queen of Bonfire? Is that an appropriate title?

KK: She was always smiling. When we were out there she would kid Kim, tease Kim. Kim's Bonfire pot was cluttered with so much stuff. Miranda would tease her about it all the time.

IT: *Was she out there at the stack all the time?*

KK: She was the times that I went.

IT: *How did you react to the Bonfire tragedy and her death?*

KK: That was really rough. I know she and I weren't very good friends. But it still struck home when I realized that it was somebody that I knew. It wasn't just a faceless number, it was a real person. You would have to have been out there. And read that diary entry that took twelve pages.

IT: *After the accident, you wrote a diary entry of twelve pages.*

KK: Yes.

IT: *What did you see when you got there?*

KK: Fire trucks and ambulances had recently showed up, and they put up the first of several barriers. They'd eventually put up more.

I showed up with several friends, and on the way somebody told us that Bonfire collapsed, and we thought we would be doing Rebuild, and we saw the fire trucks and ambulances and I realized that, Oh my God, there were people under there.

We had just assumed that they would need people for Rebuild. We didn't think anybody would be hurt. It just wasn't quite believable at the time.

When I showed it was a solemn disbelief. I walked around and I felt kind of useless. The only thing I could do was I gave them my flannel. A paramedic walking on the inside was taking up coats and things like that, and I gave them my favorite flannel. And after that I walked around. When I saw people that were about to lose it, I'd ask them, "Hey, do you need a shoulder?" and I'd hold them when they cried. That's what I did for several hours.

I helped with RHA, compiling lists of who were known to be out. And I ran an errand and got breakfast for everyone, and I ran another errand. And I went to check the whereabouts of a girl named Holly. Her name showed up that night on a list of people who had been released from the hospital.

I was supposed to be at work at around 7:30 [in the morning]. I was going to take a shower and go to work. That's when I heard from inside the perimeter, "We need twenty pots right now to help!" There were five of us dressed up for Bonfire work. I couldn't leave. I didn't show up for work. I instead carried logs for eight hours.

IT: *And what was that like?*

KK: It was hard sometimes. Physically it wasn't that difficult, because we weren't concerned about that. It was scary sometimes. They would tell us to push back. Whenever that happened, it was because they were uncovering someone from the Bonfire. I think the hardest part was watching them remove some of the people who didn't survive.

Overall, we were carrying logs and helping each other. You know that is what Bonfire was about in the first place.

IT: *What did you do afterwards?*

KK: I went to a lab. By the time it got to be four in the afternoon, there was a faculty member out there. I asked the faculty what the general rule about going to classes was. He told me that he'd seen me working for a long time. And he wrote an excuse for me on the back of his business card. I ended up leaving anyway, because there was a line of one hundred Bonfire workers waiting to get on crew. And there were fifty outside. I was just dehydrating myself, and I needed to go to class.

IT: *You must have been in shock that first day. Did it finally hit you?*

KK: That was the time I was walking across. And I heard somebody make some comment. I think I saw people carrying flowers to take to the Bonfire site. And I started crying. A random girl stopped me and held me and talked to me about it.

IT: *I hope that we can be honest today. I know that we protect our traditions here at Texas A&M.*

KK: I'll admit that right after Bonfire fell, I wouldn't watch the news because it made me mad.

IT: *Well, what made you mad about it?*

KK: Well, they did a lot of misquotes. Or they would only say the negative parts, you know. Like I'd say, okay, I can admit that part of it, or I'll accept that, but they wouldn't explain things fully. Like they said that we broke regulations by having freshmen and sophomores on stack. Well, that whole regulation book thing, from what I understand it, was part of a class the Redpots did one year way back in the early nineties or the eighties or something like that. Several years ago. And they wrote up this safety handbook, but it wasn't official, and it was more written as a joke. Like, they put a bunch of . . . of bullshit in there cause it was something that they had to do in order to get class credit.

KR: From what I understand, back when it was a Corps thing and not a Corps, non-reg, all-Aggie thing . . . you weren't allowed because you were a fish. You were an underdog. You had to work your way to that privilege, but now when people go out to stack, it's a matter of, you don't actually get on Bonfire until you have been out here long enough so that you have been shown how it works. And then you work your way up to first stack, and then you work your way up to second, and then maybe if your lucky you get on a swing.

KK: I was only actually on stack once, and that was after I'd been out there several times. All the other times when I went out there to help, they either had me doing scarecrow duty or . . . okay. Carrying the log duty.

IT: *What is that called?*

KK: Fuck duty. Fuck crew. It's what it's called when you carry a log.

IT: *(laughter) I've heard of that already.*

KK: Or I was on the base of it doing wiring. In order to climb up, they have to know that you know how to wire. And to be on the swings . . . the only people I saw on the swings were at least sophomores, if not juniors, like the co-chairs. Miranda was on the swing the night before it fell. I saw her up there.

IT: *It seems from the reports that we've been getting that the wiring on the first stack seems pretty important. Now how much training did you get before you started wiring logs on the first stack?*

KK: In order to do the wiring when you show up there, they had the specific people that were in charge of training everyone from Mosher, the co-chairs were in charge of making sure that we knew what was going on. Now in order to participate in Bonfire, you were supposed to take the Bonfire safety course.

IT: *The cut course, right?*

KK: You go out to like cut class, and they explain everything about Bonfire.

IT: *Do they still give you the cut card?*

KR: It's not a card anymore. It's a sticker.

IT: *Okay, on your i.d. card? Okay, so what kind of training did that involve, being trained by your co-chair?*

KK: My entire first semester, any time I went out there, I had a co-chair who was out there. "Okay, Karen," [she would say,] "I want to make sure you know what you're doing. This is how we do it." And then they'd watch me, especially the first few times. I was next to them, and I was wiring next to them. And that's how it was. They wouldn't send me off with another group and go wire somewhere else.

IT: *They would look at your work.*

KK: Mm-hm.

IT: *So it was like on-the-job training.*

KK: Yeah.

IT: *Although I'd heard people say that they had gotten on the upper levels basically without any experience at all up there.*

KK: Um, that wasn't my experience. Of course, I had different co-chairs my freshman year. And I'm from this dorm. And I know that as far as that goes, to use your words, it's like on-the-job training. I guess some other leadership positions perhaps might not do it the same way.

IT: *So how were you involved in building Bonfire 1999?*

KK: I went to cut once, and I went to stack twice. But I was out there the night before it fell, and I went up to the co-chairs the night that it fell and told them that I was going to go out there, and I told them the time that I was going to show up. And I knew that I had to finish this biochem chapter, so I was reading, reading it, and then I said, "Oh, my God, I'm supposed to be out there," and I closed the book, and I got all suited up to go to stack, and then I was like, "Oh, if I don't finish this chapter, I'm never going to," so I finished reading the chapter, and then I headed out there. When I got out there, it had fallen fifteen minutes ago.

IT: *Oh, my God.*

KR: Yeah, no kidding.

IT: *You were involved in Bonfire both your sophomore and your freshman years. You were pretty intensely involved?*

KR: Our fish year, we were both out there almost every time.

KK: Every weekend.

IT: *Every weekend for cut?*

KR: Oh, yes. My arms remember that.

IT: *Now, why were y'all so intensely involved as freshmen? Was it because people woke you up every day?*

174

KK: The grunt work of Bonfire is all done by freshmen.

IT: *What do you mean by the grunt work?*

KR: Cut is the big grunt work. Going out there and actually swinging the axes, carrying the logs out, it's sort of a . . . it's not a rite of passage. It's an Aggie thing.

IT: *Yeah. Pay your dues.*

KR: Kind of.

IT: *This year, it seems like there were a lot of freshmen involved in stack as well. Like 85% of those killed or injured were underclassmen.*

KK: I guess the reason why I didn't get as involved this year or last year as I did my freshmen year, is because the sophomores and juniors that get really active in it, or stay active in it, usually have leadership positions. I wasn't in a leadership position, and I wasn't a freshman, so I was kind of in the middle. So I'd still go out there, and hopefully my old friends would still be out there, and we'd be like . . . but it wasn't quite the same thing.

IT: *What is the general atmosphere out there at the Bonfire stack and cut?*

KR: Speaking from the girls' point of view, we, I guess, lucked out. I heard some weird stuff, about girls and other guys' dorms, the guys giving the girls some hard problems, but with Aston [Hall], they treated us with respect because we put in our full due, we worked our butts off, and we were right in there with all the guys.

KK: They expected us to work just as hard as them. They'd come over and make fun of us if we weren't swinging the axe right [laughter].

KR: A lot of times, it was just a good comradeship. It pulled us together. It made us feel more a part of the community.

IT: *Was it kind of like, sometimes when I read about it and listen to other people, it sounds like, kind of a party.*

KR: Not at cut. I mean at lunch time and we're all taking a break, it gets a little silly . . . but the pots that are from Aston or your co-chair, they come around and see you're screwing around, they get mad, like, "You have axes in your hands. That is dangerous stuff."

KK: Now at stack, they play music and stuff. It's got more of a festive feel to it. I remember the last night that I was out there. I specifically remember one point in time, and I wish I could tell you all the other specifics of it, but there was some guy who didn't quite listen to something one of the Redpots said, and the Redpot got really mad and said, "You're off! Go! You listen to what I say when I tell you to do otherwise. And this is not safe. You get off of that right now!" So, from my experience, yes it, it has kind of a, like they'll play something, "Honey, why don't we get drunk and screw," and all the boys are up there whoopin', and all that jazz, while they're wiring.

KR: As far as the music they play, it's kind of just to help keep everybody moving, keep you awake [. . .] the music helps people concentrate [. . .]

IT: So, do you think that discussing the problems of Bonfire in public forums like books and articles will help to make sure that nothing like this tragedy will ever happen again?

KK: I believe in freedom of the press, and I believe we should look at what happened, and figure it out. I think the best way to discover it is a real investigation.

KR: What they're doing now.

[. . .]

IT: What is the biggest misconception that you have encountered about Bonfire?

KR: I guess from the mass news networks, I get the impression more that they really don't know why we do this.

KK: I think most people think of it as a big pep rally for a game.

KR: It gets hard to explain. Part of being at A&M, being in Bonfire, going out to watch it, it's part of being an Aggie. It's part of the culture. It's part of the community, the family that bonds you together.

IT: Okay. What does being an Aggie mean? What is the Aggie Spirit?

KR: To me, it's a sense of pride, that as often as you hear the classic Aggie jokes, oh, look it's those dumb Aggies. You have to be highly intelligent, no matter how you may act sometimes, to even get into this school. To stay in, you have to have something upstairs, and I hear people talking about, they're engineering majors, and business majors. And I'm in wildlife, and I hear all the things that these people do to become an Aggie and make it through, and graduate with a diploma that says, "You're from Texas A&M University."

KK: If you go to a job interview and they notice you're wearing an Aggie ring, and they're an Aggie too. Then you have an automatic comradeship . . . like you meet someone on the street, it's like, "Oh, you went to A&M?" I went to Colorado earlier this month. And I met a few people that graduated from A&M. I was wearing my Aggie sweatshirt. They were like, "Are you a student there?" And automatically, I had a friend in the middle of nowhere.

KR: The person you're interviewing with, you may not get the job, you may get it. But it also confers a sense of, "They had to have accomplished something to make it out of that school with that ring, with that diploma." It's just a really big family community. In my grandparents' hometown, there's this guy Mr. Holsonbake. He's ninety-something years old, and he's an Aggie, and he comes down to every game. I've talked to him, and he'll tell me about all these Aggies that I should go talk to, and it's just, it's a family.

IT: *Okay. Okay. Now one of the students who died in the collapse was a Brownpot. He was also legally drunk. How often have you seen alcohol at Bonfire cut or stack?*

KR: At cut, if they ever find somebody that's come out, especially if it's one of the higher-ranking guys, the other pots I've actually seen them pull him aside and say, "Hey, man. You're not doing anything today. You're going to sit on the side."

KK: I can tell you what I've been told about that particular situation. That it was pass-down night. That he was on stack, but he wasn't working. That he climbed up there, but he wasn't actually wiring or anything like that. That's what I've been told. Now that could be completely false, and I don't condone that action.

IT: *What other incidents of drinking have you seen?*

KR: Only when it burns, and then that just makes me angry. Bonfire is so much more than just for the students. It's for all the old Ags that come back with their families. I'm like, if you want to drink, drink afterwards, after it's fallen, or when you go home, but not out here.

KK: I must admit, when Bonfire burned the past two years, a bunch of drunk people wander around, and then there's the block parties across from campus and stuff.

IT: *Yeah. So you haven't seen any drinking out there at stack.*

KK: Not that I can remember.

IT: *Some of these people actually drink before they go out to stack.*

KK: I assume that there's always going to be stupid people. But I don't particularly note those particular stupid people. (laughter)

IT: *Are those stupid people usually caught and shuffled away?*

KK: From what I can assume, from what I've seen, if you were in a drunken state, where someone can tell that you're drunk, they're not going to let you up on stack.

IT: *We're going to go through some negative aspects of Bonfire here. What about hazing activities at Bonfire?*

KK: The only hazing activities I've heard of was Walton got suspended for what they did to what they call the New Boys, and that's the Bonfire leadership. Like when they pass down their pots, they made them hug a tree, and then they'd take off their hat, and then had to go run and get their hat, and all the time they're saying, "Get back on the tree!" You know like that kind of thing. That's the only real hazing personally that I have ever heard of. And other than that, I haven't heard of anything.

IT: *What about groding?*

KK/KR: (laughter)

KR: It was our sophomore year, we were out there, and we were with some of our friends. And there were two guys, and all day we were wanting to take them to this spot on the dirt road. Dirt roads out at cut are normally this powdery, thick dirt. And there was a spot where one of the water trucks had dumped some water, and it was really muddy, and we just . . . wanted to get them muddy! And groding is more of a just fun way to pick at your friends.

IT: *What exactly did y'all do?*

KR: We ended up getting pulled in the mud instead of them.

KK: Here's a picture of us (shows me a picture of them muddy). It's not like a thing where we pick on a cute little innocent freshman. The groding thing was more like a practical joke.

KR: Everybody knows after lunch groding is going to happen, and that if you don't want your friends to get you, you kind of go hide for a minute. And if you want to grode them, you wait 'til everything starts and then you run out there and you get them.

KK: There were some people I know that if I groded them, it would have offended them, or hurt them, but I know Kim, and I know that she would grode me back. (laughter) It's not a big deal.

IT: *So, is there still a great deal of sexism at Bonfire cut or stack?*

KK: I think that we were very lucky to get to cut with the group of people that we did . . . cause they treated us like equals.

KR: They saw that we knew what we were doing, and even though we couldn't cut as much as they did—

KK: Even if we couldn't carry those big logs—

KR: We put our full heart into it—

KK: I think there's sexism in the way that they structured in that the leadership. You know how female halls have co-chairs, but the co-chairs are not technically recognized by Bonfire leadership. They're part of the hall council. They're only recognized if the crew chiefs from the male hall that you cut with, if the crew chiefs *let* them have any leadership. And then all the other leadership positions, unless there's a co-ed hall, and there's a female crew chief, all the other positions are male. Except for the Pink Pots, which are Women's Bonfire Committee. And Women's Bonfire Committee is in charge of water and cookies and punch. And to me it seems incredibly sexist. And the Red Pot shack, don't even get me started on that one.

IT: *What goes on at the Redpot shack?*

KK: Well, it's not anything that goes on at it. It's just that the only way you're allowed to be in there is if you're sleeping with one of the Redpots . . . and, oh, that's for females. For men, it's a different story.

KR: Even if you're a guy—

KK: You either have to be a Redpot, or an old Redpot, a Dead Pot, then you can go in there, or if you're sleeping with one of the Redpots, and you're a woman, you can go in there.

IT: *I've heard things to do with perimeter that had something to do with that. This was in the past, of course, that women couldn't enter the inner perimeter without having fun with one of the Redpots. So, what about that woman that got beat up last year? Do you know anything about that?*

KR: Which one?

KK: I met her.

IT: *"Which one?"*

KR You hear rumors all the time. I do know this one gal. And her name was Andice. And, I'm trying to remember what it was all about. I hate to say this, but she was in the Corps, and I think that that had a very large part to do with it.

KK: I think it was a thing between her outfit—

KR: That was a part of it. She was on one of the ropes with her outfit, and guys from another outfit came and grabbed her off. It's been so long since it happened.

IT: They grabbed her off, and what did they do to her?

KR: I'm trying to remember if they actually hit her or not.

KK: Well, it was one of those things where, I guess it's like centerpole or something, they tell you, "Take a piece of the log," which basically means, touch the part which you're going to try to carry. It's kind of like a sense of pride if your dorm or, since this was like a Corps thing, your outfit, if your Corps outfit has the more freshmen on it, then it's something cool, I guess. She was hanging onto it, and they'll pull each other off, and stuff like that.

KR: Her major antagonist was someone she was having problems to begin with. The major guy that initiated the violence was somebody she was having problems with, personal problems on a whole other level, way outside of Bonfire. And he decided to, just take the opportunity out there, and do what he did.

[...]

KK: She wouldn't have been able to stay on it anyway. Cause they don't let women do perimeter pole. I did it my freshman year. One of the Redpots go up and down. If you're a girl, and they can see, like your pigtails or something, they take you off.

IT: Were they standing on centerpole or something?

KR: It was one of the perimeter poles.

KK: It was when they were putting them up, in order to erect them and add them to stack. They have them laying down, and then they tell everybody to like cover down and then they all lift it up.

[...]

IT: Anything else about male-female relations at Bonfire?

KR: I've never really seen anything, or been personal witness to it. I've never had anybody, just because I was a girl and I was out there, really say anything to me. And yeah, it kind of bothers me that there are certain things with stack and with centerpole specifically that are a male thing. But it's also a Corps thing. If you belong to a non-reg dorm, the only thing you can do is be on those ropes for perimeter pole. It bothers me a little bit, but I also see that it's tradition. And that so many things a part of Bonfire that were once male-only, Corps-only have gone over to male-female, non-reg and reg, and it, it takes time, you can't always expect a massive change in something to happen overnight.

KK: I don't know if everyone had the same experience that we did. But like I said, we were with Aston [Hall]. We were with a lot of gentlemen.

IT: *Yeah. I used to live in Aston. (laughter)*

KR: They may have the outer appearance of being kind of nasty little pain-in-the-butts, but inside, they were real men.

KK: At least they were able to accept that we're Aggies too. You know, and being female doesn't make us any less of a gung ho Aggie. So we wanted to be out there working and doing the same thing, and we wanted the same kind of respect.

IT: *Is there any racism out there at Bonfire?*

KR: It sounds kind of bad, but there aren't that many people outside of whites that live in our dorm, so I really don't know. It's also a matter of some people just don't want to do stack or cut or Bonfire. They like to go out and watch it, but they don't necessarily want to be out there.

KK: I don't know that it's necessarily racist, but I've never seen any leadership that is not white, and . . . not male, but (laughter), anyway, that could also be because like she was saying, there's not a whole lot of minority population in the dorms or the Corps outfits. Now—

KR: What I have seen of the nonwhites in the Corps outfits, doing the stuff everybody else was.

IT: *Right. It's curious that . . . from what I understand, there aren't that many minorities that get involved in Bonfire at all, actually.*

KR: Once again, I really hate to say anything like this. It's just, I don't know if any of them are interested in it in the first place.

IT: *Right. I'm wondering, why?*

KR: It just may not be their thing. I mean, a lot of people that I've known—white, black, purple, yellow, red—didn't really like the concept of physical labor outdoors. And I think that may have a big thing to do with it. There are certain people that don't mind getting outside and cutting wood, and getting poison ivy.

KK: It's the same reason why a lot of women choose to be the ones that serve the water. We're in the minority when it comes to that, that we're actually out there swinging an axe, carrying a log, and wiring in logs on stack. It's that, because that's what their used to, and that's what most women are comfortable doing, is being the one in the back serving the water to all the workers.

IT: Now, what about academic performance. Does Bonfire affect students' academic performance?

KR: I know, my freshman year, I kind of used Bonfire as kind of an excuse. But it was completely my fault. The co-chairs, and the crew chiefs, if you had said, "Hey, I can't go today. I have to work on some stuff," they would have been, "Hey, that's cool." But I never really thought about it, so I just said, "Well, I just want to go, so I'll just not do it."

KK: To work on Bonfire, like if you were one of the Mosher co-chairs, that better be your only outside activities 'cause that and school is going to be enough.

KR: If their GPR isn't high enough, they can't stay co-chairs.

KK: You can do Bonfire and still excel in school, but you're going to have to realize that if you want to do it full-blown or be a leader, then it's gonna take up a lot of your time, yes. You just have to balance your time. So I think that it could affect academic performance, but—

KR: It's dependent on the individual.

KK: Yeah, you can use it as an excuse.

KR: I've known several people that work Bonfire that have 3.0's and higher. And they weren't like the, "I go out once a week." They were very gung ho—

KK: I'm a very gung ho person. I was my freshman year. At the end of that first semester, I had a 3.4. And I was out doing Bonfire just about every time.

IT: Now, do y'all think that the Administration really knows what goes on at Bonfire stack? Do they have a real good understanding of how the whole thing works, and what goes on at stack and cut?

KK: I don't know that I can answer that question, only because I'm not one of the leadership people. So I don't really deal with the University. The only thing I know about that is when I saw the occasional faculty member. I never saw anyone out at cut, but like, whenever I was out there carrying logs, I talked to several faculty members.

IT: What were they doing out there?

KK: Well, this was, I saw several faculty members after it'd fallen, and we were carrying logs. And I talked to some of them. And that's the only contact that I know of.

IT: So, before that, you'd never seen any faculty or administrators out there.

KK: Not really, save like the time when our hall directors were out there—

KR: But they're more, as far as Bonfire is concerned, just like the rest of us.

IT: Right.

KK: They're graduate students.

KR: Mind you, the times that I'm assuming Karen goes out there are like really late at night in the early A.M. hours, whereas, the normal person working for the school works eight to five, and may not be able to get out there at the early A.M. shift. So if you only go out there at early A.M. shift, you may not see them because they go all during the day. But, like I said, I don't really know because I've never really been out to stack.

IT: There's effectively no faculty or administrative supervision.

KR: No, there is Rusty Thompson. He works very religiously with them. And it's his baby.

IT: How often is he out there? Have you ever seen him out there?

KK: I don't know if I've ever met him. I don't know if I've personally met the Redpots either. Like I know who they are, and I recognize their pots, and when they tell me to do something it's, "Yes, sir." But I don't know that I actually know those people.

IT: Okay. Do you think that the tragedy could have been prevented?

KR: It's kind of hard to say because we don't know really why it fell. I mean it may be a matter of . . . I talked to my dad, and he was here at A&M in the early seventies. And it may be the way they were building it. I know he was talking about how they [the students of the 1970's] lean the logs actually in. Like they tip them. I'm not too sure what that's all about because I couldn't really figure out, well, if you did that on first stack, how would you really build on top of that? But it may have been, they thought that they had something going on, it could have been just centerpole itself—

[. . .]

IT: Do you think that someone should be held responsible for not having this whole process examined over the past several years or decades?

KR: It's kind of hard to say that because the administration's changed hands so many times. Different officials have been in and out and—

[. . .]

IT: Do you think there should have been some sort of overhaul of the process [in 1994, after it leaned]?

KK: That would have made more sense. I think it's a little late now to point fingers. I read in the Battalion today that some engineering professors are talking about Bonfire and saying how this and this and this was unsafe. But if that's what you felt before, why didn't you tell someone?

KR: You hear about all these professors and people who have been saying, "For years and years and years, I've been saying they've been doing it wrong, wrong, wrong." And you hear them now so vehemently now that it's happened, but you never heard more than a teeny little peep once in a while from them before. I mean if they felt so strongly—

IT: Why do you think that is?

KR: I think it's more of a, they're trying to get attention.

KK: They're trying to save face, so that they don't actually have to be responsible for it either.

KR: If they felt that badly about how we were doing things oh-so-wrong, if they felt that strongly, you'd've thunk they'd been a bit more insistent about people hearing what they're saying.

IT: Do you think that people who speak up against tradition here at A&M are sometimes censured for it?

KR: Well, I'm a part of a group here on A&M campus called Cepheid Variable. It is a sci-fi(science fiction)/fantasy/horror group. If anything would be out of the norm, it would be my group, and we've never run into any real problems. People may give us weird looks, but then again, I'll admit, we're kind of weird.

KK: The only thing that I know of is that, you know there's a professor that's like opposed Bonfire for just years, and he has signs up in his window, and you can see them, and you can see also that there's been things thrown at his window and stuff. Yes, like anything where you go that has that kind of strong of a tradition, it's going to be a group-think mode. So, if your going against the flow, you're going to have opposition. But, you know, that's natural. That's a normal part of the process . . . I don't think it's a bad thing to have opposition.

IT: Opposition meaning dissenters?

KK: Opposition to the tradition. If you're going to oppose A&M tradition, just be forewarned. (laughter)

IT: *I see. I see. Be forewarned.*

KK: It's not, it's not like a bad thing—

KR: This is A&M, a lot of people come here *because* of the traditions.

KK: People feel strongly about the traditions, and I'm not saying Bonfire. I'm saying Silver Taps and Muster. If they suddenly said, "I'm sorry. We've booked this, and you can't have the hall for Muster anymore, so we're just not going to have it this year," you would have people coming out of the woodwork saying, "I'm an Aggie. I can't believe that we're not going to have Muster."

IT: *Yeah, yeah.*

KR: I think as far as Bonfire goes, maybe it turns out that it was a single person or a group of persons' fault. Instead of laying blame and saying, "Oh, let's punish you," figure out what went wrong, and let's get it right next time.

KK: That's what I'm saying. I think it's too late to point fingers.

KR: I think we need to figure out, say, what we did, we kinda was doing something bad on the design, if that's what it turns out to be, and do it right for the next Bonfire. Don't end this because it wouldn't be fair. It wouldn't be right because it's not like every single person that was out there did something wrong. Taking something like Bonfire away from all the students here now and every future generation of Aggie, it would just take a part away from the Aggie soul.

IT: *Do you think that there can be an alternative to Bonfire?*

KR: No. Nothing would really compare. Bonfire is a project year-round. It starts with finding the land, finding the trees, getting the centerpole. It's a build-up. It's a part of who we are and what makes us Aggies.

IT: *What about the suggestion that Aggies could, say, build houses for local people that needed them?*

KR: We already do that.

IT: *You have the first Habitat for Humanity built by only Aggies.*

KK: I think what you're thinking of is finding a cut site and using that wood for houses.

IT: *No, no, no, no. That's . . . funny to me.*

KK: That wood is either like plywood or firewood. That's house wood. Not lumber.

IT: What do you think about that . . .

KR: I think the program we already have (Habitat for Humanity), just build it, but as we've said, if Bonfire turns out to have been some fault on humans' part, fix it, don't just destroy it. I mean, I've talked to so many people that were dear friends to the ones that died, that are very close to the families because they're a part of their family. They don't want Bonfire to stop. I don't see why it should. Just fix the problem.

KK: I have a good metaphor here. It's like the Christmas tree. When they started doing Christmas trees way back when, they used to put little candles on them, which was very dangerous, and it would light the tree on fire and burn the house down, and it was like a very dangerous tradition, but it looked pretty and everyone wanted to have one still, and—

IT: Yeah.

KK: And they found a safe way to celebrate that tradition. This is a tradition, it may not make sense to everyone, but this is a part of Aggieland. And as soon as we find a safe way to celebrate it, I mean, if that means that we have a stack that's only like twenty feet tall versus the fifty-five feet. If that means that we have to totally re-engineer it, and we have to start building it in August, you know, and go piece by piece, and have someone come out and inspect it everyday—

KR: Well, fine.

KK: That's the way it works. But I don't think that we should just trash it. I think there's too many things in this world that we say, "Oh, you know, instant gratification, we need it right now, let's just trash that." That's part of A&M is learning to appreciate things that we've had, you know, the traditions, our heritage. That's part of A&M culture.

IT: What kind of meaning do you see in Bonfire?

KR: It's a hard thing to put into words. It's something that you feel inside. A lot of my friends, they're what you would call your two-percenters. However, they're still like, "Hey. Bonfire is Bonfire." And it means something. It brings a certain pride, a feeling of love and happiness. And feeling as if you know forty thousand other people even though you may not have ever said a single word to half of them.

KK: I can read you the last bit here.

IT: Last bit of what?

KK: This is the account I wrote. It's like nine pages. And this is from the point in time when I went up and I told Miranda I was going to meet her out at stack until I finally got home. This was the night that stack fell. [Reading from her journal] It's been a roller coaster of emotions since that Wednesday night-Thursday morning. For a while I felt guilty for not having gone out there and having been there when it fell. Even though I could have been a victim, or that even I couldn't have done crew since no eyewitnesses were allowed to help. I began to cry once walking across campus. Another girl saw me and held me. She said that her church group would pray for me. It's just like the Aggies to just help a random stranger. I also went to Miranda's funeral and spent a great deal of time defending the Aggies. The Arizona newspaper printed a derogatory cartoon, an Austin DJ made some hurtful comments, and twelve victims of the tragedy were nominated for the Darwin Awards. None of us, me or my friends were going to accept that. We stood up for ourselves by responding to every single negative, inaccurate, or insensitive gesture. Bonfire is how I met Kim, how I met Stephen, how I found my space at A&M my freshman year. It helped bring me closer to my dad. This was more than just a fire for a football game. It's about Aggie Spirit. Our family. Please find a way to celebrate it again. Safely. Then it can burn again. But this time also as a memorial to the twelve Aggie victims. The true Twelfth Man.

Dr. Wendy Stock

There are few professors in recent times who have impacted the Aggie culture as much as Dr. Wendy Stock. When Wendy Stock first came to Texas A&M in 1984, there was no campus National Organization for Women (NOW), women were not allowed in the perimeter of Bonfire, and sexual harassment was of unknown proportions in the Corps because no one knew about it. She changed all of that. Dr. Stock left Texas A&M in 1993 and now teaches at the University of California Berkeley.

Irwin Tang: . . . Yes, so I graduated from Texas A&M in 1992. I'm working on a book about the Bonfire. I am concentrating on the cultural aspects of Texas A&M that may have contributed to the collapse of the Bonfire.

Wendy Stock: Mm. The physical collapse?

IT: Yeah. Yeah. The way Texas A&M operates, you know, this Bonfire tradition was basically left on its own, sort of run on its own, by students who oftentimes were more concerned about hazing and having fun or drinking—

WS: Urinating on each other and so forth.

IT: Right.

WS: (laughter) Oh, so you're saying, because the university had such a laissez-faire attitude, and kind of made such a religious ceremony out

188

of Bonfire, and they left the management of it alone, that it was inevitable that at some point perhaps an accident would occur because it was not subjected to the same level of scrutiny maybe that some other organizations like Gay and Lesbian Student Services might be.

(laughter)

IT: Exactly, exactly. In fact there were accidents going on every year.

WS: Yeah, people were hurt, cutting things and so forth, more minor, I think, up until now no one was ever killed, were they?

IT: The three deaths that occurred before the collapse involved motor vehicles. That may show some negligence on the part of the university as well. Tell me a little bit about yourself and your association with Texas A&M.

WS: Okay. I'm a clinical psychologist. I'm now 46 years old. I did my undergraduate at UC Berkeley in Psych [in 1976], got my doctoral degree from State University in New York at Stony Brook. After a year in private practice, I ended up at Texas A&M to work with a sex researcher, actually, that I had done my dissertation with. My area of research was women's issues, gender issues, and sex research. In general, human sexuality. And pornography was an area that I did research on. I've always defined myself as a feminist, and I define that as simply wanting equal access for everything. Equal treatment, equal access. I have never thought of myself as a man-hater. I'm a feminist in the sense of wanting political equality. I came to A&M, started out as a research scientist for two years, and then became an assistant professor of Psychology.

I got to Texas A&M in 1984. In 1984 or 1985, I was contacted by the Texas National Organization for Women. She was the campus coordinator. And her job was to contact NOW members who lived in parts of Texas that may have had chapters of NOW that weren't active or where they were trying to start them. And they tried to have them on most large campuses. There was a Brazos County chapter, and I actually attended that for the first year I was there . . . Maybe it was '86 or 87. I had been active in the Brazos County Chapter, but it wasn't doing anything. They had meetings every once in six months or something, and they were really not doing anything political. They were actually concerned with not getting bad press. They were very conservative for a NOW chapter in terms of addressing anything. And when they did have a president who was an African-American woman, who came in at the end of my time at that chapter—she wanted to do some community surveys, I think to look at lighting in the community, getting better lighting for women, so they wouldn't be at risk at night as much—and some people got really uncomfortable because she was actually doing something. So I was kind of disappointed with the level of activism, so I said, okay what the heck, I'll try to start a chapter at A&M. I think that at that point I was a visiting assistant professor or something. I asked a faculty friend of mine if she wanted to be co-faculty sponsor because I wasn't sure if I had that much time and everything. She declined because she was afraid she wouldn't get tenure if she was really involved with NOW, and associated with it. I thought about it because I was hoping I would eventually get tenure as well. And then I realized, that could influence it, and if it did, then this isn't the kind of place I'd like to stay the rest of my life anyway. And so I made that kind of a judgment that, it could hurt me, maybe, maybe not, but that I never run my life like that, even in graduate school. And I just decided that's too high of a price. Nationally, NOW is a very middle-of-the-road feminist group. They're not out there tearing things down or anything. They're just basically middle-class white women.

IT: Right. They're not the Lesbian Avengers.

WS: No, they're not. Absolutely. Starting the chapter at Texas A&M, that's kind of what people thought. Oh, man, man-haters, radical man-haters, lesbians, blahblahblah. I did start the chapter, and had a pretty good response considering it was a fairly conservative area. We had about fifteen women. I have to look back. I have a newspaper file. I think this might have been fall '86 [. . .]

Our second action was the Bonfire thing . . . Some of the women in NOW, including the president of the chapter at that point, they were, a lot of them were really good Aggies. And their brothers had worked on the Bonfire. Their fathers had, and their family members were in the Corps. And they really felt like true-blue Aggies, and I thought the whole thing was a very strange custom. And I thought a lot about Aggies was kind of strange, and sort of like this, strange religious cult. There's certainly more tradition there than at any other college I've ever been, in terms of a school. So I had already seen, that that was really important to people, to participate. And for some people, it was like a family tradition.

IT: Do you think that at Texas A&M, that traditions are stronger, or that there are simply more rituals?

WS: I think there are more rituals, and I guess that's how I would define having traditions. You know, they stand during the football games, they have the Redpots and the Pink pots, the perimeter, and the Bonfire, and there's a lot of lore, different events, jokes, and customs and slang terms and so forth. More than at any other school than I've ever attended or taught in.

IT: What was gender relations like at Texas A&M in 1987? Were we kind of behind the rest of the nation in the sort of feminist point of view?

WS: I think the students were probably more conservative and not as supportive of feminism. The place where I noticed it, was, there was more homophobia there than at the west coast at Berkeley and the east coast in New York. I also was active as a member of the gay and lesbian group even though I was faculty. I was at the time living with a woman. I was involved with a lesbian relationship that was a five-year long relationship. And I've always been politically active in that area too. I've defined myself as bisexual and am currently married to a man, and have been with him for eleven years now . . .

I was in a monogamous long-term relationship with a woman, and so I encountered a lot of negativity and hatred and hostility, just walking around with her, and, more fear in that town because people I knew were beaten up if they held hands on the street and stuff like that. So, in terms of conservative values about sexuality, I noticed that.

In terms of heterosexuality, I think there were more traditional attitudes about rape. I felt like there were more sexist jokes. And the thing that really stood out was things that I would hear about the Corps of Cadets. I had had no interactions with the Corps, but I heard—Women would come in my office who were in the Corps and tell me some things that had happened to them from the beginning, from as long as I was there. But they just wanted to talk about it; they didn't want to report it because they were afraid of the consequences. And it was only later, when Carolyn Muckley came to my office, I think in 1992, and she did want to report it, and there was that big— then three others came forward, and they actually did get an investigation by the university that found sex discrimination in the Corps and sexual harassment in the Corps, both. And then the Justice Department came in and did its own investigation, had the same two findings, that it was widespread in the Corps. Not just a few bad apples, as the Corps had kept trying to say. And they instituted a set of recommendations, and my understanding was that the Justice Department was going to come back on a yearly basis and check to see if they were doing more education in terms of educating them on sexual harassment, not allowing the kinds of practices that was going on.

A number of women had come to me confidentially and told me about being raped by upperclassmen in the Corps. And as well as the usual kind of hazing that could happen to anybody. It was a sexual harassment component on top of it. So I think that other military schools like the Citadel and VMI have had the same kinds of problems, and the same kinds of lawsuits that eventually came up.

IT: *When you say "a number of women" what do you mean by that?*

WS: Three a semester.

IT: *Three a semester?*

WS: Two or three a semester would seek me out and tell me these horrible stories.

IT: *That's pretty amazing considering that there weren't that many women in the Corps back then.*

WS: Right. So, a lot of them were experiencing this, not everybody 'cause some didn't. And they felt like there was no problem and were quite adamant about it, that there was no problem. But others did. A fairly high proportion. Actually, we did some research on it during the year that Carolyn had come forward, and a fairly high percentage had experienced some kind of harassment. So, I knew there was a real problem, and I knew that the university, within the Corps they were aware of it, some of it, anyway, not all of it. And that things were not done that could have been done earlier to address the problem. And that the Corps was, like with Bonfire actually, was allowed to go on its own and conduct its own affairs without interference from the outside until this huge bru-ha-ha happened where some women really were willing to speak out publicly. [. . .] Not everybody, I think, was intolerant of women's rights, and sexist, but there was more tolerance in the university system for that type of behavior, and more of a permission for that to exist without being confronted or to test it by the administration or by other students. So that's where I noticed it, so I wouldn't say every single student was like that, 'cause many students, maybe the majority, were reasonably liberal.

But a number of them were not, and maybe there was a reluctance to speak out against it.

IT: *Why do you think the administration, as you say, let this go on?*

WS: I think it is because they were sort of bound with Aggie Tradition, and kind of in love with their traditions, and many of them actually are former Aggies. And also if they're not, there's a financial element. As you probably know, the Former Students Association donates quite a bit of money to the university—like millions. And a lot of these people are also dyed-in-the-wool Aggies. And so if you start messing with traditions like

Bonfire, you know, I think that there would be a very negative reaction, and in fact, I and two faculty members who were involved, jumping back to the "cadets" issue, we were kind of vilified in the Former Students Association newsletter as being part of a homosexual conspiracy against the Corps. And we were targeted in a way that was kind of frightening, and viewed as enemies, and viewed as undermining the Corps as kind of hostile forces, when what we were doing was, we didn't want any more women to be hurt.

IT: Right.

WS: We were trying to get attention to that. But none of us cared much about the Corp one way or the other. If they want to wear uniforms and march around, fine. If that makes them happy, you know, it was sort of irrelevant. We didn't want them to stop doing that, you know. The women wanted to do that too! Some of those women wanted to do that military thing. And so people thought that we wanted to stop the Corps, and they reacted very angrily and viciously at times, to anybody that was trying to stop it. So I think, because those people donate money, the administration may also be reluctant to throw a monkey wrench into any of these traditions or to be too heavy-handed because I think that it would anger some of the more traditional former students.

IT: Yeah. The thing is, though, rape, attacking women at Bonfire, and letting kids work on Bonfire while they're drunk are not traditions at all. But I suppose your saying that the administration didn't want to touch any of it, to [avoid offending] any of the former students at all.

WS: I think that's part of it. I don't think that's the only explanation.

IT: Right.

WS: I'd say that contributes, and say, a tolerance for that sort of thing going on, that "Boys will be boys," or "They're just kids, and they're just having fun," but I think there's a lot of entropy at Texas A&M towards change, like resistance to change. I think that anyone who tries to mess with any type of longstanding practices, even if not verbalized as a tradition, it's a practice, that those people do get a lot of flack. And nobody wants to be in that position if they don't have to be, and it's easier to go along. It's sort of benign neglect and fear of public censure.

So, originally, with the Bonfire thing, some of the women in NOW wanted to participate, and there were other women they knew that wanted to help build it. At that time, women weren't allowed beyond the perimeter.

IT: So these women were really fired up to build the Bonfire.

WS: They really wanted to do it. And I thought this whole thing was just ridiculous and also unecological, and a waste of resources, and it put a lot of smoke in the air, and it sent burning cinders out landing on roofs of people nearby. I thought it was excessive. I didn't know it was really dangerous. And it was celebrating gearing up for a football game, and this is probably offensive that I don't like football. I think it's a violent sport . . . anyway, I don't like football. It's kind of barbaric.

IT: So, uh . . .

WS: So, this whole thing is to gear up for the big game, and I just thought the whole thing was, it certainly is not my cup of tea. But the underlying political issue was equal access. These women felt that they should have a chance to do this if they wanted to, and I supported that even though I wouldn't have wanted to be anywhere near the Bonfire thing. I supported their right to participate equally. So I, and a couple of other faculty, I think the dean of students—Linda Parrish, whatever her title was, she was in administration—and one other faculty member from the English department went to the Bonfire. And our NOW students went to the Bonfire and met with the Head Redpot and some of his crew and discussed some of the issues. And the news were all over the place. Channel 3 people were there [. . .]

So that was basically the motivation. I personally was not into the Bonfire thing, but I wanted my women in NOW—my students in NOW—to do it if they wanted to do it. So I supported it. They went there, they initiated the action. I approved it, I went with them. I wanted to make sure that nobody was hurt because there had been a couple of women reporters from the Batt who got roughed up there, I think right before that.

IT: Right.

WS: They got dirt thrown on them, and names called at them, and stuff like that, when they went over the perimeter. I mean the whole thing is just so childish. Like you can't cross this line if you're a woman. For cry—I just really thought that was unfair. So, anyway, they did get some attention, and afterward, I recalled that students from NOW did help build the Bonfire. I forget if it was that year or later, I recall that they did change it such that women from some point on after that were able to participate in building it if they wanted.

IT: Now, when the NOW women went out to work on it, did they end up in crews, and did they work the six hour shifts and what not or was it sort of a demonstration of what they wanted to do?

WS: I don't know the specifics, but when we went to meet with the people, they weren't planning on working on it at that moment. When I was there on site, it was to have these initial dialogues with the young man who was in charge, and I guess his crew. This is vague, but I recall that they had some kind of training, that the women who did do it, that I knew, from NOW, that they went out I think in an organized way, with other people, you know, guys working on the Bonfire. I don't think they just went in there for show. So that's my memory, and I'm even recalling visually the news clipping of the NOW vice-president at the time hauling a log with a bunch of these guys, and I believe that they integrated themselves, they who were really were there and wanted to build it. That's my impression, though, I don't have absolute facts on that.

IT: *The whole scene, when I saw the pictures of it in the old Battalion clippings, the whole thing looked pretty surreal to me, actually, these Redpots and NOW members lifting logs together, very stiffly and sort of uncomfortably. I couldn't help laughing. And also the letters that were published during that time, they were pretty funny. I mean, it sounded like a bunch of junior high school students, you know, snubbing their noses at each other or something.*

WS: Which letters, by who? There were a lot of letters in the Batt, and there were a lot of people who were angry about the whole thing.

IT: *Yeah, it was amazing. There was one that really was interesting. The guy said to someone who had written previously about women belonging at the Bonfire, and that the boys should let them in, and all this and that. He said, well, you know, "a well-placed backhand" would keep women in their place.*

WS: (laughter) So things like that, there were a lot of letters like that. And comments and stuff. I guess it was very threatening for them in some way, that they would have to change something and have women on site. Maybe they were concerned that they weren't going to be able to engage in the same kind of antics with women around. What I heard is that it hasn't changed, that they were still doing those same things, women or no women (laughter).

IT: *Yeah.*

WS: Being drunk and acting like goofballs or whatever.

IT: How would you put Bonfire in the context of gender relations? Was it basically a male game?

WS: More males were interested in participating in it, and it had kind of a macho image, I guess, of hauling around these logs and doing rugged kinds of activities.

IT: To me it seemed like a demonstration or a proving of manhood, the original Bonfire.

WS: You're probably right. I haven't ever really thought of it in a cultural way, but kind of like a manhood ritual, like this is one of the ways we can be these rugged, macho men as we help build the Bonfire.

IT: Do you have any comments now as to what it might be now that women have become a part of it?

WS: I think it's the same as most other areas that have been male territory. Males are socialized that they have to prove, repeatedly prove that they're male, and that they're good representatives of maleness. And so, even if you've won at a sport, or won a fight, or done something masculine, and successful in some way, it doesn't last. You have to re-prove it again. You can't just sit on your laurels. And part of the definition, as far as I understand, at least from the research and reading that I do and teaching, is that the very traditional definition of being male is being different from female and to a certain extent superior in some way, you know, having power over women, and certainly not being like women in any way. Differentiating themselves as men from women, and not just on the basis of, well, our bodies are different. It's all these other traits that go along with the traditional masculine definition. So when women move into a territory that's been traditionally male, it's not just changed. It's threatening. It's seen as taking away a means of defining oneself as a man, and rendering it as not different from women. And being viewed as like a woman is like being one down for men. In fact, when kids are growing up, when boys want to insult each other, they call the other person a girl, or sometimes a homo, a queer, a fag. So being called a fag or a girl is about the worst thing. Girl might be worse than fag, I think. When they have children rank order, I think the girl is at the bottom, for boys.

They learn early on as part of our culture that being a girl is a bad thing, and that other men will laugh at you and call you a pussy, and really ridicule you, and you'll lose social status if you're like a woman in any way. The more that you're like one, the more risk you run of being called a wimp or a girl. And so, when women move into male territories

196

like work, like construction for example, or medical sciences, like surgery had been a male domain, those women got the worst kind of harassment.

[. . .]

Going back to Bonfire, I think that this was going into this male preserve, male domain that would take away what, something that they thought was very meaningful in terms of defining themselves as he-men.

IT: So, I'm trying to reach some sort of understanding of what the meaning of Bonfire is now, then. If it isn't a way to prove one's manhood, then what is it to these men and women who work on it?

WS: That's an interesting question 'cause I don't know whether the women have sort of joined in, defining that kind of work also as something that they define themselves as—maybe they define themselves as good Aggies or something. Committed Aggies. I wonder if they see themselves also as sort of macho and rough-and-tumble. They're certainly not baking cookies, you know, the women who are doing the work. And whether men feel that something's been taken away from them by having women there is a good question. If it's diluted in any way, or whether the women have sort of been absorbed into it. Like when there's a small number of women who enter a male institution, they don't necessarily change it. Like the small number of women who started out in the Corps, initially, their presence didn't change that culture. They actually, they had to fit into the culture.

[. . .]

IT: Historically, Texas A&M, its culture has been based on gender roles. This is similar to most of the old cultures of the world. Do you think that gender roles are necessarily wrong?

WS: To the extent to which they restrict people's options, in terms of how they can behave and how they are trained to think about themselves. Women are trained to think, oh, women aren't good in math. Or a woman can't run a marathon, which people used to—everyone believed. Then it's kind of a limitation because the person grows up thinking they're not capable of something they are potentially capable of. Or males grow up being told, men don't cry. That's very actually damaging, and it's not even healthy. Actually, physically, it has consequences to repress a lot of feelings, so there are ways that gender roles hurt both genders by restricting their range of emotions, and access to all of their abilities. And so I think that any kind of role that causes someone to only be able to utilize some part of their ability is probably not a good thing.

IT: In that case, Texas A&M culture may be extremely limiting for some of its men, since we are often expected to be, especially if we belong to certain organizations, ultra-men.

WS: You know, I think it hurts both genders a lot. Men who are brought up in that traditional way don't even have access to some of their feelings. They're trained to think those aren't important anyway, but, from the outside that seems like a terrible deprivation. When men work on those things in therapy, they often are pleased when they are able to be in touch with a full range of emotion. And they have better relationships. Actually research shows that they have better relationships when they become more emotionally expressive, not just being able to express anger, but being able to express the whole palette. It's kind of like gender deprives people of half of their palettes. We only get half instead of the whole range.

IT: So, tell me about the Corps controversy of 1991-1992. What was your role in it, and what was your interpretation of it?

WS: Like I said, I'd been hearing these accounts for years, but not able to do anything about it because nobody wanted to report it. And some woman had actually reported internally in the Corps, that they'd received sexual harassment of some sort, or sexual aggression. And nothing had apparently changed or been done with it. And so I was aware of the situation for years, but Carolyn called and said that she sounded very tentative, and she said that she had been—I didn't know her at all—she said she had called a number of people and sought help, assistance, or support in bringing these charges against the Corps. I believe she experienced some harassment, although I don't think that she had been raped. But she knew people who had been, and had been in the Corps the whole time. I think she was a senior at that point, and finally had just had enough, and felt like she had to do something. She just felt compelled to do something to change the situation.

So she asked, could I help her to do something. And I said, well, I don't have any power. You know I'm the faculty advisor [for NOW], but I certainly don't have influence in high places. I would support you. I would stand with you. I would help you do whatever you need to do. But you would have to be making the decisions. I really made it clear that, it wouldn't have any credibility for some outsider to lead any charge, that she would have to do that if she wanted to. So she came to my office, and she had this four-page handwritten account of what kind of things had gone on in the Corps. And she let me read it, and I talked to her about it. And she said there were a few other women who were ready to talk about it. And she, I think, contacted them, and at least one of them came and spoke with me also. I asked, you know, what do you want to do? How can we help you bring this up in a way that will be helpful?

She had written the head, General Darling, and she hadn't gotten a satisfactory response . . .

IT: So did she talk much about the Bonfire beating that she had?

WS: Yeah, that was actually into the thing. They had a press conference. The press jumped on it. Dallas and Houston and a lot of large papers, the L.A. Times covered it, and then the New York Times covered it. Then CNN came and interviewed them in my office, as a matter of fact. So the women in the Corps were the ones interviewed about the situation. So this got lots of publicity, and so this campus committee was appointed to investigate the charges, and around that time, you know, after it had been going on for a few months, Carolyn got kicked in the back when she was, I think, leading a drill, as I recall. And she was kneeling over watching someone do push-ups, or counting for them. And some member of the Corps kicked her in the back really hard in the kidney area. She was in a lot of pain. It was a bad kick. She showed me the bruise. She had a bruise all over her back. People wear protection over their kidneys when they play football. So it's a vulnerable area.

IT: Was this the Bonfire, uh—

WS: Oh, that was actually Jennifer, who received it, who was asked to bend over, and was hit with a, smacked on the butt with some kind of a—

IT: An axe handle.

WS: Axe handle, right. That didn't happen to Carolyn. That happened to Jennifer, one of the other women who came forward reported that. She was Asian as well as Carolyn, actually, who was half, I think, Vietnamese. And Jennifer was uh, I think, Filipino or Japanese, I can't remember, but she had been subjected to all kinds of racial slurs as well as gender-related. So, that was her letter, Jennifer's letter, where she reported having bent over, and all that stuff. So there was a combination of things that probably happened to males as well. But sort of on top of it, in addition to it, there were extra things that happened to the women, specifically gender-related.

IT: Was there a lot of racism reported to you in the Corps? You don't hear a lot about that.

WS: Men from the Corps didn't come to me and tell me things while I was there. And the first I had heard of it was with these women where they had been subjected to racism. So these were two Asian women, and they said this was fairly common. I don't ever recall hearing an account, say from an African-American person in the Corps, but I know that in the military in general, that this is very common. These racial words—slurs—are used in boot camp. Anything they say that can bring you down or get you angry, they try to provoke you in that situation. If you're a person of color as well as a woman, they'll use whatever's handy. I wouldn't be surprised if that was part of it for other races, but I know they mentioned some real anti-Asian terms being used on them.

IT: Like the usual "gook" and "chink" and all that?

WS: Uh-huh.

IT: Anything particularly interesting?

WS: I'd have to look back at Jennifer's letter. She did mention some terms. I think they also mentioned things like "bitch," "whore," gender-related. I'd have to look back—

[. . .]

IT: What's interesting is, all this racism, this violence, this sexism is happening—sure it's happening in the military, maybe that to some people is acceptable—but it's also happening at a university.

WS: Right. And the university has an obligation not to tolerate that kind of thing. Racism, sexism, any kind of discrimination. And to work to change it, and eliminate it when that happens.

IT: And also, most of these kids in the Corps are not even on ROTC contracts. They're not contracted to become officers in the military.

WS: That's my understanding. So they're not even real military. So why are they allowed to—

IT: Yeah, I mean—

WS: I'm really glad you're asking these questions, and I really hope you ask them in your book if you don't get good answers. Why do they tolerate it has to do with the culture of Texas A&M, as we talked about before. The glorification of that culture and lack of courage and responsibility on the part of the university as an institution to address those things.

Dr. Hugh Wilson

Dr. Hugh Wilson has been a professor of Biology at Texas A&M since 1977. He served as an Air Force medic in the Vietnam War and tells me that he was in Saigon during the Tet Offensive. Dr. Wilson began publicly opposing the building and burning of the Bonfire in the early 1990's, earning him a great deal of notoriety on campus. He has been managing the "Dumb as Dirt" anti-Bonfire website for several years.

Irwin Tang: What is your specialty?

Dr. Hugh Wilson: Systematic Botany or plant taxonomy.

IT: I guess that's the classification of plants or something.

HW: Basically. The classification, evolution, mostly of flowering plants that I deal with.

IT: How did you begin opposing the Bonfire?

HW: You know, my personal history is kind of hard to recollect. It's been a long time. You know, I think it was originally expressed by the signs that currently sit in the windows here in Butler Hall. And my desire to counter pro-Bonfire sentiment on campus with another perspective.

IT: [You put] some signs [up] in Butler?

HW: Yes, they were featured actually this fall in the Battalion in a short opinion article on suppression of opinion on campus. And the author pointed out that the signs had been obliterated or masked by debris that'd been thrown on the window, and used that as a hook into the notion of suppression. But at any rate, I think my initial effort to publicly voice my position on Bonfire relates to those signs and the presence of pro-Bonfire signs on campus. And then after that, the establishment of the university web site and the positioning of a pro-Bonfire web site on campus stimulated me to counter, I believe, with an opposing web site that functioned to, you know, establish a dialogue. It seems that in both instances, whether it's signs or web sites, the dialogue was one-sided. And that the position was one-sided. And as a biologist, I think most biology faculty see the Bonfire as something that produces a negative result, that has a negative aspect.

IT: Do you think that there was a fear? Why wasn't there balance to the debate?

HW: That's a good question, and I think to appreciate the dynamics of that question, you really have to be at Texas A&M, and feel the weight of the local culture basically. And this weight is encompassed by the term, "Tradition." And the traditions, whatever they may be, are deeply embedded in the local culture. And as a result, any criticism, any critical comment relating to the traditions, is not looked upon in a friendly way. I think it was interesting that Dr. Anderson, an engineer, came out shortly after the collapse, pointing out that the fundamental structure of the Bonfire stack, from an engineering point of view, was flawed. That was an article, I believe in the Houston Chronicle. And they asked him about this dynamic of being critical, and he said that you tend to be vilified, I think is the term that he used, and isolated, if you are critical of fundamental traditions like Bonfire. And I think that's true. I think people fear, to a certain extent, anyway, this process of Route 6 goes both ways, a general vilification of opposing positions.

IT: Well, let's just jump to the question of tradition, then. This university obviously values tradition. Do you value tradition yourself? What do you think of the university's valuing or consistent serving of tradition in sort of a very energetic manner?

HW: I think every organization is founded, at least to a certain extent, on tradition. In fact, this episode has resulted in discussions of faculty and students at Duke and Berkeley, two highly esteemed academic institutions, both of which have had bonfire traditions of a sort. And discussion of these in the media has been very interesting relative to the bonfire tradition of A&M. I think any institution is going to have its share of traditions that are dearly loved by those involved, and they function to allow those involved to be identified with the institution. And they serve a function, and I have no personal anti-tradition tendency. Sometimes I think they can be frivolous. Sometimes I think they can be counter to the academic mission of the institution, and all of these institutions, fundamentally, do have an academic mission. That's what we're supposed to do. That's what we're paid to do. And when this business of rah-rah or tradition or what have you conflicts with that, then those of us who are paid to do academics, I think, are reasonably concerned.

The fundamental difference with A&M is the magnitude of the traditions. Physically, Bonfire exemplifies that. Compared to bonfires of other institutions, it's just several orders of magnitude greater. And the general notion of tradition on campus, I think, as part of the campus culture, is several orders of magnitude greater. An interesting tradition of many, is Elephant Walk, which just occurred here last Tuesday.

IT: *Right.*

HW: And to me that is a tradition that is harmless. It allows students to be students and youngsters and engage in various sundry exercises that are interesting and part of the dynamic. And as a result, you know, it's unusual. It's unique to the institution. I see no harm in it. However, if they had Elephant Walk every Tuesday, it would be a liability, as far as our academic mission is concerned. Bonfire represents, in my view, that extreme. Where you're devoting, essentially, an entire semester. Again, it's a small percentage of the students, but those students bear the burden of building that structure during the semester. And just that act has an impact on the academic mission.

IT: *Do you have any anecdotal evidence of how Bonfire affects students' performance in the classroom?*

HW: To be honest with you, I really don't. Student attendance is hard to quantify or assess. I have a feeling that it probably could be assessed if someone took as a basic premise that a good portion of the work in constructing Bonfire is accomplished by the Corps of Cadets, which represents a defined student group. And one could, with that assumption, probably look at the grade point average of fall semester versus spring semester within the Corps of Cadets, to assess quantitatively, the impact. If you assume the hours given, that is, over 120,000 man-hours involved in the enterprise, is true. If you take that at face value, then it's hard to imagine that it hasn't impacted the academic performance of those students that are directly engaged.

IT: So how did you react to the Bonfire tragedy?

HW: With amazement to be honest with you. When I went to work, I noticed the helicopters flying over campus, very early in the morning before dawn. The first thought that crossed my mind was that UT had managed to get to the Bonfire site and ignite the Bonfire. Something of that sort. The idea of the stack collapsing had really never entered my mind as a likely event. Well, it entered my mind as a likely event, but I was unaware that it was so heavily populated by students during construction. So the whole dynamic of this thing hadn't crossed my mind, and I was very surprised to see it happen.

IT: What followed surprise? What did you say to yourself?

HW: Well, I don't have this buttressing element of school spirit and tradition to more or less color my view of this situation. My first response was this was an accident, this was an accidental occurrence, and that it resulted in fatalities. And initially, it was four or six, I believe was the body count. And in walking over, I immediately walked over to the site, and looked around and it was evident that they were working pretty intensely to uncover possibly more casualties. And it just suggested to me that this, given the magnitude and the size of Bonfire, that it was probably an accident waiting to happen. And it's unfortunate that it happened. And the first thing that crossed my mind, given the nature of the media coverage, was that this will be something that will basically stigmatize Texas A&M, on a national, perhaps global, level for many years to come.

IT: You say that the victims, the twelve victims thus far—hopefully it will only remain twelve—didn't give their lives for Bonfire, that their lives were taken. How were their lives taken, and by whom?

HW: Their lives were taken by an accident. I think it's interesting the way that this has developed, is that the symbolism associated with these casualties on campus, is symbolism that we have associated with violence enacted by people of some sort. The analogy with the Vietnam War memorial and the materials that are placed around the site—the ribbons. The connection with the Murrah Building (in Oklahoma City) explosion. All these things are events that are human-perpetrated. Violence, human violence. Whereas this Bonfire collapse is an accident. There was no intent. It was simply an accident. The lives were taken in an accidental event. So to me, it's comparable to a large traffic accident, or something of that nature, a very unfortunate situation.

But in this particular case, the event occurred on state property, associated with an enterprise, an event, that has been promoted and supported by the state of Texas. And one could reasonably argue that the students were involved in doing basically what they were encouraged and instructed to do by higher authority. And the first question that would come to mind in regards to them giving their lives, is that, I believe, had they known that they were involved in a life-threatening enterprise, that they would have willingly given their lives. And in fact their lives were taken by an accidental occurrence, that, from a certain perspective, was not their responsibility or not their doing. In the sense that by Texas law, most of them were under 21, and if they aren't of legal drink under Texas law, then you have to assume that they aren't fully adults yet. And as a result, one would expect on this campus, with an enterprise of that magnitude, that there would be supervision and direction from those responsible on campus to ensure that these students were not in a life-threatening situation when they did that.

IT: Who is responsible?

HW: That's a good question. And I'm sure that's a question that a lot of people are trying to answer. I think from the administration's point of view, a student organization is responsible. And whatever the student organization is that builds Bonfire. And it may be left at that. There have been other untoward events associated with Bonfire, and usually when this happens, the responsibility lies, in some way, with the students. But I think in reality, the university, given the fact that it was on campus, should bear some responsibility. Responsibility should be tracked to responsible individuals on campus.

It may be the faculty senate is responsible. The faculty senate has spent a lot of time discussing Bonfire. If you query the senate minutes on the web, using the query term "Bonfire," you'll get a lot of responses from various meetings of the faculty senate. If the faculty senate is a responsible body on campus, then indeed, that group might be responsible for Bonfire. It could be student government. If student government is a responsible entity on campus, a powerful entity . . . To me, knowing the structure of the organization, the structure on campus, I would assume that the administration of the university is responsible.

IT: Do you think there should be some punishment of administrators? Some sort of resignation or reprimand of administration officials?

HW: Oh, yeah. We're talking about an accident. We're not talking about an act of malice. I think the primary concern would be just to discern responsibility. And then, depending on the nature of that responsibility, if there was negligence involved, that's one thing. If on the other hand, it turns out that it was normal course of operation on campus, then it would be very difficult to sanction [someone]. But then you certainly could sanction the normal course of operation. I guess my point is, the reason for assessing and appointing responsibility is to ensure that this sort of thing doesn't happen again.

IT: Do you think that George Bush, as governor of Texas, has any responsibility or had any responsibility over the tragedy, and the future of the Bonfire. Do you think he has any say over the future of the Bonfire?

HW: Well, that's a good question. The connection between Texas A&M, the university system, and the state has always been an item of curiosity. In many ways, the way things operate around here, you can envision A&M as an autonomous entity. Recently there was an effort to circumvent the Higher Education Coordinating Board and develop an alliance with a law school down in Houston. And that episode demonstrated that indeed A&M is a state agency, and there are policies associated with this operation that involve oversight at the state level. In this case, the coordinating board. And A&M must comply with the coordinating board for its academic actions. As a state agency, it's certainly part of the state governmental system. And there's no avoiding the fact that the buck stops with Governor Bush, considering A&M is a state agency.

Now, in this instance, you certainly can't expect Governor Bush to be cogniscent of all the activities on all the campuses of the state schools. In this particular case, it's complicated by the presence of the Bush Library here. And I think to a certain extent, complicated by the fact that we're looking into a presidential campaign, a national campaign that involves Governor Bush. So his association, in my point of view, with the Bonfire collapse, is more or less tangential, in that you can't anticipate that he would be able to know what was going on on campus, but with regard to the chain of responsibility, the buck definitely stops with Governor Bush.

And I was impressed by his initial announcement of the collapse, which was more or less tearful and emotional, dealing with the fatalities. But coupled with that was the comment about the "great tradition" of Bonfire. And to me that was an anomaly. To have a catastrophe of this magnitude, even though the full magnitude wasn't appreciated at the time, and describe [Bonfire] as a "great tradition." I think at that time, it was time to consider it possibly as something other than a great tradition.

IT: You say Texas A&M has the tendency to act autonomously. Is that something that has been going on for a long time, in your view? Do you have any other examples, or—

HW: Well, it's just the sense that the A&M culture which has been discussed greatly here, as the nation's become aware of the A&M culture, the culture on campus, it seems to be localized and parochial relative to the state of Texas. And in that sense, A&M can be thought of, or has the aspect of an autonomous, more or less independent state agency. But in the real sense, it is obviously a state agency. Its uniqueness is just based on its unique historic history. But there's no doubt about the fact that it's not an independent entity, that its controlled by state government.

IT: *Two of the dead of the Bonfire were discovered to be legally drunk. How much drinking occurs at cut and stack?*

HW: I'm not a good person to ask that question. I've been to cut. I made an excursion to cut one time just to see what goes on. And I have to say that was four years ago. I didn't see any drinking at cut, although I was keeping hidden. But I really don't know. I have no first-hand information with regard to cut or stack or what have you. I think I'm like many faculty on this campus, and that is, this activity goes on kind of on the periphery. You really have no knowledge of what happens at two in the morning right here on campus, you know. I think that everybody that's familiar with campus and lives here is aware that drinking has been associated with Bonfire, all aspects of Bonfire, traditionally. The administration's efforts to make rules and regulations to minimize that over the past several years—there's been some pretty nasty episodes of drunkenness and what have you associated with Bonfire—so the fact that some of these students were drinking I don't think was a huge surprise for most people familiar with Bonfire.

IT: *On your website, you said that you walked to the scene that morning—*

HW: That morning about 8:30, yeah.

IT: *And you saw beer cans.*

HW: A small stack of empty beer cans, definitely.

IT: *About how many beer cans?*

HW: About half a dozen.

IT: *Oh, really?*

HW: Really didn't give it any thought. But they were there.

IT: *Where were they?*

HW: They were beyond the taped off area. They were not within the taped-off area. They were within view of local police, who were at that time standing, patrolling the taped off area. I'd say, maybe thirty, fifty yards towards the systems building from the tape that demarcated the stack.

IT: And you think those cans were left over from that night's drinking, building the Bonfire.

HW: I would guess that's the case. But all I know is the cans were there. And I mentioned it only in reference to comments from Bob Wiatt, director of campus security, who indicated there was no evidence of alcohol use at the Bonfire site. And certainly, I saw those cans, and I would guess a lot of other people saw those cans. To me, that was evidence suggesting the use of alcohol at Bonfire site.

[...]

IT: Have you been harassed in any way by the supporters of Bonfire? And how?

HW: I've been protesting, complaining about Bonfire for a long time. And to a certain extent, people are used to my position. It isn't as if I just suddenly popped up complaining about Bonfire. I've had on several occasions most recently last week, two Corps members come in and very politely more or less attempt to quell my objections to Bonfire. And actually, immediately following that, a young lady came in and really reamed me out in no uncertain terms in regards to my objections and their lack of taste relative to the catastrophe. I certainly had the email that in many cases has been kind of threatening. In some cases, it's been polite, again, discussion in attempts to either dissuade me that this is an honorable tradition, or tell me to leave town if I don't like it, you know. But that's been about the extent. I've had no formal interaction with the administration, whom I often take to task about Bonfire, regarding Bonfire.

IT: But there have been no threats of violence.

HW: Nothing really conspicuous. Again, an occasional email reference that might be interpreted as a threat to violence, but—

IT: And the Corps members were simply stating the case for Bonfire.

HW: Well, they were just, and this has happened before, where the Corps in their full garb come in, usually a pair of them, I don't know who sends them or they come on their own, and more or less, give me the business about the spirit of Aggieland, and the great tradition, and it's inappropriate to complain about it, and usually that degenerates down to specific arguments about they're going to cut the wood anyway, and et cetera, et cetera, et cetera.

IT: And what do you say to those arguments that yeah, sure, that sure, there are a lot of man-hours wasted, or used rather, and we do cut down a lot of trees, and perhaps we burn up a lot of jet fuel, but this is a tradition and it's worth it because there is a kind of bonding in the building of Bonfire that cannot exist without it, and that you cannot really be an Aggie without Bonfire?

HW: I think that's a fundamental truth, that you can't be an Aggie without Bonfire. And that's the dilemma that the university faces, that you have an indoctrination, and I think that a lot of this hinges on Fish Camp, and the history of A&M, an indoctrination that imbeds in people's minds the pivotal nature of Bonfire relative to their existence as Aggies, and it's a dilemma. And it's not something that I can easily suggest a resolution to. It's a cultural dilemma. But I have to speak as an academic. Again, I'm being paid to be an academic. I'm connected with the institution in an academic way. And my primary objection is how Bonfire impacts the institution as an academic institution. It's a matter to me of reputation, and my concerns historically have been how do people view Texas A&M as an academic institution when they know that they're encouraging its students to burn eight thousand trees on campus, is the bottom line. You can argue about the value of the trees, the time spent, et cetera, et cetera, but when that event is viewed beyond Texas A&M, the resulting perspective is not positive from an academic point of view. Now this whole concern about our reputation as an institution has been unfortunately fully realized by this disaster, where now you not only have A&M associated with a multi-death accident, but then you have the world taking a very close look at this process of burning eight thousand trees on a Texas college campus. So the negative impact in terms of reputation has been maximized. It's almost hopeless to complain about it.

IT: Have you gotten any feedback from the outside world—

HW: Really quite a bit. I, in the past, have not put online the emails that I get relative to this website. But I elected to this time put in a bracket, a window, of email that came in from November 19 through the 30th. And just screening the positive side, I kind of see that they're mostly not from Aggies. They're usually people from Texas. But it is people that have been exposed to the situation by watching the TV or listening to the radio, and their views, their outlook on the situation, is pretty straightforward, and I think pretty supportive of the notion that the positive aspects of

Bonfire are limited pretty much to the view that one has if one, number one is an Aggie, and number two might be a Texan. When you go beyond those two groups, you're looking pretty much at a negative response.

IT: What do people think about us? I mean, you're saying it has affected our academic reputation. Has anyone expressed an opinion about our academic standing in relation to the Bonfire?

HW: Well, there's just been the questions, What kind of university would have this going on on campus? This kind of a general view. And you talk about reputation, there are various ways to evaluate academic function of an institution. And I think the dilemma that has been, A&M through the years, the twenty years that I've been here, has strengthened itself in terms of academic performance. And I guess that's the problem that I see, that this strength that has been built here has been minimized by this other view of the institution, which is just not hardcore academic functionality in terms of publications or scientific profile, and looking at the organization as an organization that will promote this waste, this kind of frivolous enterprise that is really counter-academic in a lot of respects.

IT: You say on the web-site that Texas A&M per-capita funding is one of the top ten in the nation—

HW: That's definitely true. The A&M System—

IT: Which includes Texas A&M and Prairieview A&M, and Texas A&I now, right?

HW: And I think in terms of funding, the peripheral schools aren't as important as TAES and TEES—

IT: TAES and TEES?

HW: The experiment stations.

IT: Oh, okay.

HW: The engineering and agricultural experiment stations, combined with campus, when you look at endowment, and these criteria refer to private endowment, public support, especially through the federal agencies, A&M is up there competing with the best, or the richest, I guess you could say.

IT: Right.

HW: I think any measure would put A&M up there.

IT: But as far as what we're getting for our bucks. How much bang are we getting for our buck? And how does that relate to Bonfire?

HW: That's the dilemma that I try to point out, is that if you look at those schools, the top ten schools with regard to wealth, private endowments and federal funding, there's only one that doesn't make the top fifty of *U.S. News and World Report's* ranking of national schools. And that's Texas A&M. Specifically the A&M system, but basically Texas A&M. And to me that points out a dilemma that A&M has to confront. And that is this translation of resources both public and private is not working well. And some of it has to do with our reputation as an institution, at least that's an area that people interested in A&M could pursue, is to try and make A&M a place that would look reasonable as an academic institution from the outside, for people from California to New York to Oregon.

IT: *So you think our reputation has affected the rankings or the reputation has caused quality faculty to look somewhere else?*

HW: Well, I think both things come into play. But if you look at the rankings, *U.S. News and World Report* is probably not the best ranking system to cite, but it is handy because it's quantified. And that is, you can go through the numbers and sort by the numbers. And reputation, although ill-defined, is a criteria that they use. And I think we could improve our reputational score. And one way we can do that, unfortunately, is really again, kind of a moot point now in regard to this disaster because the media has just impacted this disaster, or connected this disaster with Texas A&M. But prior to this disaster, certainly doing something about Bonfire, I think, would have had a positive result.

IT: *Has there been a university cover-up with the Bonfire, and its role in the building of the Bonfire?*

HW: Well, from my point of view, the most remarkable aspect of the university's response, the administrative response was through the web-site. The first thing I did is check the web-site to get information on the Bonfire.

IT: *Uh-huh.*

HW: And discovered that the whole web-site had been altered. The fundamental frames-based system in place prior to the collapse was gone. And the animated image that led you to the Bonfire site, the official Bonfire site, was gone. And if you try and search for the Bonfire site, or even prior sites, of last year and the year before through the University search system, you're unable to do that. So the university responded to control its kind of content, web content related to Bonfire immediately.

IT: Why?

HW: I don't know why. I think one could look at the situation and say, get into the area of good taste relative the victims and their families. Having a big promotional web-site for Bonfire after this disaster would be an anomaly. On the other hand, wiping out all the pages, through all the prior years, suggested to me that something was going on beyond simple tasteful presentation of Bonfire through the university web-site. And I have a feeling that's the case. I have a feeling these pages that they've developed in the past are very promotive, encouraging everybody to get involved in the tradition and what have you. Even from the straight point of view of litigation, it was probably in their interest to put that away.

[...]

IT: In the past, the administration seems to have been extremely concerned about the opinions of students and former students. They seem to want to avoid any protest against [any] reduction of the Bonfire. In a recent article in the Statesman, *it showed that some of the administrators said to people who wanted to lower the Bonfire, "Well, there's going to be lots of student protest. You may not want to do this."*

HW: And I'm sure that's the case. The faculty wanted to slowly, incrementally, decrease the size of the Bonfire ten years ago. And there was resistance to that, and I think this business of indoctrinating people, and embedding this in the local culture has been very effective, and as a result, we have a base of current students and former students that have this in their heart and their mind, the significance of this thing. It's a real thing. And the position of A&M as a well-endowed university is in good part based on former students. And administrators are very sensitive to former students, from that point of view, as donors. So if they were to arbitrarily minimize Bonfire, it could have a negative impact financially for Texas A&M. Now I think now with this disaster, they're presented with an opportunity to adjust, and the interesting question is, will they do it?

IT: What about the argument about university democracy? If most of the students want the Bonfire, why shouldn't there be a Bonfire? They pay their fee bills after all.

HW: Well, I suppose that's a good question. And I think the answer would be, first of all, that I don't think there's ever been a university referendum relative to Bonfire. Do we know in terms of the numbers of faculty, the numbers of students, or even the number of administrators, what the relative positions would be, positive versus negative? I know those positive would be very vociferous and maybe unusually powerful. But does that translate in a democratic way to real numbers? So the first thing with regard to that question would be to assess via a referendum, which I guarantee you will never happen (laughter), and then indeed if the weight of student opinion, faculty opinion, administrative opinion is for Bonfire, then you have to ask that question. And I suppose you get what you deserve if everybody wanted Bonfire, and knew the full dynamic of Bonfire, that is there was dialogue prior to the vote, I would be in no position to complain about it, to be honest with you.

IT: Hm. That's gonna turn a few heads. They're gonna say, let's have a vote then—

HW: I've always thought that would be interesting—

IT: —partially just to get you to shut up, I suppose.

(laughter, Wilson nearly spills his coffee)

IT: What is the total monetary cost of Bonfire for the University?

HW: That I can't answer, in monetary terms. It's very difficult, I think, to answer, in that, well, just the quagmire of the bureaucracy, and the various inputs involved. How do you quantify the involvement of the Office of University Relations? Or the Office of Student Activities? And the administrative folks there who deal with Bonfire, or have to deal with Bonfire. The logistics of Bonfire are such that it's very difficult to dump off the whole thing to a student organization. There has to be involvement, support. But how you quantify that support, how you figure the electric bill and all this stuff, this is difficult. So in terms of monetary cost, I really have no notion. It would be interesting if the investigation got into the detail that they would at least be able to estimate how much the state— the taxpayer—is involved for the Bonfire.

[...]

IT: Was your original opposition to Bonfire related to an endangered species that was further endangered by Bonfire?

HW: As I creep back through history, I think my first resistance was to put these signs to counter the Bonfire, but very early on, I was directly impacted by the Bonfire cut, in that the cut site in one year occurred in an area where I was surveying for an endangered species. I complained. These surveys for an endangered species federally listed involved federal and state sanctions against those who would eradicate an endangered species. And these sanctions are only applicable when there's federal funding in the enterprise, whatever that may be. And I've done many impact assessments. For instance, when they built the new sewage treatment plant here at A&M, I was involved in making sure that this endangered species was not going to be impacted because there was federal money involved. And given the nature of that protection, kind of the spirit of the Endangered Species Act, I thought it was untoward for a state agency, A&M, to be promoting eradication of an endangered species locally by cutting the Bonfire.

IT: *Was it actually affecting the survival of the species?*

HW: Definitely. There were populations of the plant in the cut site. And when you remove the forest, you remove the habitat for this particular orchid.

IT: *Can you describe the orchid?*

HW: Its technical name is Spiranthes Parksii. It's called the Navasota's Ladies' Tresses. And it's one of forty-six vascular plants listed by the U.S. Department of the Interior as endangered in Texas.

[...]

IT: *Is there any benefit to cutting? There have been arguments made that when the Bonfire cutters go in and chop down trees, they leave the crooked ones, and that benefits the ecosystem. There's shade involved, there's room for more trees. There have been arguments in the past, and there have been memos within the administration trying to develop an ecological argument for Bonfire.*

HW: I think if you look at literature associated with the timber industry in general, there's always a scientific, how can you say, "prostitute" is the word that comes to mind, but I'm sure there's some more humanistic word, that's willing to come up with a scientific justification for just about anything. And the timber industry certainly has quite an array—increasing diversity by bringing in lots of weeds or what have you, or whatever—of justifying clearcutting. But from an ecological point of view, especially in a part of the world like south-central Texas, it's pretty hard on ecological grounds to justify clearcutting. Clear-cutting is clear-cutting. That's it. You're eliminating the natural vegetation. You're eliminating the natural habitat. If you don't have a good reason to do it, you're probably doing something wrong with regard to the local environment.

IT: *Did the students know about the endangered species, and if they did, did they care?*

HW: That's a good question. I don't know. I don't know if the word was passed to the cutting crews or what have you. I certainly did my best to let those people who I thought were responsible know what was going on, both on the university side and the regulatory side. And it was an interesting response, the lack of response. And it encouraged me to just quit working with endangered species because it was evident that it was pretty much spitting in the wind in terms of trying to preserve some of these plants while the state is actually actively pursuing eliminating their habitat.

IT: *How has [Bonfire cut] affected the local ecosystem, seeing how every year, we go out and cut large swaths out from the local area?*

HW: Its effect on the local ecosystem has to be— the context has to be established. That is, the local ecosystem is pretty much eliminated right now in the College Station area. It's very difficult to find native natural plant habitat. The native vegetation, if you drive down the Brazos [River] bottoms here to the coast, you're going to find a flat plain where once huge forests [stood]. So the impact right now is extensive. So additional heavy impacts are just adding to that problem. And to be honest with you, it's going to happen. As human populations increase, it's just going to happen. The problem is, should the state be supporting this activity? If it's going to happen, let the businesses, the developers, what have you, let them deal with it. I think the state really opens itself to charges of hypocrisy when you have one agency, the Texas Parks and Wildlife trying to promote native Texas vegetation and habitat, and another agency, Texas A&M, encouraging its students to go out and clear cut the local forests.

IT: *Did anything come out of your exchange with the authorities on the legality of Bonfire?*

HW: Well, the only legal issue relates to air pollution, and the Texas Natural Resources Conservation Service and the EPA, and it introduced me to the complexities of air quality code, both federal and state, and pointed out that the Bonfire, ceremonial bonfires, are exempted from all regulations.

IT: *All regulations?*

HW: All regulation . . . For instance, if the donor knocks down all of its trees with a bulldozer. They're all piled up and he wants to burn them. How he can do that is specifically regulated with respects to time of day, how much propellant he can put on it, et cetera. Very detailed. But if it's a ceremonial bonfire, it's open. It can be burned at any time. You can put as much jet fuel on it as you want. Et cetera, et cetera.

215

After the December interview, Dr. Wilson mentioned his experience as a medic in the Vietnam War, and said that if the students could have seen what had happened physically to the twelve victims of the Bonfire tragedy, it would change them. He implied that just as those who fought in Vietnam don't glorify war as much as they may have before their experience there, students wouldn't glorify the Bonfire so much if they saw the physical conditions of those who died as a result of the Bonfire tragedy. The following is from a February 8 telephone conversation.

IT: What do you think about the email that Bowen wrote to an alumni, telling him that you were being monitored and that if you step out of line, the administration would take appropriate action?

HW: I don't worry about them getting rid of me. My tactic has been to be prominent. If they try to fire me, it would be evident why. They can exert sanctions on me. If I want to get a pay raise or have a fair shot at resources, they can exert control.

Other faculty who have spoken out talk about being vilified and attacked—these engineers who have spoken up. I think it's unfortunate. Any kind of suppression doesn't belong on a university campus. But I don't think his email can be called suppression. But the tone is of concern. You're familiar with what goes on. It's this idea of A&M being a military base with classrooms. The idea of mind control and conformity comes into play. Marching in step. The *esprit de corps.*

Wilber "Tex" Williams
Class of 1989

Wilber "Tex" Williams is seeking a Master's degree in Architecture at Texas A&M. After the accident, Tex publicly proposed an open competition to choose the design for a Bonfire memorial. Texas A&M is currently in the process of considering Bonfire memorial proposals.

Irwin Tang: Can you tell me a little bit about yourself?

Tex Williams: Well, I'm black.

(laughter, both)

TW: I did my undergrad here, at A&M. I studied environmental design in the architectural department. I graduated in '89. And I was pretty disillusioned by the experience here, being not one of the good ol' boy Aggies, stereotypical, you know. I was disillusioned by the experience of being African American and being here in College Station, studying at A&M. I didn't feel comfortable. So, anyway, it was a pretty difficult experience for me. And so I graduated, and as soon as I graduated—I graduated on a Friday night—you know, Monday morning, the following Monday morning, I moved out of the country. I moved to Europe, to Paris, where I lived for ten years. And I just moved back from Paris a couple of months ago. So I have an interesting perspective on A&M and

217

its changes, and what it meant, and what it means, and what it could mean in the future to be an Aggie.

IT: Why did you attribute some of your alienation to being African-American?

TW: [. . .] Why I attribute it to my African American heritage is because for me, the Bonfire tradition and the way that it has been, has been—me as a two-percenter on the outside looking in, as a two-percenter because I felt I was forced to be one, I didn't feel like there was a place for me in a lot of the Aggie Traditions to be involved. Me looking from the outside at that tradition of a bunch of Texan men running around, chopping down wood and building symbols to burn them, with some kind of confederate flag imagery on top of the—what do you call it, the hats—

IT: The pots—

TW: The pots, hats, you often see confederate flags on those. To me a bunch of Texan men running around burning symbols, based on a tradition that's ninety years old; ninety years ago, in Texas, you had men running around building symbols, burning them, in my ancestors' front yards and back yards because they didn't want to beat the hell out of t.u., they wanted to beat the hell out of my ancestors. (laughter) Just that whole idea of that tradition alienated me. And I see how the tragedy just happened as an opportunity actually, for the tradition to evolve, and for the tradition to be more inclusive for people like me. I don't want to be a two-percenter. I want to be a hundred-percenter Aggie. I want to participate in all the traditions. I want to be a part of what goes on at this university. And I think if I can—if nothing else, by participating in your book, and talking about some of my issues as what I consider as part of the future of this university, if it wants to be a world-class university, which I believe that it honestly does, they would have to take into account voices like mine. Voices like mine would have to be completely integrated into this university, into how it works, into the student body, we have to be taken into account.

IT: What kind of tradition would make you feel like a hundred-percenter?

TW: What kind of tradition? I love the Bonfire tradition, but I think that it could be opened up or evolved in a way that it could be more inclusive of different cultures. I think that it could be opened up in a way that students of African descent, students of Asian descent, students of American Indian descent, all different types of students, who aren't even at this university yet, but who are of high quality and who are being recruited by universities all over the world to be students. Some of them could be at A&M, and be participating in a Bonfire event, tradition, where they *want* to work to create this symbol, of, of what, a new type of symbol. Or maybe refocus the direction of all this intellectual and physical energy that has been going into building the Bonfire, refocus it on a different type of tradition. So, I'm not exactly sure what it could be, I don't have the answer, but I think that if you come together as a student body to talk about different possibilities, maybe some answers could come out of it.

[...]

IT: Talk about your project.

TW: The project is to create a Bonfire memorial student competition for students, only students, because the Bonfire tradition has been a student-run tradition. It's students out there doing everything. To get students involved in making propositions as to where the Bonfire tradition could go. Whether it takes the form of a memorial or whether the Bonfire tradition continues exactly the way it has continued, but evolved somehow. I think we should take advantage of this tragedy to let the tradition evolve toward something new. I know a lot of students have something to say about that, whether it take the form of a memorial, which could be, whatever, an eternal flame or something. I have personal views on that. I know other students do. I'm trying to get the architecture department and other departments across campus to become involved in an idea like that so that we can look at these different propositions and ideas and make a judgment on which ideas could be looked at closer, which ideas could possibly evolve into a memorial, I call it a memorial, but it doesn't necessarily have to take a physical form. I consider what you're doing to be a memorial to the Bonfire and also a way for the tradition to evolve. I mean when your book comes out, it will stand as a testament to the lives, these twelve lives that were lost, and will definitely provoke some thinking.

[...]

IT: How do you think your project will affect the evolution of the tradition?

TW: I think it will cause some awareness. I think the fact that we're beginning to talk about concrete propositions of what could possibly happen, publicly, through the Battalion, or through a competition, that will force people to think in ways they haven't necessarily thought about.

They will be forced to listen to ideas coming from students that they don't necessarily . . . listen to . . . all the time because they're not part of the mainstream university.

IT: Interesting. Do you think that the Bonfire should continue in its current state? And if not, how do you think it should change, or what do you think should replace it?

TW: Obviously, through the tragedy, the Bonfire cannot continue the way that it has been continuing for the past ninety years. Obviously we're moving into a new millenium very soon, and with this happening six weeks before the year 2000, we have exactly twenty years to achieve our Vision 2020. I think these things come together to make an opportunity to really make some change, which is what A&M is obviously looking for by their Vision 2020.

[. . .]

IT: How did this project originate?

TW: Through a graduate 601 design studio. After the tragedy, we had planned on doing some stupid design project [. . .] of creating a lifeguard house at the beach in Malibu, which is like, so far removed from our experiences here, also a lifeguard house, I mean I was pretty upset. I didn't want to do a lifeguard house. Anyway, [the professor] came up with a way at the last minute, after the Bonfire tragedy, to give us an opportunity to work on a memorial for the twelve victims, and I was very excited about that because I think architecture is partly social and psychological. It's not just space trusses in structural steel. It has a lot of components other than that. And those other components allow you to think about issues like memorials and how architecture can actually affect people emotionally, socially, psychologically.

And so this Bonfire project was extremely exciting. We only had one week to think about it. And so we did. I gave it a lot of time and energy because I felt so strongly about it. Even before the idea had been proposed by our professor, I had already began to think about, wow, what a horrible tragedy, and what, what does it mean? I mean, how can this be turned around and made into something positive for the whole world to see about A&M, its values, its traditions, where its trying to go. I thought I saw this opportunity to really make something beautiful out of this tragedy.

[. . .]

IT: So, assuming the Bonfire itself is an act of architecture, that it is a work of architecture, what do you think of it as an architectural structure? You say that architecture can affect people's psychology.

Photo credit: Wilber A. Williams

A memorial to the Bonfire victims proposed by Wilber "Tex" Williams would consist of twelve log cabins and a permanent Bonfire stack topped by an eternal flame. Students would be able to climb a spiraling staircase around the stack to reach the flame.

TW: Sociology, yeah.

IT: *Your symbolic standing in the world, and so forth. What do you think of the Bonfire as it still is?*

TW: What it was before the tragedy?

IT: *Right.*

TW: It was an incredible piece of architecture. It was evolved, it was always changing, every year. It was living. It was a living piece of architecture. It was a great piece of architecture. That's why I'm so excited about the idea of memorializing a great piece of work. It's like, right now, there's a competition to form a memorial for Martin Luther King in Washington, D.C. There's a competition to memorialize his life, his work. That's a great project because Martin Luther King was such an important person, symbolically for the culture, that to memorialize him is like the greatest project. Same thing with the Bonfire. The Bonfire, up until the tragedy, was a great piece of architecture, a great activity, socially, psychologically, architecturally. So the idea of trying to memorialize that is great.

IT: *From an architectural viewpoint, then, why did the Bonfire have to be what it was? Fifty-five feet—used to be over a hundred feet tall—tower of burning logs? Why do you think that had to be like that? What does it represent?*

TW: Like I said, I'm a notorious two-percenter. I never got into the history of the A&M traditions. So that would be more up your alley to answer that question. I don't know why it had to be like that. For me . . . it goes back ninety years ago, Texan men running around gathering wood, building symbols, and burning them. To me, it's directly related to that. Other than that, I don't know.

IT: *You're referring to the crosses that used to be burned in front of the houses of African Americans.*

TW: Right.

IT: *By the KKK, usually, or just local—*

TW: Local people. (laughter) These are all local people running around.

IT: *You were talking about Vision 2020. Can you talk about your view on that for the readers?*

TW: [Vision 2020] is A&M's attempt to bring Texas A&M up to the level of one of the top universities in the country, top public universities in the country, which it isn't right now. It could be. They have all the resources, they have all the space, they have all the people, they have all the money to do that. They just need to implement it. They've written a document that tells how they plan on doing that. And that document is called the Vision 2020 . . .

IT: *How do you think Bonfire affects the possibility of our achieving that vision?*

TW: I think that if the Bonfire is opened up as a tradition where people all over the world—talented people—can participate, then—we'll just take that tradition as an example—where people all over, whether they're African or Asian, or from where else—

IT: *Latin America—*

TW: Latin America, thank you. (laughter) Whoever they are, if they feel like there's a tradition happening on this campus, a major tradition on this campus, where they come and participate, and in effect, they're making some positive social change through that tradition, instead of building a symbol and burning it, to represent our burning desire to beat the hell out of t.u., if they even know what that is, or even care. That could be a way to bring in more diverse people, more talented people, more people willing to invest their time and energy into the vision of the university, just taking the Bonfire as a symbol of a way we can move to our Vision 2020 through our traditions.

IT: *Do you think there are talented people out there who are not coming to A&M in part because of our image?*

TW: Yes, of course, of course. I mean, I'm one of them. If I'm back here after ten years, it's completely against my will. I didn't want to be here at A&M. I planned on going into film, into graduate film at NYU. I was in Paris working as an artist. Environmental design, installation work, a lot of photography. All the different arts. I tried everything. In order to express myself in one media, I decided to go into film. And there was only one film school I wanted to go to if I came back to America, I only wanted to go to NYU. So I only applied to NYU. I reached the last cut-off point, where they chose only twenty-nine students, and I was not one of those twenty-nine. And I found that out only in May of last year. And at that point, that brought me back to my original passion, my original love, which is architecture. Which I'm very happy about, but when I was in Paris deciding how I was going to come back to America, I was thinking of NYU, or UCLA, it was on one of the major coasts, it was not in College Station because of the experience I had before leaving A&M ten years ago, in '89 when I graduated. So I was definitely not interested in coming back to College Station.

IT: *Can you give me a couple of specifics as to why your experience was so bad in Texas A&M in College Station?*

TW: Um, well, a couple of specific examples . . . Hm.

IT: *I know it's been a long time.*

TW: No, it hasn't been that long, but some of them are so personal, that I . . . I'd rather not give specific examples. I'm not trying to focus on that. I'm trying to focus only on the future. I'm trying to focus on where the fact that I'm back, is the fact that I am one of the students the university probably wouldn't have access to if destiny hadn't put me here. What can I do to help the university evolve towards this Vision 2020? What can I say? How can my voice be heard, so that people can understand that there are other voices out there that do have things to say, they're not necessarily absolute truths, but that we can talk about, and that will help us grow and move towards Vision 2020?

IT: *Has the university changed? Do you think that the African American students can feel more at home now than ten years ago?*

TW: Let's not even focus on that. Let's just talk about the different students. Here we are, Irwin Tang, from Asian descent, writing a book on A&M's traditions, interviewing Tex, who's an African American, and we're sitting here, talking about A&M's future . . . that's different from ten years ago when I graduated. We didn't have this kind of thing going on. So, it's definitely changed. I know I have. (laughter)

IT: *It seems like, despite these improvements, people of color are still not involved in the Bonfire. Particularly, Caucasian women have gotten more involved with Bonfire, and there have been violent incidents against them. As far as people of color are concerned, you rarely see them involved in Bonfire activities.*

TW: I agree. In many of the Aggie traditions, you rarely see people of color involved . . . I agree, and I believe it could and should change. If A&M is really serious about moving towards this world-class status—I know that there are ways to move toward that status. I'm not saying that I know which ways, but I know that there are ways. I think we need to talk about that publicly as a university, as a student body, as administration, and faculty, talk about how we're going to move forward towards that.

IT: *Do you think there are reasons why people of color are not involved in Bonfire?*

TW: Well, did you notice? I think that the most people of color I've seen involved in the Bonfire tradition happened the moment that the tradition fell. The moment that it collapsed. The moment that there was tragedy, I saw more people of color involved. Me, I mean here I am talking about spending so much time on the tradition, where I've never been to a Bonfire. I've never been to a Bonfire. I've spent six years at this university, no, five-and-a-half now, and I've never been to a Bonfire. So here I am, now that the institution has collapsed, which is unfortunate that lives were taken, but I think it's fortunate for the University because it allows it to think about traditions in new ways and maybe to evolve towards somewhere else.

IT: *So, in a strange way, it allows people of color—*

TW: To become involved. Did you see all the football players out there moving logs? I mean I saw football players with logs above their heads. These were African-American men who were willing and ready to help re-direct this tragedy, re-direct this tradition. I didn't go out and pick up logs, but I did go out and spend quite a bit of time by myself walking around, a lot of time crying, a lot of time thinking about this tragedy and where it could go. I spent a lot of time on my thoughts, and putting my thoughts into architectural form. On this memorial idea, yeah, I spent more time on this tradition since it fell, than I spent in the past five-and-a-half years altogether. (laughter)

IT: *So it seems that more people have gotten involved because they have found an opportunity to help people, and to help Texas A&M instead of simply building a bonfire.*

TW: Building a symbol, with a lot of men running around, Confederate flags, building a symbol, and saying beat the hell outta who cares, but let's beat the hell out of somebody. That is not inclusive of me. I do not, I do not want to think that way. I do not want to participate in a tradition like that. There's no place for me to participate in a tradition like that.

IT: *How should the Bonfire evolve then and be all-inclusive? Can it still remain a burning Bonfire?*

TW: I think we have to try to figure out what the essence of that tradition has been. We have to really think about it long and hard, really talk about it loud and strong, and come up with this idea that's new and improved. A new and improved Bonfire tradition. I think its possible . . . I think it can still be a burning symbol, and still, and now through its evolution, be more inclusive. Because a burning symbol is not necessarily what its been in the past. It could be something different. It could definitely evolve. It should evolve. It shouldn't die. The tradition should not die. The tradition should evolve.

The DAN Books

On the day the Bonfire fell, Bonfire Adviser Rusty Thompson told reporters that there was no written blueprint as to how the Bonfire is to be constructed, that the information is passed down from one generation of Redpots to the next. If there were building instructions, Thompson said, they would be in the little notebooks that the Redpots carry with them all day and night.

Those notebooks are called General Dan Faires Communications, and each Junior Redpot carries one. All of the 1999 Communications were turned in to investigators of the accident and made public. Although the books are not particularly informative about the nuts-and-bolts construction of Bonfire, they do provide a great deal of insight into the Redpot culture.

Each book contains a condom taped into an inside divider. Each book contains a section of quotations and sayings of various bonfire workers. Some of the books contain the imperative, "Don't be gay." Others contain the acronym, "NTAFB" and its explanation, "Never trust a Fucking Bitch. Don't tell them anything." One book uses a racial epithet against African-Americans.

Negative comments are made against Pink Pots and Band members. One wrote, "We fuckin hate BQ's [Band Queers] except Mike Ruscek. He will save my ass." The Redpot may have been referring to the student crane operator, Mike Rusek, who was also a band member.

Some books write something similar to this quotation: "It's not about building a goddamn fucking Bonfire. It's about being a fucking Aggie." This demonstrates the common theme among Aggies that building the Bonfire has little to do with simply building a big fire. Building the Bonfire expresses the Aggie Spirit.

The work ethic of the Redpots seems to concentrate on the intensity of one's exertion and the dedication to, even obsession with, building the Bonfire. "Nobody ever drowned in their own sweat." "Never let anyone work harder than you." "Running saves an hour a day." "Eat Sleep Drink Shit Aggie Bonfire." "There is a purpose to everything. It is not a glory job. You want glory be a Yellboy (yell leader)." "Step up intensity—do job better." "Pain is weakness leaving your body."

Safety was a concern, at least on paper. "People not wearing pots we are responsible." "Safety, motivation, key." Safety, however, may have been compromised by such ideas as the one presented in this quotation: "Be decisive even if it means being wrong." Did the Junior Redpots continue building a leaning Bonfire even though it could be "wrong"?

One of the reasons why very few people knew about the many violations of school and Bonfire policy occurring at Bonfire events may have been the apparent distrust of the outside community that Redpots encouraged with each other. "Don't tell nobody nothing." "Never talk shop on campus walls have ears."

And of course, there was, "Aggies Against Bonfire = Aggies Against God."

Watch What You Say

Within the first week of Bonfire, some Texas A&M faculty who had been opposed to the Bonfire long before the accident spoke to reporters. Biology professor Hugh Wilson and chemistry professor Danny Yeager were the most active dissenters, their voices and opinions airing on CNN's TalkBack Live, National Public Radio's "All Things Considered," TIME magazine, and The Bryan-College Station Eagle.

Although all of those opposed to Bonfire were saddened and shocked by the tragedy, they perhaps found more reason to oppose the Bonfire as a result of it. Traditional dissenters to the Bonfire tradition believe Bonfire is a tremendous waste of natural and man-made resources, as well as a waste of 125,000 hours of labor. They think that the time and material could be better applied on something constructive. They also see the Bonfire as environmentally irresponsible.

Two professors who have not been as outspoken as Wilson and Yeager, but who spoke to the Eagle were philosophy professors Steve Daniel and Colin Allen. On the day of the tragedy, Allen told the Eagle that "even people who have been critical of Bonfire hate to see what happened today."

However humane these bonfire dissidents seem, apparently they are still a threat to the Texas A&M Administration, specifically to President Bowen.

L.A. gangster-rapper Ice-T says in a rap song, "Freedom of speech, just watch what you say." Such is the case at Texas A&M University.

Obviously, there is no prohibition against speaking one's mind. But speaking publicly against the University's traditions often draws a backlash. The punishment may be as innocuous as a colleague saying, "Hey, Highway 6 runs both ways," which is the Aggie version of "Love it or leave it." Other times, a dissenting comment draws more serious consequences. Most people in the Aggie community understand this, but do not know exactly what those consequences might be.

When the University released thousands of pieces of its email correspondence for the Bonfire, a revealing exchange was made public. On November 22, four days after the Bonfire collapse, a former student emailed President Bowen, asking him to remove Dr. Hugh Wilson from his position as professor. The former student wrote that Dr. Wilson's "Dumb as Dirt" anti-Bonfire web page charges Texas A&M and other public bodies with illegal activities, and that the page calls those who disagree with Wilson "dumb" and "irrational." He felt that these methods of argument warranted Wilson's removal. Bowen answered the former student two days later with the following email.

> Subject: RE: Removal of Dr. Hugh Wilson
>
> Dr. Wilson has spent years criticizing the bonfire. He thrives on controversy and feels rewarded when he is attacked by someone he has offended. We do monitor his activities and he is working within his constitutionally protected rights of communication. If he should cross the line, we will take appropriate action.

The email makes the not-so-implicit threat, "We are watching Wilson closely. Once he takes an errant step we will use it as justification to dismiss him."

recommendations as to the future of the Bonfire or assigning responsibility for the collapse. Bowen stated that the commission would be expected to turn in its report by March 31, 2000.

By the end of the week, Bowen announced that he had chosen Leo E. Linbeck to organize and chair the commission. Linbeck is the chairman and chief executive officer of Linbeck Construction Corporation. John A. Weese and a team of university staff members were chosen to help Linbeck in his investigation.

Bowen said that he chose Linbeck "because of his reputation for integrity and openness and his vast knowledge and experience in various aspects of construction." Linbeck stated that the investigation would be impartial, open, and thorough. But his integrity was called into question when reporters brought up the fact that Linbeck is the chairman of Texans for Lawsuit Reform, which lobbies the state legislature to limit punitive damages in civil injury and death suits. Further muddying the separation of interests is the fact that Bartell Zachry is also a member of the board of Texans for Lawsuit Reform. Zachry is the head of H.B. Zachry, which may be a target of civil suits because it volunteered a crane and three workers to help build the Bonfire.

December 1999

On December 1, Linbeck chose the other four members of the investigative commission. Allan Shiver, Jr. is the son of the late governor of Texas, Allan Shivers Sr. He runs a consulting and investment company in Austin and helps run an orchard in the Rio Grande Valley. Veronica Kastrin Callaghan of El Paso is vice president of KASKO Ventures, an industrial real estate company. She works in the area of industrial warehouse construction. Hugh G. Robinson is the CEO of a construction management firm called The Tetra Group. He also serves on the board of directors of Belo Corporation, the parent company of *The Bryan-College Station Eagle* newspaper. The final member of the team is William E. Tucker, chancellor emeritus of Texas Christian University, having served as chancellor from 1979-1998. Linbeck, Callaghan and Robinson have all served on the board of the Federal Reserve Bank of Dallas.

According to Bowen, "The commission is to satisfy itself that the truth about what caused the accident is known as far as it can be discovered and to report its findings and conclusions with recommendations for corrective action."

The future of the Bonfire (whether the tradition is to continue and in what way) is to be decided by the University and its students, but soon after the accident, Bowen already had thoughts about that. On November 19, Bowen told *The Eagle* that "it's highly probable bonfire will continue. I can't be more explicit at this point." On November 30, Bowen wrote an email to alumnus Malcolm Hartman Jr. saying, "If I had to bet, I would bet that it continues." Bowen also said that safety issues had to be addressed.

On December 3, the investigative commission met at Texas A&M and came up with a set of preliminary questions that it wanted answered, including:

- Were specific structural designs used to build the bonfire, and was outside expert advice sought?

- What equipment was used, and what kind of training did operators have?

- How were students selected and trained to work on the bonfire—and what role did A&M administrators play in supervising them?

- Who in the A&M administration was responsible for ensuring safety at the site, and what was the attitude of students toward safety concerns?

On December 10, the commission assigned Kent Lietzau and Jon Zagrodzky of management consulting firm McKinsey & Company to assemble the professional investigators and technical experts for the investigation.

Packer Engineering, based near Chicago, was assigned the job of discerning the exact cause of the 1999 Bonfire collapse. They will look for differences between the 1999 Bonfire and previous ones. Fay Engineering will study the evolving structure of the current Bonfire structure, which originated in 1946, when a center pole was first used to build it. Fay Engineering will analyze the materials used and conduct stress tests on the different designs used over the decades. Kroll Associates specializes in business investigations, forensic accounting, security consulting, crisis management and electronic systems protection. Kroll will coordinate investigative teams, maintain a communications and information-sharing system between teams, and conduct interviews.

January 2000

In early January 2000, the commission and its hired investigators announced that a report may not be ready by March 31, 2000, as Bowen had requested. Investigators also estimated that the total cost of the investigation could be $500,000 or more. Linbeck encouraged investigators to not speak to the public during the investigation.

Official Reaction

November 18, 1999

On the day of the accident, most of the important officials under whose jurisdiction the Bonfire is constructed each year made statements to the press. All of the statements expressed sorrow at the accident, but some revealed other concerns.

Texas A&M University President Ray Bowen announced that the 1999 Bonfire burning would be cancelled. "It is only fitting that the Bonfire not be held next week," he said. "Will it be held next year? That will be answered in the coming weeks or months after careful review of what transpired. We don't have all the answers today. Our primary concern is getting those students all out from underneath the stack."

Bowen also stated that he was "99 percent confident" that safety measures had been adequately carried through. He said that future Bonfires may be different. "It may be a small bonfire. You can imagine where it's actually built by professionals but cut by students, just to be sure that what's up there is meeting every standard."

Rusty Thompson, the Bonfire adviser for the 1998 and 1999 Bonfires, said that although Bonfire is built only by students, three volunteers from construction companies were serving as advisers at the Bonfire site when the accident occurred. It became known later that there was only one volunteer crane operator. Thompson countered rumors of horseplay by saying that the students were not playing on the stack, and he called the Red Pots "true professionals" who "know exactly what they're doing."

When asked why there was so little adult supervision in the construction of Bonfire, Thompson answered that the students are adults, which brought a big "whoop" from the crowd of students. Thompson was active in responding to the media for the first few days after the accident but then grew extremely quiet with the media purportedly because he was busy dealing with the accident aftermath itself.

Bob Wiatt, the University Police Chief, stated that "from what we have gathered at this point, there is no indication that anything inappropriate occurred at Bonfire site the night of the accident. That includes alcohol, rough-housing or careless behavior."

Governor George W. Bush choked back tears at one point as he spoke, "I just can't imagine what that means to have that happen to them. It's sad, it's tough . . . But the university will rally and recover. Right now it's a time of chaos at Texas A&M, but things will be fine." Later, Governor Bush would call Bonfire "a great tradition."

On Friday, the day after the accident, Governor George Bush was asked whether he thought the tradition of Bonfire should continue. He answered, "Absolutely." About the memorial service that had been held the day before, Bush said, "Nobody was urged to come, nobody was told to come and it was a turnout that was unlike anything I've ever seen. People just praying and crying and sharing their grief and concern about the fate of these people, those surviving and those who passed away."

November 22, 1999

On Monday Nov. 22, University administrators met with local law enforcement, fire and rescue organizations, and the U.S. Department of Labor's Occupational Safety and Health Administration (OSHA) to figure out who would conduct the investigation of the accident, and how it would be conducted.

On the Saturday before the meeting, Lieutenant Governor Rick Perry had already said that he and other Senate leaders preferred that the investigation be handled by Texas A&M. "No one has more interest in finding out what happened there than the University," he said. "I have every indication that Texas A&M will look at every aspect of this and do it in a full and proper way and disclose all the facts that need to be disclosed."

George W. Bush decided to let Texas A&M take care of its own business. After a weekend of funerals, President Bowen announced that the university would choose a qualified person to head an independent commission to investigate the Bonfire accident. The commission would be charged with finding the cause of the accident but not making for bonfire. Furthermore, even official university sources acknowledge that a maximum of only 20% of the trees survived.

The student replant committee and Texas A&M apparently were aware that with such a low tree survival rate replant was a potential public relations disaster. In April 1999, in quite a reversal of direction, only 300 trees were replanted. Instead of the usual one-to-two year old trees that had been standard in the past, three-to-five-year old tress were planted in the cities of Bryan-College Station and not out around Lake Somerville (20+ miles away) as had been typical in the past. Replant committee sources indicated that they expected 80% to 90% of these 300 trees to survive—in large part because they would be watered and looked after by the cities' workers at, of course, Bryan/College Station's expense.

Another replant is scheduled for March 4, 2000. This time only 214 trees are being replanted at Bryan Regional Athletic Complex (BRAC). This is to replace the old growth forest of 6000 - 8000 trees cut down for the 1999 bonfire stack that collapsed. Replant this year (and in previous years as well) would be a joke if it weren't so sad.

Some people have argued that trees donated for the A&M bonfire stood on land that was to be cleared anyway. Perhaps—perhaps not. Certainly, a few fanatical A&M loyalists would feel some sort of special calling to donate the trees—even if they had not intended to clear the land. Even if they had, should Texas A&M be providing a free land-clearing service for local landowners?

Then, of course, there's the role model that A&M should provide to its students as well as to others in the state. When I first came to the area over 20 years ago and would travel to Big Bend National Park, on most days the limit of sight was over 100 miles at the south rim of the Chisos Mountains. Now when I go there, it is unusual for the limit to be more than 50 miles. Typically, it's well under that. Once recently I even saw it officially listed in the teens. Some of this air pollution is from new coal burning power plants in Monterey, Mexico—several hundred miles away. Much of it is from the industries on the Gulf of Mexico near Houston. Houston and Dallas both have tremendous air pollution problems. EPA sanctions are threatened for both. This past summer Houston replaced Los Angeles as the most polluted large city in the U.S. for ozone. The atmosphere in Bryan-College Station and much of Texas and the U.S. was hazy for months nearly two years ago from forest fires in Mexico and Central America started to clear the land for farming. It seems that Texas A&M's role should be to encourage preservation and conservation rather than wanton, needless destruction of the environment and pollution of the air.

IT: What is the Aggie Spirit and how is it manifested or not manifested by Bonfire?

DY: Certainly there is much pride, spirit and unity among the students at Texas A&M concerning bonfire. These attributes can only be considered positive if the ultimate goal is something beneficial. In this case the goal is the building and burning of bonfire and, of course, having a good time. Once the burning is over—that's pretty much it except for the clean up of quite a mess. Because of the dangers involved, the environmental impact and bad examples the forest destruction and bonfire burning set, the disruption in students' academic lives, and the crude behavior during the construction and at the burning itself, the Texas A&M bonfire is not beneficial. There have been many examples throughout history where pride, unity and spirit have been generated for something we consider negative or even evil. Bonfire is certainly not nearly as bad as or on the scale of Nazism, the World Church of the Creator, the Jim Jones cult, the Ku Klux Klan or Aum Shinri Kyo—and I'm certainly not comparing bonfire supporters to members any of these groups. The point is, however, that pride, unity and spirit by themselves are not necessarily virtues.

Matt Carroll
Class of 1970

Matt Carroll was commander of the Corps of Cadets in 1969-1970. He was the top student officer during the construction of the tallest Bonfire of all time. Upon graduating with a degree in architecture, he served as the atomic demolitions tactics coordinator for the Eleventh Armored Cavalry Regiment on the East German border. Carroll led the regiment in developing a way of hand-placing nuclear bombs anywhere in the world. Over the last two decades, he has been involved in the management of over five hundred million dollars in construction projects and earned a Ph.D. in Architecture from Texas A&M in 1999. The following is an amalgamation of conversations and email exchanges from December 1999 to February 2000.

Irwin Tang: Tell me about yourself.

Matt Carroll: I arrived at Texas A&M in September of 1966. I came here because, in the old days, at least, it "was" THE "poor boys' school!" This was where "working class" kids came with their "callused" hands and their "hard earned" money! It had real "salt of the earth" quality in those days!

IT: What was Bonfire like in those days? You must have worked on the largest Bonfire ever, the 110-foot Bonfire of 1969. Were you pretty excited about building Bonfire?

MC: By the time it comes around—Have you ever talked to anyone about what it's like being a fish in the Corps?

IT: *What's it like?*

MC: I don't know how to respond to a question like that. You just about have to go through it yourself to know. It's something that's going on twenty-four hours a day, seven days a week. It goes on when you first walk into the place and doesn't stop until you go home for Christmas.

IT: *What happens in a typical day?*

MC: (laughter, long pause) A typical day. First of all, every company does their own thing. I can only speak about what happened in my company.

IT: *Which was . . .*

MC: G-1, which meant company G, first brigade.

IT: *Specializing in anything in particular?*

MC: Architecture. It was an architecture company, back then. When the corps became noncompulsory, the school of architecture left the Corps quicker than any other school. Students in architecture left the Corps, and those who remained in the Corps changed majors. But there was a number of us who stayed in the Corps and architecture.

It's been since 1966 since I was a freshman. There's something called a whistle jock, a freshman. They blow the whistle, and the freshmen stand against the walls in the hall, with their heels to the wall. Sophomores come out and start hazing the freshmen. Quizzing them about campusology. Different statues on campus and their inscriptions and this, that, and the other.

And after the third whistle call, freshmen stand outside in formation. The freshmen are inspected to see if their shoes are shiny enough, their brass is shiny enough, is there a little thread sticking out of a seam in your sleeve or something? So on and on it goes.

IT: *What happens if you have a thread sticking out of your sleeve?*

MC: I don't know. You might have to do some push-ups.

IT: *How many?*

MC: Each freshmen is supposed to be able to do their class. So for me it's seventy. But most of the time it would be less than that. Most people can't do their class. But eventually, the upperclassmen filter out. And the Corps staff comes out, does the first call, brings the unit to attention. We're in formation and we do a left-face or a right-face and we march down to the mess hall.

When in 1970 Texas A&M President James Earl Rudder asked Corps Commander Matt Carroll to "save" the Corps (which had been losing membership for years), one of Carroll's ideas was to allow upperclassmen to have longer hair.

There's a formal thing for everything. When I first got here, they had waiters. All the freshmen had to speak in unison to the waiter. And the waiters were often harassed. Maybe I shouldn't use the word harassment. Some of it was friendly. The waiters knew it was coming. Sometimes the freshman would come up with some smart aleck remark (laughter).

You can't eat until you memorize what everything's called. You also have to learn a whole lot of people's names real fast. All the sophomores, juniors, and seniors. There's a lot more to it.

IT: *Was there ever any malicious harassment?*

MC: Where do you draw the line? What's malicious and what's not? I mean, it's *all* harassment. I don't know if it's the same now, but when I was there, you said howdy to every single solitary person that you passed anywhere on campus.

If you had met the person before, particularly if they remembered your name, then you had to be able to speak to them by name. And if they were with someone you didn't know, you had to run over there as fast as you can, and whip out. You have to run over to their right side, and you have to stand at attention and stick out your right hand and say, "Howdy. Fish Carroll is my name sir." And then they'd say their name, Jones or something. "I'm glad to meet you, Mr. Jones, sir. Where are you from, Mr. Jones, sir?" And then, they'd say where they were from, and then they'd ask you where you're from, and you'd say that. And then you'd say, "What are you taking?" Those are the three things, their name, where they're from, and what they're taking.

Now if he's a sophomore with two of his friends or three of his friends, you'd have to do it with all of them. And maybe be late for class. Now this was more important than being on time for class.

IT: *What would happen if you decided to get to class on time?*

MC: Then you'd get harassed, and it would be mean. If you didn't like it, it was Highway 6 runs both ways. Leave. That's why they made Corps membership noncompulsory. Too many people were leaving. They wanted growth. They wanted national football teams. You're not going to get national football teams from a tiny little military school.

IT: *Did Bonfire push people out of the Corps?*

MC: By the time Bonfire comes around, it's just part of the harassment.

If they don't have good enough grades, the university's not going to let them stay. They're not going to re-admit them. There's a line right there. And anyone who's near that line is going to get pushed over. Even if they can make it to class, they're going to be so dead tired, it's gonna be hard for them even to stay awake, much less get anything out of class. You weren't going to get much out of class even if you were there. You're tired and sleepy. You're hurting. Your whole body is in pain.

IT: *You worked on cut for four years. Where did you cut?*

MC: I don't have the slightest idea. You get up early in the morning, you get on a flatbed truck. You're linked by arm with the guy next to you. You just hope and pray you're not on the outside. All you got between you and the ground at whatever speed you're going around the corner is one linked arm. There's no seat belt or safety belt or anything, just an arm. And they've got us as tight as possible, row after row. Nobody's out there with a book, telling people how to do things. It's all passed down from the year before.

IT: *What was cut like back then? Was there a lot of horsing around?*

The only horsing around was at lunch-time. I was isolated in my one spot in the woods, but I never saw any alcohol at cut. The rest of the time, it's just God-awful, horrible manual labor to where all your clothes are soaking with sweat.

We were lifting and moving trees all day. For some of those trees, they were so big, we had to roll them over a line of smaller trees, and then use the smaller trees as leverage, lined up three or four deep on each side of the larger tree, and we lift the large tree by lifting each side of the smaller trees.

IT: *These must have been the thousand pound trees of old.*

MC: By the end of the day, every muscle in your body is aching. You just lay on your bed until the whistle jock blows the whistle in the morning.

IT: *You've been involved with construction for some decades now, either studying it, or organizing private construction projects. What kinds of regulations regarding design and worker safety would apply to a project of the magnitude of Bonfire, a structure of several stories?*

MC: First thing, you want to build something out here? You've got to get a permit. If you're in the city of Bryan-College Station, you've got to go to the building permit office, and you've got to get a permit. Well, they're not going to just give you a building permit, so you give them a set of drawings. Now if it's a commercial project, you've got to have a registered architect and/or a registered engineer stamp on there with their signature. And they take liability if something happens. Got the picture?

Now they are not so strict with residential structures. You don't have to hire an architect, but you're going to have to give them a set of plans. And they're going to look at your plans, and they're going to compare them to their codes in their code book, and if there is anything on there that isn't according to code, then they're going to take a little red pen and they're going to say, "Irwin, here's your drawings, you're going to have to make these changes. After you've made the changes, give them back to us, and then we'll give you a building permit.

IT: Do the regulations allow for wooden pillars or logs wired to each other, tied around a center pole?

MC: I don't think, and I'm 99.9% sure, there are no registered professional engineers that would put their stamp on a drawing of that thing and sign their name (laughter). There aren't any. I mean, unless it was some kind of bogus thing. Find someone who was fixing to die in a year and doesn't care.

IT: There seems to be an inherent instability in standing up a log on its end, even if it is wired to other logs.

MC: Any engineer worth his salt would say that that thing should not be going on. It's not safe. It's not safe for human beings to be hanging off the sides of the darn thing.

IT: What is the heart of your criticism of the structure of the Bonfire?

MC: C'mon, you got to go over there, and you've got to take a whole lot of classes a whole bunch of years, and then take a long drawn out test to get your professional engineer's license. And what does that involve? It involves a whole bunch of sophisticated, complicated formulas to determine, in this case, what is the size of the columns, the size of the beams, based on tested, scientific formulas. These professional societies have taken for example, wood, and all the different shapes and sizes, and they have tested them to see what their strengths are. And different kinds of trees are given different strengths. If you're going to span so many feet, if you use two-by-sixes, then you're going to have more of them, closer together. If you're using two-by-eights, you're going to have a little larger spaces, but if you're in a building, you have to realize it's going to take more space vertically. If you want to use a smaller vertical dimension, you space them closer. But there are standard sizes, so that you can calculate their strengths. The same is done for steel. The same for concrete, and every other structural material.

Well, you're out there with who-knows-what. And the other thing is there are standard methods of attaching wooden columns, steel columns, concrete columns to the bases where they're sitting, okay? And everything has to be plumb, perfectly vertical. And all of this is checked by an instrument that makes sure that it's plumb. They have different kinds of levels. Nowadays, they have very sophisticated laser levels. And all these things are tested. There's usually an independent company that comes around and tests all that stuff. They don't take your word for it. And they of course record everything that they're doing.

IT: Even for a residential structure?

MC: Yes. An inspector for each discipline, each craft, from the city, will come around and inspect and sign off. The first thing they do is the structure, the frame. And yeah, when you say you're finished, an inspector comes around and inspects everything. To make sure you have the proper sizes, the proper spacing, everything is put together correctly. They do this for electrical, plumbing, HEAC, insulation. Okay. If you miss an inspection after you put the drywall on, they're going to make you tear it down, okay?

IT: What would the inspector say if he saw thousands of logs stacked on top of each other like in Bonfire.

MC: Let me see your drawings. Let me see what engineer put their stamp on it, and signed their name on it. Where's your specs? You know, these big commercial projects, they've got a book of specifications, for each and every one of these disciplines that tells you, like, exactly how many pounds per square inch the concrete has to be, what the standards the steel is supposed to meet. Or the lumber or whatever it is.

IT: Did you think about this when you were working on Bonfire?

MC: No, no, no. When you're a freshmen, they wake you up, tell you to get in such-and-such a formation, and you go out and work.

IT: What about when you were Corps Commander?

MC: The command structure has nothing to do with Bonfire. When I was Commander, and Bonfire came around, I just went back to my unit and did cut. I was just a senior in my unit. Every unit had a specialty. There were units that did all the unloading. This was all done by hand back then. I don't know when they started using cranes. Maybe that was the mistake. Cranes enabled them to do stuff that was more dangerous. If they were limited to what they could do by hand . . .

IT: What position did you attain in the Corps of Cadets?

I was President General James Earl Rudder's last hand-picked Corps Commander. When I became Corps Commander, President Rudder asked me to save the Corps. Just do what needed to be done. Membership was going down quick. I helped to carry his coffin when General Rudder died.

IT: In a lot of ways, it seems to me, that Bonfire culture is driven by Corps of Cadets culture. When I started reading the 1950's Bonfire history, I started to understand why people walking across the Bonfire site get beat up. The cadets are under U.S. military order to protect that piece of land, and it's like treason if they don't. So I see the Bonfire as coming out of a military tradition in the Corps.

MC: I think of the Corps, back then, as something like the movie "Boys' Town." About the only thing really "military" about it was the uniforms. It was actually more like a big "fraternity." There was a considerable amount of horse-play, otherwise known as "good-bull."

Most people look at the uniform, and they think "military." It's not that way. People don't obey orders. They don't have a chain of command. The people at the unit level are to a great degree independent. The Corps is not like West Point. A lot of these boys don't even have contracts to go into the military.

IT: Most of them.

MC: It's a gang hiding behind the uniform. People don't know how fiercely independent some of these units are. Sending orders through the chain of command? Forget that. You got to talk people into it. What makes good leaders at A&M? Why do good leaders come out of A&M? Because they have to talk people into everything.

IT: I guess you would know, being a former Commander.

MC: Everyone on staff is called a staff rat. And so there's resistance. "Those people are teaching bull classes." The regular military personnel at the Trigon [military sciences building] are called "bulls." They rarely if ever come over to the Corps area. There was no direct contact with freshmen, sophomores, or juniors. The only senior who had contact with these people were commanders.

Each unit would have an adviser. But there is this culture of independence. There's sometimes unbelievable rivalry between different units. Certain units had real bad relations with the Band. So rival units had to be housed at separate parts of the Quad. It was a thin veneer of being military. It was far from military. More of a fraternity than a military organization.

IT: So there was a lot of independence, or the units would strive for independence from the Corps staff. It seems like there was a pronounced dichotomy between most of the student body and the Corps leaders and university administration.

MC: A small number of students ran the whole campus. In the old days, the perfect corps staff would be Corps commander, deputy Corps commander, president of the student body, president of the student class, president of the MSC, editor of the Battalion, head yell leader, and RV [Ross Volunteers] commander. All the top positions. So they all eat breakfast, lunch, and dinner together, and run the whole place together.

IT: So all the top positions on campus were held by the top people on Corps staff. A very top down hierarchy. Every thing was run—

MC: A very elite clique. Like how society really is.

IT: So there were a few major leaders and a lot of followers who have an independent culture, trying to get away with whatever they can.

MC: You have no idea what you're going to do as sergeant-major of the Corps until you get there. And then you find out it's just a dirty detail. Because you're going to spend most of your time chasing down bad boys. Because there's a level on which that "Good Bull" stuff is not looked on as Good Bull. It's only looked on as Good Bull from the bottom up. When one unit steals another unit's flag, if you're the unit that steals another unit's flag, hey, that's like a coup. The freshmen have to clump around these flags, and protect these flags. That's one of your major jobs as a freshman. They get the biggest strongest ex-lineman football player to carry the thing. And all his fish buddies get around him. Cause they're all trying to steal each others' flags. This is just one of the games that go on over there.

Well, this is great for the fish that stole the flag. But it's really bad if you're the unit that had it stolen, cause then you're at each other's throats, particularly if the unit who lost the flag doesn't know who stole it. Then they start trying to guess who's got it. Then they start doing stuff to the units around them. And it creates a big mess. So the Corps sergeant-major gets a call from the vice president for student affairs—Malon Southerland at the time was the special assistant to the Commandant. So I would get calls on the phone from Malon early in the morning or late at night, "So-and-so lost their flag. Whey don't you see what you can do to find it." Or, "Such-and-such a unit got their showerhead stolen." These various and sundry pranks. So that's what the Corps sergeant major does with his time, he tries to figure out who done it and go after them.

IT: What's Malon like?

MC: Malon is a guy who smooths the water, or tries to.

IT: Sometimes it seems like Malon Southerland and the top adminis-
trators must not know what goes on at the ground at Texas A&M, as if they
are out of touch with the grass-roots.

MC: Anyone who's been in the Corps should know. But the campus
was different back then. There wasn't as much drinking back then. Alcohol
wasn't allowed in dorms. There weren't all these bars around campus.
Beer in pizza places had just started when I was there.

IT: And hazing wasn't as bad either, as far as Bonfire is concerned?

MC: If someone came in from the outside, to them it would all be
hazing. But people in the Corps don't think about hazing as hazing. It's
just part of being in the Corps. There were freshmen who would "fart-
off" to upperclassmen knowing they would be run around the Quad or
something. They would do it just to show how tough they were. You could
avoid that if you wanted to. You could be quiet.

IT: Someone died in 1984 from being forced to run around in the middle
of the night.

MC: There was an RV junior from Washington D.C. He was assigned
to say the prayer for dinner. He got up there and said, "Good food, good
meat, good God, let's eat." So the RV seniors ran him around the golf
course till he dropped. They took turns. It took a whole bunch of them.
Cause the first one, he ran the senior until the senior couldn't go anymore.
Got it? That's how tough this guy was. It took half a dozen of them to run
him until he dropped. Those guys were in pretty good shape.

He knew something like that was going to happen. But everyone
in the Corps heard about that. So this guy had a fantastic reputation
as a result.

IT: So in what ways did this culture impact Bonfire? One obvious way,
it seems, is that the Bonfire chain-of-command is nonexistent. The Redpots
don't listen to the Bonfire advisor or university administration. And the in-
dividuals don't necessarily follow the orders of the Redpots. No wonder there's
such a lack of discipline. Then you've got dorms and Corps outfits and the
Band all rivaling each other.

MC: They say, "It's time to do the Bonfire. Formation is going to be
such-a-such a thing." You go out there not knowing what is going on.
There's no rules or regulations written down. You learn from verbal

communication. The rule book, when I was there, was known as The Standard, and every member of the Corps had a copy which they had to keep on their desktop. One of the first things you're told is not to open it or quote it, especially to an upperclassman. Officially, it says one thing, then you're told to do something else.

IT: I wonder if anyone recited university alcohol policy to the Pots.

MC: Everyone learns their position from the person before them. At the end of your sophomore year, you write up a dream sheet. You write down what positions you'd like. Then interviews start. Each level takes their pick of who they want. They start looking at people when they're freshmen.

Certain units ran certain things. Some units were heavy into politics. Two or three units put on SCONA, a student group that sponsors issue forums. Some units were known for running the Battalion. The freshmen do all the work. The seniors sit back and watch.

IT: Just like in Bonfire culture. The senior Redpots direct the Junior Redpots, who do all the work. The late sixties was a time of social and political upheaval in the United States. College students all over the country were becoming radicalized in droves. What was the attitude of A&M students in the late sixties?

MC: During the late sixties, the environment and all of the subjects involved and related to it were beginning to become front page, head line issues. The first "Earth Days" were being held all over the country. During my fifth year, '70-'71, I had time to become a serious student for the first time. I wrote papers on resource depletion and recycling. During "Bonfire" that year, I "rescued" some wood. I turned it on the lathe in the Architecture shop to create a set of bowls for a project in Architectural Design. "Bonfire" was obviously a grotesque waste of natural resources and human labor. That was the only logical and reasonable conclusion that any thinking person could come to under the circumstances.

IT: Minorities, especially Blacks and Asians tend to avoid getting involved in the Bonfire tradition. I still have not seen a picture of a Black or Asian carrying a log.

MC: There was an article in the Battalion. As a result of Hopwood, universities are using a system where they automatically accept the top ten percent of any high school. The only university where [minority enrollment] went down was A&M. Why's that? Because people are self-selective. They choose to come here. And of course, this is an unattractive place for minorities. What self-respecting "brother" or "sister" is going to come to "White Flight U."? Come on.

They were trying to stop this, when I was still there, but it was still going on. Every upperclassman had a "nigger," to clean his room, to polish his shoes, to polish his brass, to pick up his laundry, to take his laundry.

IT: Was that—

MC: This is the term that was used. Now, most of these people were apparently European Americans. I used to think it was a good thing for those people to experience that so they could see what some people experience in their life, had to put up all their life. That said, it is amazing how well African Americans and Mexican Americans did in the Corps. I worked with several African American and Mexican American leaders in the Corps, including a Corps Commander named Guttierez, and Henry Cisneros, who was Band Commander. They really did well, especially in what most people would call a racist environment. They would come in and prove themselves to their peers, to the class above them and the class below them.

The first African American commander was, we used to call him "Fast Eddie." Eddie Taylor. He was commander of the First Battalion, which if you had to point to a major unit, and say which was the most racist, you would have said the First Battalion was.

IT: I heard that some corps units would do chants that had racial epithets in them.

MC: If a racial epithet was heard by a bull in the Trigon, or somebody on staff, action would be taken. All right? It would be rare for someone at the unit level would report something like that because people just don't do that. It's kind of staff versus unit level, with the staff being the enforcers. People on staff get less serious about enforcement as you go down. People on Corps staff are very serious, people on brigade or wing staff level are pretty serious, battalion or group staff are less serious.

We took the units we considered the most trouble, and put them in our dorm with Corps staff and battalion staff. So that one of us could at least get out the door and see what was going on. To a certain extent it's like a big game.

IT: You think that's how it is now.

MC: Yeah, pretty much. There are certain things that get started, and then continue and evolve. That business with Fish Drill Team [the violent hazing episodes publicized in the nineties], I mean, I was shocked. It was bizarre. I mean, who ever came up with that? None of that went on in Fish Drill Team when I was here. We had four guys on Fish Drill Team in our unit, and none of them said anything like that.

You come back after so many years, and they're doing stuff that they never did when you were here. You don't know where it came from.

IT: It seems it got a little relaxed in the seventies, eighties, and nineties, as far as hazing and alcohol are concerned. But it seems like they're trying to crack down in the last couple years. No more than forty push-ups, and absolutely no Confederate flags. No tolerance for sexual harassment.

MC: This was not a refuge for die-hard Southerners.

IT: It was a serious university.

MC: There wasn't any air conditioning. And it was not a freshman privilege to have a fan. Every single solitary sophomore is watching as many freshmen as possible. Anything they can see to criticize, boom! Whatchoo doing this for? Whatchoo doing that for? Why'd you do this? What is this? Go over there! And it's all day long, like that. And it's all night long. You go out in the hall, if there's ten upperclassmen in the hall, you got to speak to them by name, if there's twenty, you got to speak to every one of them by name. If there's some upperclassmen from some other units visiting, you got to run over there and whip out. And then that guy's going to expect you to know his name if you see him anywhere on campus! Can you imagine? Can you imagine trying to study in that kind of atmosphere?

IT: (pause) no.

MC: You're sitting there studying your chemistry. You got to go the bathroom. You walk out into the hall, you've got to rattle all these names off right off the top of your head. Then you go back to study.

IT: Should Bonfire be abolished, reformed, or kept as it is?

MC: [. . .] Why are we wasting our time talking about Bonfire when we should be talking about universal health care or something? Or campaign finance reform. It's like clutter. They're filling the pages of newspapers and magazines with this Bonfire stuff, I mean— Of course it should be gotten rid of, it should've been done away with a long time ago. Of course, it's . . . it's a *sinful* waste of resources. And now it's been a grotesque waste of human life.

It's a God-awful, horrible, crying shame that twelve young people had to die to finally bring an end to this Bonfire thing. Personally, I believe that it's a case of gross criminal negligence on the part of the Texas A&M Administration. This was the proverbial "accident waiting to happen!" It was inevitable. It was just a matter of time. Every year they have crossed their fingers and rolled the dice. It finally caught up to them!

However, it's not only the Texas A&M Administration! Other entities in the Texas State Government bear responsibility for this criminal negligence. Texas state law enforcement authorities should have shut the thing down at least as soon as federal and state environmental and pollution laws were enacted. The "executives" of every Texas state agency with such responsibilities are also "responsible."

What about the Legislature? The A&M Bonfire has been going on for a long time. It's not as if they didn't know that it was happening. I don't think that they can be excused. The Legislature should have taken action to have the laws enforced long ago.

With so many "state" government entities bearing various degrees of responsibility, it should be very obvious that the "state" government of Texas, as a whole, is responsible for the deaths. This brings us to one of the major problems with government today, Sovereign Immunity. In the late 1800s the judicial branches of the state governments followed the lead of the Federal Judiciary. They resurrected the archaic monarchial idea and declared that under this concept, Sovereign Immunity, the state could not be sued without its permission. The states and their entities became immune from the law because it is virtually impossible to get the required permission.

Obviously, the Bonfire thing should not and cannot continue as before. Unless and until it can become something truly creative and constructive, as befits the third or forth largest institution of higher education in the United States, it must be abolished. If the students and faculty are truly serious about honoring those who have died, they can, in memoriam, reform the "tradition"!

IT: What do you think of the Bonfire debate?

MC: Nobody will speak their mind. Nobody will say what they think. There is an underlying atmosphere of fear at Texas A&M because of all the stuff they've seen and experienced. One faculty member I spoke to recently had a son who was a freshman in the Corps. He would complain loudly about the Corps. A year later, he said to me, "We have to be careful about the traditions of the University." It took only one year to change his position.

IT: The people who oppose Bonfire do so secretly out of fear, you're saying. The Corps would certainly be upset about an end to the Bonfire.

MC: A lot of people say that it would be really bad for the Corps. Abolishing Bonfire would be the best thing for the Corps. The Corps loses more people to the Bonfire than anything else.

IT: *The time and energy they have to devote to it contribute to their dropping out of the Corps. What do you think should be done instead of the traditional Bonfire?*

MC: Professor George Mann, who has been on the A&M faculty since I was an undergraduate, suggested that a memorial with an everlasting flame be erected at the Bonfire site, that the natural resources and human labor be invested in Habitat for Humanity, and that the houses built be dedicated as part of a ceremony at the memorial each year. There have been similar recommendations by other individuals. Such an approach might even act as a catalyst to inspire similar activities on other Colleges and Universities across the nation.

IT: *What do you think are the chances of anything like that happening at Texas A&M?*

MC: It seems to me, if it was put to a vote, I think a majority of students would vote to change it to a Habitat for Humanity effort. And why is that? Because most of them don't work on Bonfire. Most of them are not that emotionally attached to it. Okay? You have 43,000 students here. How many work on Bonfire? Two thousand, three thousand, four thousand? It's really a rather small minority. So I think the more people that can be brought into the discussion, the debate, it would be best. I think it would be best if it could be taken out of the realm of emotionality, and into the realm of the kind of reason and logic that's supposed to be being practiced at an institution of higher education. Especially one of the flagship universities in one of the biggest states in the country.

IT: *What needs to be done?*

MC: Have you seen the new statue of General James Earl Rudder? Have you read the inscription under the statue? Go read it.

[The new statue of President General Earl Rudder (who climbed the cliffs of Normandy on D-Day) is located to the west of Rudder Tower. On the main campus, only the statue of former President Sul Ross compares to the Rudder statue, the inscription of which reads:

Heroic Soldier and World War II Military Leader
Commissioner of the General Land Office of Texas
Sixteenth President of Texas A&M University
Third President of the TAMU System

At a critical juncture in the history of Texas A&M, President Rudder's vision, leadership, tenacity, courage and commitment to excellence in education caused the university's doors to be opened to women and established the foundation for Texas A&M to become an institution of national and international prominence. Major General Rudder demonstrated an uncommon ability to inspire and lead people to exceptional achievement, and with an uncompromising dedication to integrity.

MC: They've made a hero out of him. He made membership in the Corps of Cadets non-compulsory, and he allowed women into the university. When he was the president of Texas A&M, the majority of the cadets hated him. Since I was Corps Commander—the top student commander—I was the one who had to take the Corps to hear his speeches.

Whenever they heard they were going to go hear Rudder, the cadets would complain and holler. And during his speeches, they'd fall asleep. He's the type of person, when he's talking across a conference table, when he's talking one-on-one, he's really good. The speeches were not the greatest, but a big part of his job was just to get people to listen to him.

IT: *The students hated when he announced that women were allowed at A&M.*

MC: Now he's a big hero. The kind of leadership needed now is the real leadership that President (General) Rudder displayed when he made the decisions to admit women to the University and to make the Corps noncompulsory. Certainly, they were very unpopular decisions at that time. It is highly probable that a large majority of Former Students were adamantly opposed to such policies.

We need the leadership to say, "It's time to put an end to Bonfire as we know it, to take that energy, excitement, and material and turn it into something constructive."

Introduction to the Conclusion

The final section of the book includes four chapters. The first chapter sums up the debate about the Bonfire's future using a "For" versus "Against" format. The second chapter talks of the cultural collapse represented by the Bonfire collapse, and how various aspects of the Aggie culture have contributed to the collapse. The two conclusive essays consider the possible meanings of Bonfire and the Aggie Spirit, and ask how we might stay true to that spirit in the years to come.

The Bonfire Debate

The arguments for and against Bonfire hinge largely on the assumptions one makes about the purpose of Bonfire and of higher education. Presented here are some of the arguments for and against the continuation of the tradition. The arguments are divided by subject, and each includes an analysis.

Education and Academics

Against Bonfire

Legend has it that a Redpot once earned a 0.00 grade point average during the semester of Bonfire. There are no statistics for it, but it is common knowledge that some students drop out of school as a result of spending too much time working on Bonfire. Many professors notice a lowering of grades and attendance during Bonfire-building season.

For Bonfire

The extracurricular activity may force students to manage their time better. Furthermore, the leadership skills learned while organizing one's dorm or Corps unit for Bonfire construction are invaluable. And if one is not learning to lead, one learns cooperation. Besides, every extra-curricular activity requires time and energy, so why should Bonfire be singled out?

254

Analysis

Bonfire teaches leadership skills to its leaders. Traditionally, those skills sometimes include safety enforcement, inspiring others to work hard, and organizing large groups of people to perform complicated tasks. Other "leadership skills" learned through the Bonfire tradition have included encouragement of hazing, ignoring University regulations, and ordering acts of violence on the disliked.

Of course, it is the responsibility of each student to make choices about his or her academic career. But corps outfits are required to work on the Bonfire, often making the Bonfire a required detriment to their studies. Although it is the responsibility of the student to take this into account upon entering the Corps, it is also the responsibility of Texas A&M to make academics its first priority, even within the ranks of the Corps of Cadets.

Texas A&M aims to become one of the top public universities of the nation by 2020. Traditionally, the University has used the Bonfire in its promotional materials. The Bonfire helps to attract a great number of students to the university, some of whom are of the highest academic standing. Some of the students who died building the Bonfire were attracted to A&M because of it traditions and rituals.

But the Bonfire also adds to the image of Texas A&M being a university that puts a disproportionate amount of student resources into the maintenance of tradition and the improvement of athletic performance. This helps to shoo away some academically gifted students. Texas A&M prides itself on the number of merit scholars it attracts, but it does so largely through doling out huge scholarships. Of course, improving A&M's academic standing has more to do with concentrating resources on faculty, research, and teaching than on ridding the university of Bonfire.

Nevertheless, abolishing Bonfire would increase studying time both before and after the year 2020.

The Environment and Waste

For Bonfire

A Redpot in a debate about the Bonfire said in 1994, "What's the purpose of keeping old growth forests around if you can't use them? Why not get them out of the way and plant forests you can use and are worth something to the population?" All the trees cut down for Bonfire would almost certainly have been cut down in the first place, and always for an economic purpose (benefiting the owner of the land). Why not use the trees for an important tradition? Every tradition and every mode of entertainment requires the sacrifice of time, energy, and natural resources. Using thousands of trees and hundreds of gallons of fuel on a Bonfire is not a waste when it is an important tradition involving tens of thousands of people.

"Oh, hell," said a 1978 Redpot to Texas Monthly in 1990, "if they want to build houses [instead of Bonfire], then they can get their butts over there and haul their own wood. No one's stopping them. Just don't try to push our butts around." If people wish to apply local resources to social needs, they should do it themselves.

Against Bonfire

Scott Spitler of Aggies Against Bonfire was quoted in the Austin American Statesman in 1991 as saying, "Using all these trees is such a waste. People have the attitude, 'They're going to be cut down anyway, so let's have a party with it.' There are people in Bryan-College Station five miles away who don't even have enough heat for the winter to survive. They have to go to the church to stay warm." Because Bonfire uses trees that would have been cut down anyway does not free the major local economic entity—Texas A&M and its student population—from its responsibilities of using local resources wisely. Hundreds of gallons of fuel used for burning and transport would not have been used "anyway." Over 125,000 labor-hours would not have been used "anyway." And various fingers would not have been amputated, and bones been broken, "anyway." The University directly or indirectly spends tens of thousands of state government funds on administrative, material, labor, and insurance costs for the Bonfire. A state-sponsored undertaking as large as Bonfire should somehow benefit the larger community; Bonfire workers could build houses or clean up the environment.

Analysis

The point may be moot in a few decades. Forests are growing thinner and farther between all over the country. Accelerating development, disappearing woodlands, and endangered species laws will make the hundreds of acres of forest (within an hour's drive and close to a highway) needed for Bonfire harder and harder to find.

In 1996, Texas A&M had to advertise to find a landowner to volunteer his forest. In such a scenario, the University risks violating its "rule" of clearing only forests that would have been cleared anyway. How long will it be until the Former Students Association will have to raise money to pay a landowner for his forest's trees? And how long after that will forested land be so rare and valuable that landowners will refuse to have their precious trees cut down for any price?

Having grown up in Bryan-College Station as it has doubled and re-doubled and doubled again in size, I have watched the forests, range land, armadillos, turtles, rabbits, frogs, unusual insects, and trees steadily disappear from my hometown. Aggieland's environmental degradation is real and accelerating. The question in the long run will not be whether burning 8,000 trees is a waste or an environmental hazard. It will be, "how do we manufacture or hydroponically grow 8000 trees for Bonfire?"

Safety

Against Bonfire

Twelve students have died building Bonfire. We should not risk any more lives.

For Bonfire

We can build a steel centerpole. Our best engineers and construction experts can help design and oversee construction of the Bonfire. Students can go through extensive training before cutting and stacking.

The tradition of the running of the bulls in Spain often results in runners being gored. Traditional Southern food often makes people fat and gives them heart attacks. Many traditions are "dangerous," but that does not mean we should stop them. People die driving to a college football game. Should we abolish football?

Bonfire can be made safer than a college football game.

Analysis

Although it took the death of twelve students, Aggies now know Bonfire construction is extremely dangerous. What precautions will the University take to protect students from themselves and from Bonfire accidents? If the University is prepared to invest the tens or hundreds of thousands of dollars each year to hire the engineers, foremen, and training specialists to properly design and oversee the construction of Bonfire, then perhaps construction can indeed be made safer than a drive on the freeway.

Safety is the simplest issue that Texas A&M has to tackle. Unfortunately, the University has waited until now to tackle it. However directly the University may be able to solve the safety problem, it may not be wise to trust the University to do so.

Tradition

For Bonfire

Bonfire is a tradition. It should burn on.

Against Bonfire

The all-log Bonfire was created in the 1940's. The multi-layered Bonfire came into being in the 1960's. Before 1943, Bonfires were relatively short heaps of trash. Before 1909, there was no Bonfire. If students wanted to be true to the original tradition, they would burn a small trash bonfire or none at all. The point is that traditions are created and destroyed by people. Traditions evolve. The Bonfire tradition should not be sacred simply because it is a tradition. The more important question is, what purpose does it serve?

Analysis

Traditions evolve, but they do so for reasons. If there is no need to destroy Bonfire, why can it not evolve into a safer, alcohol-free, hazing-free Bonfire? Such a Bonfire strips the tradition of almost everything that makes it fun—everything except for the camaraderie and unity involved in hard work. Wouldn't such a Bonfire then be evolving into an even more purified manifestation of the Aggie Spirit?

Traditions evolve according to those who make them evolve. And traditionally, it is the combination of red-ass students, University administration, and former students that "evolve" or reform the Bonfire in reaction to pressure from students, faculty, and community members. The process of tradition-evolution, then, has traditionally involved many people who are supposedly "anti-tradition."

There is something to be said for tradition. Just what it is, must be said and said now, without fear and without holding back. The tradition of Bonfire will evolve, and the greater the diversity of voices "evolving" it, the better. Get your two cents in, Aggies.

Cultural Collapse

Aggie culture was the central contributing factor to the collapse of the Bonfire. As we have seen through the histories and interviews presented in this book, the Aggie culture not only contributes to making the Bonfire more dangerous and divisive, but also contributes to a more dangerous and divisive Aggieland in general.

Student Independence

In the interviews with former Corps Commander Carroll, we see a Corps of Cadets in the sixties that is downright hostile toward efforts at being controlled and dominated by Corps staff. We also see and administration that takes on a "crisis management" approach of handling things. As the Wendy Stock interview showed, this crisis management and damage control method of managing the Corps allows for problems to fester—such as sexual assault and harassment—until they boil over into embarrassing national spectacles. Bonfire was a Corps-dominated tradition until the 1970's. The Bonfire adapted all of the misogyny, hazing, violence, rowdyism, and anti-authority attitude from the Corps while becoming more and more independent from the behavioral constraints of Corps staff. It became a student-run operation while maintaining and perhaps embellishing upon the more dangerous traditions of the Corps of Cadets. In the past three decades, the Bonfire could have used a military-styled crackdown on discipline, but it had become independent of such constraints and was run by an A&M administrator who respected a hands-off tradition. As the interview with students Karen Kortum and Kim Ryle showed, the average Bonfire worker rarely sees this administrator.

Furthermore, the "boys will be boys" attitude that has accompanied the culture of student independence does not work when there are girls around because the boys often forget the rule about not hitting girls (or harassing or insulting them for that matter).

The dedication to student independence allowed for the degradation of the design and construction of Bonfire without the safeguard of faculty checks and balances.

Corps of Cadets

The driving force behind mainstream Texas A&M culture remains the Corps of Cadets. Commandant Ted Hopgood has attempted to reform the Corps in recent years by limiting the number of push-ups a cadet can be punished with and outlawing the Confederate flag. But A&M history shows that the traditions of hazing, violence, and misogyny come and go like the tides. Matt Carroll was shocked by the Fish Drill Team's hazing practices of the nineties, which were not present, according to him, in the sixties. But they were present in earlier decades.

If the A&M administration wishes to restrain Aggie culture, it would be wise to keep vigilant watch over Corps of Cadets culture.

Misogyny

Former Corps Commander Matt Carroll said that after I mentioned the word misogyny to him, he had to look it up in a dictionary. According to him, there was little hostility towards women in the times when Bonfire and the Corps were purely male domains. Wendy Stock mentioned some reasons for male hostility towards female "encroachment." Whatever the reason, women are here to stay. Many of them enjoy immensely the Bonfire building process. It is unknown how much of the misogyny at Texas A&M spills over into the surrounding Aggieland community.

Racism

A few years ago, I saw a truckload of Corps members driving through my neighborhood screaming racial epithets at people's houses. As the interview with Tex Williams shows, such images make going out in the woods under the direction of "Texan men" unappealing to many minorities. As the Bonfire history shows, there have been racial incidents during construction and burning that could drive minorities away for years at a time. As late as 1998, anti-black racial epithets were spotted on helmets of Bonfire builders who were regulating onlookers during the burning of Bonfire 1998. From the history of Texas A&M, with one of its legendary coaches apparently belonging to the local Ku Klux Klan, one might deduce that racism in Aggieland is an organic mass shared by both the university and the community.

Suppression of Dissent

As Bonfire history and the interview with Danny Yeager show, the suppression of dissent and the self-censorship of those wanting to criticize the university and its traditions does spill into the surrounding community. No Aggieland resident wishes to be ostracized or to lose business.

The structural engineering professors of Texas A&M may have wanted to avoid the consequences of criticizing a University that won't listen anyway. Among the many engineers who thought the Bonfire structure unstable, only Teddy Hirsch went through the trouble of suggesting changes to the Bonfire structure, and he failed to get the administration to listen.

Tradition

The greatest tradition at Texas A&M is tradition itself. Aggies will go to great length to protect a tradition. Such protection and rigid codification of rituals often betrays the very spirit of the tradition. More practically, in the case of the Bonfire, protection of it – along with its auxiliary traditions of hazing (often involving alcohol), drinking alcohol in and of itself, and the protection of Bonfire workers from troubles with the law – has led to the devolution of the tradition. More public scrutiny would have surely forced Texas A&M to more strictly enforce its own regulations.

Zealous protectors of tradition have made it taboo to criticize Bonfire. According to Mike Ward of the Austin American-Statesman, some of the investigators have met with resistance from student interviewees, who may be protecting the tradition. Such secrecy and stonewalling as well as the stigma attached to criticizing Bonfire may have led the Bonfire Commission to establish a Bonfire Hotline where callers can confidentially reveal what goes on at Bonfire cut and stack, and what may have gone wrong in 1999. It is sickly ironic that those who claim to love tradition the most may be at fault for contributing to the endangerment of themselves and others who stack and wire Bonfire.

The collapse of the 1999 Bonfire represents a collapse in the Aggie culture. No longer can we go on blindly, unquestioningly following tradition. No longer can we sing the "boys will be boys" chorus and crack down only softly on violations of school policy and human dignity. We can no longer do so, because, in the heart of every Aggie, it would seem, such acts of negligence and ignorance would betray the twelve young people now committed to the ground.

The Spirit of Bonfire

From the outside looking in, you can't understand it; from the inside looking out, you can't explain it. And so the saying goes. What is "it"?

It is the Spirit of Aggieland. What, then, is that? According to "The Spirit of Aggieland," a favorite Aggie "fight" song, "there is a spirit that can never be told/It's the spirit of Aggieland/We are the Aggies/the Aggies are we/True to each other as Aggie can be/We've got to fight, boys/we've got to fight/We've got to fight for the maroon and white!"

The spirit can never be told. Anything larger than life itself cannot be explained by words. Words, after all, define, they limit, they reduce. They are finite and to a certain degree mutable yet mechanical. They mean different things to different people, and thus expressing something with words can distort it, even if it can be put into words. The Aggie Spirit is beyond words, and words should not be applied to it, lest its inexpressible organic infinitude be limited or distorted.

Although the Aggie Spirit cannot be told, manifestations of them can be. The tradition of Bonfire is considered a manifestation of the Aggie Spirit. The way some people describe it, it may be the ultimate manifestation of Aggie Spirit. If so, then examining the spirit and symbolism of Bonfire may lead us to a truer understanding of the Aggie Spirit. Of course, the Bonfire spirit may not be the Aggie Spirit. The utlimate goal, it seems to me, is to grasp, feel, and internalize the Aggie Spirit, the true Aggie Spirit, so that Bonfire can be changed, reformed, destroyed and remade, or preserved as it is, in order to more sincerely serve this spirit.

Bonfire as Family

When asked what Bonfire was all about, one co-chair began with one simple word: family. Bonfire co-chairs, crew chiefs and pots can trace their families back more generations than the average monarch. The co-chair went on to tell me that she could name all the co-chairs that preceded her. She told me that, like a family heirloom, the co-chair pot is passed down from "mother" to "daughter" each year. And each year, the co-chair writes something on the pot, something meaningful or humorous, and so this history is retained literally on the head of the current co-chair as she works at stack or cut.

The seminal mother—the first co-chair of this lineage—even telephoned the current co-chair after the Bonfire tragedy to ask if she could help them in any way. Such are the admirable qualities of any family. Family takes care of family. And in this way, Bonfire does do what it espouses to do – unite Aggies. The only catch is, of course, that it unites only the Aggies that work on Bonfire, and those that feel part of the Bonfire tradition.

Bonfire, then, is a family tradition. Even if some students begin building houses instead of Bonfire, it must still be built. Builders cannot forsake their ancestors.

Family is great. But family is simply the form of the Bonfire hierarchy. Form follows function. What is the function of the Bonfire family?

Bonfire as War

Bonfire is the burning desire of every Aggie to beat the hell outta t.u. It is also the ever-burning flame of love every Aggie holds in his heart for his university.

His university—Texas A&M—has traditionally been largely a military institution, in practice and in spirit. The Bonfire is the manifestation of both sides of the A&M-UT war. We love A&M and we will beat the hell outta t.u. Like in any war, such a dialectic instills an us-versus-them attitude that builds great camaraderie between one's comrades. But Bonfire is not only war-like in its sense of enmity, but also in its dangers. Aggies are not only fighting Longhorns. They are killing trees, weathering the elements, enduring the dangers of axes, driving back to campus under precarious circumstances, and dangling from ropes at dozens of feet above the ground as they wire logs. Aggies must rely on each other to survive in this war, which has real dangers (sometimes involving other Aggies). The closeness such cooperation fosters must be similar to that which veterans feel (more intensely perhaps) with the soldiers with whom they fought side by side.

Bonfire as an Expression of Manhood

Although most Aggies would rather not lose a finger or break a leg, as sometimes occurs while building Bonfires, the possibility of mutilation, immolation, or amputation is exciting and produces rites of passage that may not exist for young American men anywhere else. The Bonfire rose out of a military tradition wherein cadets had to prove themselves. Bonfire at one point was one of the many rituals through which young Ags proved their manhood, or tested it, or simply became a man. After all, Texas A&M's job, and the Corps of Cadet's job, was in part to make Texas farm boys into disciplined, logical, intelligent, respectful law-abiding men who could and would die and kill for their nation. And Texas A&M was good at it, in part because of the rigorous training, exertion, and leadership involved in building the world's largest fire. Those who couldn't handle cutting and stacking a seventy, ninety, or one-hundred-and-ten foot Bonfire in the span of two weeks dropped out, failing as military men. Those who could, could graduate both as soldiers and men of learning.

Now that most of the boys of Bonfire come from the city, it is perhaps even more important as a rite of passage. A city boy who drives a pick-up truck but hasn't loaded a bale of hay or broken the neck of a single chicken may need to prove that he's more country than the rural boy who has been digging in the dirt all his life, wishing to move to the big city. The suburban kid, in agricultural terms again, may need to prove that he's as tough as that immigrant kid who breaks his back in the fields picking Texas grapefruits all day.

Now that Bonfire has become co-ed, Bonfire is also about girls proving their womanhood. But it is a different kind of womanhood. Building Bonfire, for some, shows that they can play with the big boys. Bonfire is a man's game, and women can prove, at least to themselves, that they are as tough, strong, and perhaps even callous as men.

Bonfire as "Something Bigger Than Us," or is it a Party?

Students have described Bonfire as "something bigger" than themselves, meaning they have found deeper symbolic meaning and historical or cultural significance in the annual building and burning of Bonfire. Indeed Bonfire has a history older than most students' grandmothers. And the mythology of Bonfire has included trials, tribulations, controversies, and threats to its existence that may be compared to the convoluted struggles of Greek gods.

Most rituals have to do with God, survival and life events having to do with growing up and reproducing. They include planting and harvesting rituals, marriage, birth, and death rituals, and religious ceremonies. Bonfire is a war ritual before a football game, and a celebration of the unity and brotherhood between Aggies. In some ways, its most significant meaning is circular. It is a celebration of being an Aggie, and being an Aggie means being, among other things, "as true to each other as Aggies can be" while doing such things as building Bonfire. In other words, being an Aggie means loving one's university and its students. But for what purpose are we being Aggies? To continue traditions. What purpose do those traditions have? To show that we are being true Ags.

Why have students chosen to project their sense of meaning on the building and burning of a tower of logs? Because we are Aggies, and that's what Ags do. But also because it has little obvious meaning. Or, rather, it has a meaning that is not obvious at all. In a world in which human behavior can be deconstructed, analyzed, and explained in scientific terms, Bonfire holds a cryptic, secret truth. It seems silly to the outside world, but to those who build it, it is almost sacred, and inexplicably so. And that is precisely why, perhaps, it seems so magical. You can't explain it! How many things in this science-centric world can you apply such a statement?

Bonfire is not a big party. It means more to the people who build it than a party. And yet Bonfire construction takes on aspects of festivity, sometimes of a party that is out of control. And the same blanket explanation of its being inexplicable is still applied. When the "inexplicable" explanation is used in these situations, it comes off as being an excuse to do whatever inexplicable thing one desires.

Therein lies a physical and a symbolic danger of Bonfire. To lose oneself to the fun of Bonfire, and to forget that it isn't about Bonfire; it's about the Aggie Spirit.

It ain't about Building a Bonfire, it's about the Aggie Spirit

I love Aggieland. I can't help it. This love is not something I learned, so I cannot unlearn it. I was born here. I was raised here. Like so many boys before me, I learned to be a man here. I learned in healthy ways; I learned in harrowing ways. As a college student, I found my voice here. And again it was because the university educated me about an outside world I had never known (since I had never lived or traveled much outside of College Station). The university paid for my education and then some. The university challenged me to speak my piece and allowed me platforms. But the university culture also alienated me from my own love of my hometown and college. The Aggie culture often made me want to not care one way or another about Aggieland. Apathy, not hate, is the opposite of love.

But I cannot kill my heart and its feelings for my first true home. And like I said, I cannot help that because Aggieland is like blood kin. I cannot decide to not care.

I never worked on Bonfire. I never had a "father" pass down a pot to me. But I did have the university, and it passed down its own hat – a graduation cap. And with graduation from Texas A&M comes responsibilities. My first is to the truth.

And the truth is, Texas A&M is more than a university. It has its own sense of independence and unity. But such cohesiveness is largely achieved through traditional rituals and sporting events. It is not achieved through a strong sense of purpose or philosophy. The Aggie Spirit has successfully dodged definition, but as a result has too often also strayed from its true self. The ineffability of the Spirit, though, lends itself to inclusion, and I did not realize this during the time I attended Texas A&M as a student.

Indeed, the same culture that I wanted to be a part of as a child sometimes alienated me. But as I researched the Bonfire, and as I read all the letters and opinions of people who care so much about the future of the university, I realized that I am one of them. And I also thought back to my days as an undergraduate at Texas A&M, and I remember what we used to do in an active campus organization of which I was an integral part. And I remembered Eric Brown.

In our organization, we used to protest for human rights and collect money for the United Nation's Children's Fund, and do mock "die-ins" in front of the CIA recruiting table to dramatize their covert slaughter. But we also wanted to do something that would yield tangible, visible, immediate results. So we decided to help poor people fix their houses. And it was a student named Eric Brown who volunteered to organize all this. He would keep in contact with the local Social Security Administration to find out who needed help in their homes. Every two or three weeks, Eric would tell us about an old lady who needed some help, and we would all agree to meet at her house on a Saturday or Sunday morning. When we got to these houses, most of which were located in north Bryan and close to Highway 21, some us would be amazed at the degree of rural poverty these old women were living in (I wasn't surprised because I had grown up two blocks from people living in shacks, and in the middle of College Station). Some of these women we went to help didn't even have indoor plumbing. They were walking up steps without railings, and the cold Texas northers would blow in through the holes in their walls. Ironically, we would tear down outhouses for these women.

Many of these old women were lonely, and would tell us stories about their younger days, picking cotton until *and after* their fingers bled. I thought to myself at that time that these were the true Aggies, those working in the fields, and yet they had never had an opportunity to attend A&M. Also during this time, I helped an elderly homeless woman find housing and obtain food stamps. But because of her mental problems, she subsequently lost her housing and returned to the streets of College Station. The problem of homelessness struck home years later when a blood relative of mine, also elderly, who had defected from China during the Tiananmen massacre, ended up living in a homeless shelter for months as he attempted to obtain affordable housing.

So it felt good, back then, and it was good, to do something about improving people's housing. And it was made a great deal easier because Eric had taken personal responsibility for organizing all of these excursions. He would lead us to the dilapidated structures and supply or find donators for most of the tools. He was the first to arrive and the last to leave. When we didn't get the work done in time, Eric would come back the next day to finish it himself. He organized this activity (or campaign, if you will) for three years. Now isn't that the Aggie Spirit?

So when Aggies started suggesting that students build homes instead of Bonfires, the vision that kept creeping into my mind was that of dozens of Eric Brown's leading thousands of good Aggies to make things better in Aggieland. I kept asking myself, what if we had, instead of five thousand Bonfire builders, just a hundred Eric Brown's? What would Aggieland be like then?

And as the weeks passed, and controversy after controversy about Bonfire construction became public, I wondered what the Aggies were waiting for. The suggestion is out there. It's a wonderful idea. It holds components of a great Aggie tradition – acts of honor, physical and mental exertion, and something to whoop it up about. Those who wish to see an alternative to Bonfire must do as Gandhi says and live the world they wish to see.

Bonfire will stay or go, and it may or may not remain in this new millennium a valid expression of the Aggie Spirit. We must debate the Aggie Spirit. We must talk about it. But we must also vote with our feet and speak through our actions, as Aggies have done throughout history. Only through the concerted and concentrated efforts of the Aggieland community will the Aggie Spirit rise from tragedy and be reborn.

Addendum

I first printed and published this book in late March 2000. By May, the book went into a second printing to meet demand. The first two printings of this book included a bibliography in this space. I could not fit both my nine-page bibliography and this addendum, so I have made the full (and new) bibliography available at the publishing company website: www.arrriveat.com/theitworks.

Soon after the publication of this book, I hand-delivered a copy to the office of the Bonfire Commission, still working hard on its investigation. That day, I met with Kent Lietzau (of McKenzie and Associates), one of the chiefs of staff of the Bonfire Commission's investigation team. Upon examination of the book, Lietzau procured from me a total of eighteen copies. He told me after the publication of the Commission report that the books were sent to all of the Bonfire Commission members, members of the investigation team, and Texas A&M University President Ray M. Bowen.

Within the first few weeks of publication, my book was not the most popular among some Aggie readers. I had said things that many people were not prepared to hear. Both my name and my book were sometimes spoken of in a harsh light on internet bulletin boards and (I'm sure) in private conversation. My heart literally palpitated as I read some of the "criticism," and as people simply walked up to me and scowled. I am fully prepared to take legitimate criticism and to listen to logical arguments. But I have difficulties relaxing when I see my name and book distorted and misrepresented, especially by people who have not read my book.

The criticism and anger seemed to dissipate first after the Commission report was published, and then further after President Bowen made his speech on the future of Bonfire. I am grateful for the many remarks and letters I have received from Aggie readers who have understood my purpose, recognized the importance of the book, and have appreciated my hard work. As I stated in the introduction, I set out in writing this book to inform the debate on Bonfire and to ask questions about our Aggie culture. I believe I have succeeded in a most unexpected manner. In addition to speaking to everyday Aggies and Texans, this book may have influenced the Bonfire Commission itself. I have been told by both reporters and readers (and I agree with them) that the Commission's findings about the organizational and cultural roots of the Bonfire collapse, published a month after this book, are remarkably similar to my own.

John Comstock

"He came into the world two and a half month months early, weighed two and a half pounds, and he hasn't stopped fighting since," said Dixie Edwards of her son, John Comstock. Indeed, two and a half hours past midnight on November 18, 1999, John Comstock began the fight of his life. After being extricated from underneath thousands of pounds of Bonfire logs, Comstock struggled to survive, under sedation and on a respirator in the intensive care unit of the College Station Medical Center. A few days later, Comstock's heart stopped for ten minutes.

But John Comstock didn't stop fighting. "I think the good Lord has been watching over him," Ed Edwards, Comstock's stepfather told *The Eagle*, "Either that, or he was so ornery that He didn't want to keep him."

Comstock had leapt high hurdles in the past. His father passed away while he was a sophomore at Jesuit College Preperatory School in Dallas.

"And ironically, even though he's about 5 foot 6 and not very fast, he decided to go out for pole vaulting his senior year," said Rev. Phillip Postell, president of the school. "I didn't see him complete a jump over 8 feet, but he was optimistic about it." Postell called Comstock "maybe the most unpredictable, mysterious pole vaulter the school's ever seen."

In high school, Comstock served as both a "Big Brother" to younger students, and as a referee in the Richardson youth soccer league.

Aggies, Texans, and many people around the nation prayed and hoped for John Comstock's recovery. Texans donated blood to Comstock, who underwent half a dozen surgeries. People from around the country sent cards and gifts to his family. Shortly after the Bonfire collapse, I attended a prayer session for Mr. Comstock. Hundreds gathered before the Sul Ross statue on the Texas A&M campus on a cold blustery evening. After a communal prayer was said, students huddled in groups of five or seven and prayed with their hands aclasp.

After over two and a half months in intensive care, Comstock was transferred to a Dallas hospital for physical therapy. In mid-February, he began taking Texas A&M biomedical science classes over the internet. On April 14, 2000, after nearly five months in hospitals, John Comstock, escorted by his family, returned to his home in Richardson, Texas. He hopes to attend Texas A&M in the fall of 2000.

The Bonfire Commission Report

Much of the Aggieland community wanted to hear the Bonfire Commission report before passing judgment on the future of the Bonfire. Many people I spoke to put their faith in the Bonfire Commission to discover and publish the final truth about the Bonfire collapse. In the days leading up to May 2, speculation was rampant, as the Bonfire Commission had successfully kept its work secret. A March Battalion article stated that the Commission had already uncovered the cause of the collapse, but during my conversation with Kent Lietzau in early April, he insisted that the Commission was still working on the answers. Texas A&M had given the Commission 1.8 million dollars to find those answers.

On the morning of May 2, *The Battalion* published a front-page story detailing how students had broken the decree of the university administration by beginning preparations for Bonfire 2000. Dormitories had elected Traditions officers, those students in charge of Bonfire organizing. Bonfire Pots had conducted pot-passing ceremonies. And hazing was part of some of these Bonfire preparations.

In the afternoon, I drove with my mother to Reed Arena in West Campus. It was a bright beautiful day, and Aggies seemed both relaxed and anxious as they entered the arena. Near the main entrance, several Aggies stood with pens and petitions to "Keep the Fire Burning." It was hard to avoid these signature-takers, but both my mother and I did so. I had made a commitment, as the author of this book, to avoid any public commitment for or against the continuance of Bonfire.

The arena was filled with students. On the arena floor sat the families of the victims. As the commissioners summed up their findings, the students remained mostly quiet. It was during the press conference following the Commission's presentation that many students hissed and whooped in reaction to various statements. Many students cheered as Commission Head Leo Linbeck, Jr. and President Bowen implied that the problems of Bonfire could be solved. Aggies hissed whenever one of the reporters asked the Commissioners to specify who is responsibility for the collapse.

Physical Causes of the Collapse

Dr. Hugh G. Robinson of Houston presented the Commission's findings on the physical causes of the collapse. He showed a computer animation of the sequence of the collapse. The collapse began when wires on the southeast side of the first stack broke. As the logs that these wires had been holding up fell, their absence caused a chain reaction. The second stack shifted and began to fall toward the southeast, causing the third and then fourth stacks to shift and fall. As the second stack shifted and fell, it caused a break in the centerpole between the first and second stacks. As the entire Bonfire stack collapsed, the centerpole snapped in two other places. Although the guy rope pulling it towards the northwest snapped, the other guy ropes did not and pulled the centerpole back from the southeast. The stack fell toward the southeast, and the centerpole fell atop it, pointing to the northwest.

What caused the initial wire breakage on the southeast side of the first stack? The findings of the Bonfire Commission investigation show that a number of factors created an outward force within the first stack that caused the wires to break. These factors compounded each other and had a *multiplier effect* (my term) on each other.

According to the Commission, the most important factor in producing this outward force toward the southeast was wedging. Wedging is the "practice of inserting upper-tier logs into a lower tier during construction." Wedging was thought to increase the forces holding the Bonfire logs together, but it actually had an opposite effect. Second tier logs wedged into the first helped to push the first-tier logs outward. The Commission found that students practiced more wedging in 1998 and 1999, possibly because the increased number of crooked trees allowed for more gaps into which logs could be wedged.

Compounding the effects of wedging was the vertical stacking of Bonfire logs. The 1998 and 1999 Bonfires were built especially vertically. The greater the verticality of the logs, the likelier the chance that any given outward force will push the logs out so much that they break the wires and fall outward. Thus the outward force within the first stack produced by wedging was compounded by its vertical orientation. A more inward-leaning teepee Bonfire would have been sturdier.

Overbuilding of the second stack on the southeast side further compounded the outward force toward the southeast. Because the second stack was built within one foot of the edge of the first stack on the southeast side, the effects of wedging and verticality were further multiplied on that side.

The final main factor compounding the southeastern force within the first stack was the ground slope. The ground sloped slightly over one degree toward the southeast. This may not seem like much, but the Bonfire weighed more than two million pounds (more than two 747 jumbo jets), and the first stack was built perpendicular to this slope, thereby creating a slight lean of the stack, in relation to the forces of gravity. Furthermore, the second stack was built perpendicular to the forces of gravity, thereby adding force to the southeastern lean in the first stack, and also compounding the effects of wedging.

The Commission found that the wires (of .077, .084, and .105-inch diameters and made of carbon steel) were not strong enough to withstand the outward forces within the Bonfire. They found that restraining the outward forces that caused the collapse would have required "vastly stronger wiring." Compounding the weakness of the wires was faulty wiring technique. Students had not followed correct wiring techniques, had not tied enough wire to each log, and/or had not tightened the wires enough.

The Commission stated that had steel cables been tied around the first stack, as had been standard practice since the second 1994 Bonfire (and possibly earlier), the likelihood of a collapse would have been "greatly reduced."

Organizational and Behavioral Causes of the Collapse

Bonfire Commissioner Victoria Callaghan of El Paso presented the organizational and behavioral causes of the Bonfire collapse, and she did so emphatically, winning her few friends in the crowd.

Performance Improvement International (PII) was assigned by the Commission to uncover the organizational and behavioral causes of the Bonfire collapse. The investigators found that cultural, organizational, and behavioral characteristics of the Bonfire building process and the Texas A&M administration were at the root of the Bonfire collapse.

The collapse of the Bonfire was no freak event, no whimsical act of fate. It was the eventual result of a system of construction and construction management that put students at risk of severe injury every year. It was a man-made tragedy, and it could have been prevented by the human beings that organized Bonfire. The Bonfire Commission found four general human causes of the Bonfire collapse:

1. The student leadership in charge of Bonfire construction lacked the knowledge and skills necessary to build a structurally sound Bonfire. For example, Bonfire leaders employed wedging to improve structural integrity and accomplished the opposite. Steel cables

were not wrapped around the stack because they were thought to widen interior air columns and therefore quicken burn time.

2. There are no formal, written Bonfire design plans or construction methodologies. Among the Commission's quotes of student interviews was a deadly duo: "Never questioned the design or safety of Bonfire" and "Bonfire was never built the same way twice." In other words, the Bonfire design changed every year, and no one questioned the sensibility of the changes.

3. A "cultural bias" allowed for a "tunnel vision" among Texas A&M administrators. This tunnel vision impeded the administrators' ability to identify and resolve potentially dangerous construction designs and methodologies. The tunnel vision, according to the Commission, is due to "a cultural bias in which legitimate courses of action outside past experience or contrary to the University's pre-disposition are often not considered." For example, the 1994 collapse was considered a sign of the Bonfire's strength, instead of a sign that its design was faulty. The quick burn times were seen as a problem because Aggies want Bonfire to burn past midnight; the quick burn times were not seen as signs of weak wire strength.

4. The Texas A&M administration overseeing Bonfire maintained a reactive management style rather than a proactive management system. As a result of this reactive style, administrators never systematically analyzed and reformed the Bonfire building process (including its design). Rather, administrators dealt with problems as they arose, using very specific band-aids to solve very specific problems long enough so that the Bonfire could be built and burned that year. The Commission drew a table in its report showing the difference between the A&M administration's reactive style and a more ideal proactive management system. Fire complaints, excessive drinking, excessive injuries, a truck accident fatality, and harassment led to the specific administrative reactions of (respectively) a height restriction, an alcohol awareness campaign, a safety training program, rules for riding in trucks, and punishment. In a proactive management system, these problems would have led to "comprehensive action to address what appears to be a larger problem." Because such comprehensive action was never taken, the design, construction, and behavior problems that led to the collapse were never uncovered and addressed.

The investigative team discovered dozens of examples of Bonfire drinking, hazing, horseplay, and harassment. The Commission commented that

> Texas A&M is unique in allowing this level of irresponsible personal behavior in and around a construction project of this magnitude. Clearly there is potential for these behaviors to impact worker performance and thus perhaps structural integrity.

But the investigative team found no evidence that irresponsible behavior "contributed materially" to the collapse.

The Commission concluded that the university could solve the cultural, managerial, and design problems of Bonfire, but that teaching students and student leaders the skills and knowledge needed to build a structurally sound Bonfire would cost too much. The Commission also stated that students of any school, given the constraints of their academic situation, could not gain all the necessary skills and knowledge.

During the press conference Linbeck, and later President Ray Bowen, contradicted the Commission's findings by saying that a cost-effective and safe Bonfire could be built by well-trained students. Bowen, however, stated that he would make his final decision on Bonfire "with my head and not my heart." He was to announce his decision in six weeks.

The Wait

On May 29, members of the A&M faculty met in a large room in Rudder Tower. The Faculty Senate had organized the gathering to listen to opinions concerning the future of Bonfire. Only about seventy-five of the fourteen hundred faculty of Texas A&M showed up, partially because the meeting coincided with the beginning of the summer session. Dozens of faculty spoke; some were angry and some were sad, and most of them wished to see an alternative tradition replace Bonfire. The Senate Planning Committee had recommended to President Bowen that Bonfire be discontinued or radically modified because safety issues could not be resolved.

Other faculty claimed that the collapse was in part due to negligence on the part of the faculty, and that it was their responsibility to prevent any further deaths or injuries from occurring. Associate professor at the West Campus Library Rob McGeachin had the harshest words, criticizing the environmental and academic effects of Bonfire, and concluding that "the opinion of this institution in the eyes of our peers is in jeopardy if we let Bonfire continue."

Aggie students were certainly not going to sit on their hands and let President Bowen make his decision all by himself. Ryan Thompson, one of the organizers of the "Keep the Fire Burning" petition, had his organization continue collecting signatures, both by hand and through the web. The web site crashed on June 7, but Thompson organized a rally on June 10, to collect as many signatures by hand as possible. The goal of the rally, Thompson told The Eagle, was to support an on-campus "student-built, student organized, and student-run" Bonfire. When Keep the Fire Burning met with Vice-President Malon Southerland on June 13, they presented him a list of over 10,000 names of people who wished to see Bonfire burn on.

Throughout this waiting period, and beyond it, I listened to the Bonfire stories and opinions of dozens of Aggies. Through some of these conversations, I was convinced of the ability of Bonfire to erase all color and gender lines as Aggies worked together for a greater goal, even as I kept in mind evidence from other Aggies of the contrary. I spoke to Aggies of color who insisted that there was little or no racism in the Aggie and Bonfire cultures. I spoke to Old Army Ags from the late sixties and seventies who said that they never saw any alcohol associated with Bonfire back in their days. I spoke to older Aggies who said that in the fifties there wasn't even much horseplay, the environment was so strict.

I spoke to one Aggie who explained to me why the first black Corps outfit leader was called Fast Eddie. Apparently, when Fast Eddie was an underclassman, at least partially because he was black, he was especially pressured to whip out to every single upperclassman he came across in public. Thus, in order to get to class, Eddie Taylor learned to walk faster than everyone else on campus, earning him the nickname "Fast Eddie."

During the faculty meeting, I spoke to Dr. Gary Halter of the Texas A&M political science department. He was once mayor of College Station, but before that, in the early 1970s, he was the head of the Bonfire Committee. According to Halter, when Duncan Hall caught on fire during the 1972 Bonfire, a fifty-five foot height limit was imposed on the Bonfire. The next year, Halter went out to examine the Bonfire during construction. He noticed that the centerpole, as it lay on the ground, seemed longer than fifty-five feet. He talked to the Pots about this, and they didn't seem terribly concerned. In essence, he was being brushed off.

Halter went home and came back with a measuring tape and a chainsaw. As the Pots watched, he measured out fifty-five feet, and sawed off the top of the centerpole himself.

The Decision

On June 16, President Ray Bowen made his official announcement about the future of the Texas Aggie Bonfire. The following are excerpts from his speech.

Our history and our traditions are important to all of us. Bonfire is one of these traditions. It is not the defining activity of the university. It is one of many manifestations of what we call the Aggie Spirit. If somehow we did not have a bonfire, the Aggie Spirit would manifest itself in another beneficial activity just as it does in so many others at Texas A&M University. The special character of this university and its people is not, in my opinion, defined by any one tradition . . .

The character of Texas A&M University flows from the Aggie Spirit. This spirit is a manifestation of our academic strength, a manifestation of the character of the people of A&M, a manifestation of our history and those uncountable intangibles that make Aggies special . . .

It is my decision that this restructuring must produce a well-managed student project, which is forever safe, which projects a positive image for the university and which respects the academic demands on our students.

The restructured bonfire must have the following defining elements:

Design – We will have a design prepared by licensed professionals. We will have designed a single stack teepee-shaped bonfire.

Construction – We will have a construction plan prepared by licensed professionals. The time for construction will be limited to two weeks. No work from midnight to sunrise will be allowed.

Annual Compliance Review of Project – After the bonfire project is completed, the entire project will be reviewed for compliance with all design, construction, behavioral, and other objectives. A successful review will result in the authorization of allowing the following year's bonfire construction project.

Expanded University Oversight – We will augment our Student Affairs oversight with professional construction expertise.

Safety Program – We will have a safety plan prepared by licensed professionals

New Student Leadership Selection Process – We will have a more inclusive selection process.

No cut – Logs will be cut by professionals and delivered to the construction site. The benefit of this provision is increased safety and reduced time pressure on the students.

Construction Site – The construction site will be fenced, will have limited access, will have video monitoring and will have other controls characteristic of a professional construction site.

[. . .]   There will not be a bonfire construction for 2000 or 2001. If the restructuring I have described is successfully completed, we will

have a bonfire in 2002. If that bonfire construction is judged successful by the certification process I just described, then we will have a
2003 construction . . . You can anticipate important memorials and
other events to occur in 2000 and 2001. The details of these events
will need to be developed by our students . . .

This fall, we will create a working group of students, faculty and
staff to begin the planning for the 2002 Bonfire. Their task will be to
implement the conditions I have placed on the project. I will ask this
group to submit their plan to me no later than April, 2001. If the plan is
accepted, we can begin its implementation in September, 2001. This
means, for example, we can begin to identify the leadership for the 2002
project and contract for the design, construction and safety plans. We
think this phase can be completed by January 2002. At that time, the
student leadership can begin preparations for the 2002 construction . . .

[Student leaders must] commit to processes that protect not only
the students who build the 2002 bonfire, but also the students who
will build all future bonfires. It will be their responsibility to implement the cultural change necessary to see that the horror of the Bonfire collapse never visits our campus again. It is my responsibility and
that of our university administration and faculty to guide these young
people to the creation of a successful bonfire plan and, eventually, to
a safe bonfire construction.

Some of you will speculate that I have placed too large of a
challenge before our students. I do not think so, but only time will
tell. I can only remind you again that the Bonfire is a manifestation
of the larger reality known as the Aggie Spirit. It is the strength of
that spirit that will either lead our students to have the bonfire I
described today, or it will cause them to create a different tradition
that will benefit the university and the broader Aggie family well
into this century.

The Future of Aggieland

President Bowen's speech was not just about Bonfire. It was about
the future of Texas A&M, the future of its institutional character, and the
future of the Aggie Spirit itself.

The immediate causes of the Bonfire collapse were in its faulty design and construction, but the roots of the collapse lie in the Aggie culture itself. In May, the Bonfire Commission came to the same conclusion.
In announcing his decision, President Bowen made a point that was essentially the theme of my book. He said that the Aggie Spirit is the foundation of the Aggie culture, not Bonfire. The question is, what is the Aggie
Spirit, and how should it be manifested within our culture?

By radically reforming Bonfire in the way that he did, President Bowen made a philosophical shift that may or may not spread into other Aggie institutions. The changes in Bonfire represent a values-shift toward quality and professionalism without abandoning at least the symbols of our local culture. There is something to be said about traditional and local cultures. The modern global corporate capitalist culture (whew!) is swallowing or co-opting local, traditional, indigenous cultures at an alarming rate, diminishing the natural diversity of ways of life and seeing the world. But the traditional Aggie culture does not shun safety. In this sense, President Bowen's reforms do not contradict the Aggie Spirit. As in so many cases in the past, Aggies will simply learn to manifest the Aggie Spirit in a different way.

Having been born and raised in College Station, and having graduated from Texas A&M in 1992, it is the Aggie Spirit that I feel an affinity to and an everlasting loyalty to more than all of the A&M traditions and rituals combined.

Growing up Chinese American in an almost completely non-Asian environment, I was almost pathologically shy and introverted. In nursery school and kindergarten, it was quite an event when I actually opened my mouth and said something. As I grew up, I learned from Aggies and the Aggie Spirit to be more friendly, more outgoing, more effervescent, and to be redundant, more spirited. When our family car would break down by the side of the road, an Aggie would pull up and help us, and I remember either thinking or hearing my parents say, "You can always count on an Aggie to help out."

It is this spirit of helpfulness, friendliness, and effervescence that to me makes up the Aggie Spirit. For President Bowen and for others, it may also include the attributes of loyalty, dedication, tenacity, and academic excellence.

In this book, I make an argument for President Bowen's resignation. I do not budge from this position. One of the reasons why completely preventable tragedies like the 1999 Bonfire collapse occur is that those responsible are not held accountable. To this day, not a single administrator has resigned or been fired as a result of the disaster. Bowen had the guts to stand up and take responsibility, but for reasons of his own he did not resign. And he will not be dismissed. Present and future administrators learn from this that they can fail to the highest magnitude and still keep their jobs, making future tragedy more likely (whether it has to do with Bonfire or not).

But if Bowen must stay, and if Bonfire must continue, then I believe that President Bowen has chosen a prudent path. A two-year moratorium on Bonfire may seem extreme. But traditionally, the rush to build a big

Bonfire in time for the big game has been a major factor in increasing injuries during construction. After a tragedy of this magnitude, it is about time the University put the brakes on Bonfire and go a little overboard with safety precautions.

President Bowen announced the permanent elimination of Bonfire cut. It may seem strange that the twelve deaths occurred during Bonfire stack, but Bowen has eliminated cut. Most of the Bonfire injuries and deaths traditionally took place during cut. Over the decades, two students have died as a result of motor vehicle accidents involved in cut.

But if there is no cut , where will the Bonfire logs come from? According to Bowen, they will be donated. These trees, then, may come from local yards and forests. Previously, Bonfire organizers have sought land that was to be stripped for industrial purposes. Now, it is conceivable that local people will cut down trees especially for Bonfire. Long-time Aggie "Greeter" Pinky Downs, Jr. once cut a big tree down from his own front yard and threw it on Bonfire.

I've been watching the forests of Brazos County disappear for thirty years now, and I'm sure I share the view with thousands of others that Texas A&M should accept trees only from people who are already planning on cutting down their trees, Bonfire or not. Even with such a rule, though, the prestige of donating trees to Bonfire may be an incentive to chop them down.

The Bonfire will only be one tier high, Bowen announced. This means there will be little or no climbing of stack and no hanging from it by swings. This shifts the weight of priority towards safety and academics. This practical and symbolic shift will move Texas A&M closer to its Vision 2020.

Twice during the press conference Bowen mentioned "The Big Event." The Big Event is a one-weekend public service blitz during which Texas A&M students help local families clean, mow, clear, and generally improve the condition of their homes and neighborhoods. Bowen's clear implication was that the Aggie Spirit could manifest itself in community service, in addition to, or, eventually, instead of Bonfire.

And yet there is something lacking to The Big Event. And for that matter, there is something lacking to the new Bonfire. Neither of these events can truly inspire a great deal of zealousness, and neither truly exerts the body and exhausts the spirit in the cathartic manner that the Aggie Spirit desires. With the new, smaller Bonfire, each student will only be rationed a few hours of work. With the Big Event, students spend an afternoon or two making superficial improvements to the community. How is the Aggie Spirit to be sated, bonded, and united?

The Aggie Spirit can be truly manifested only by creating *permanent* changes in the Aggieland community. Of course this involves more work, more spirit, more enthusiasm, more dedication and loyalty, but that's the way the Aggie Spirit keeps its fire burning.

Aggies can build houses. Bryan-College Station has a homelessness problem. I'm sad to say that I've personally known some of the people who have ended up on my hometown streets, one of whom was my blood kin. In 1999, Aggies built the first all-Aggie Habitat for Humanity house. One construction expert told me that the time and effort put into building the old Bonfires could build a hundred Habitat pre-fab houses.

Aggies can be mentors and teachers. The new Aggie tradition may include teaching literacy or befriending misguided youths. Some Aggies may wish to be more creative and put together local literary journals, direct community stage-plays, or design safer local streets.

There are a wealth of possibilities, each of them a respectful act memorializing the twelve Aggies who perished in the Bonfire tragedy. Once the idea takes root that the Aggie Spirit can manifest itself in a myriad of ways—not only through Bonfire—the possibilities are endless. We can radiate the Aggie Spirit into every corner of the Aggieland community. Thousands of students have found a true home in Aggieland. With the Aggie Spirit, we can abolish both literal and figurative homelessness throughout our much-beloved Aggieland.